BRINGING TECHNOLOGY EDUCATION

INTO K-8 CLASSROOMS

ADVISORY BOARD

The advisory board of the project that led to this book is comprised of leaders from science education, technology education, and technology businesses.

Sara Armstrong is president of Educational Visions. She served as director of content for the George Lucas Education Foundation, where she was editor for *Edutopia: Success Stories for Learning in the Digital Age.*

William Dugger Jr. directs the Technology for All Americans Project of the International Technology Education Association. He led the creation of *Standards for Technological Literacy* and heads projects for implementing them.

Jane Lovedahl is a curriculum specialist for the Brazosport Independent Schools district in Texas. She has written about how to incorporate technology education in the elementary grades for the ITEA magazine *Technology and Children.*

Pamela Newberry is a lead curriculum developer for Project Lead the Way. Previously, she was a senior associate at the Technology for All Americans Project, where she contributed to *Standards for Technological Literacy.*

Senta Raizen is director of WestEd's National Center for Improving Science Education. She is lead author of the seminal book *Technology Education in the Classroom: Understanding the Designed World.*

Cary Sneider is vice president for educational programs at the Museum of Science in Boston. He heads development of a Web-based directory to curriculum resources for technology education.

Bernie Trilling is senior director of think.com at the Oracle corporation's Education Initiative. He previously directed WestEd's Technology in Education program.

Edward Britton • Bo De Long-Cotty • Toby Levenson

BRINGING TECHNOLOGY EDUCATION

INTO K-8 CLASSROOMS

A Guide to Curricular Resources About the Designed World

A Joint Publication

CORWIN PRESS
A SAGE Publications Company
Thousand Oaks, California

ITEA **NSTA**press®
NATIONAL SCIENCE TEACHERS ASSOCIATION
WestEd

KH

This work was supported by National Science Foundation grant number ESIE 991108. All facts and opinions are expressed by the authors and not endorsed by NSF.

For information:

Corwin Press
A Sage Publications Company
2455 Teller Road
Thousand Oaks, California 91320
www.corwinpress.com

Sage Publications Ltd
1 Oliver's Yard
55 City Road
London EC1Y 1SP
United Kingdom

Sage Publications India Pvt. Ltd.
B-42, Panchsheel Enclave
Post Box 4109
New Delhi 110 017 India

Printed in the United States of America

Library of Congress Cataloging-in-Publication Data

Britton, Edward.
Bringing technology education into K-8 classrooms : a guide to curricular
resources about the designed world / Edward Britton, Bo De Long-Cotty, Toby Levenson.
    p. cm.
Includes bibliographical references.
ISBN 1-4129-1465-5 (pbk.)
   1. Technology—Study and teaching (Elementary) 2. Technical education.
I. Long-Cotty, Bo De. II. Levenson, Toby. III. Title.
T65.3.B735 2005
372.35'8—dc22

                              2004025071

This book is printed on acid-free paper.

05   06   07   08   09   10   9   8   7   6   5   4   3   2   1

Acquisitions Editor:	Rachel Livsey
Editorial Assistant:	Phyllis Cappello
Production Editor:	Kristen Gibson
Copy Editor:	Mary Tederstrom
Typesetter:	C&M Digitals (P) Ltd.
Proofreader:	Kevin Gleason
Cover Designer:	Anthony Paular

Sample pages from the textbooks analyzed are used with the permission of the copyright holders:

Review 8.1

Gradwell, J. B., Welch, M., & Martin, E. (2004). *Technology: Shaping Our World*. Chicago: Goodheart-Willcox Company, Inc.

Review 8.2

From *Prentice Hall Technology Education Learning by Design* by Michael Hacker and David Burghardt (c) 2004 by Pearson Education, Inc., publishing as Prentice Hall. Used by permission.

Review 8.3

Wright, R.T., & Brown, R.A. (2004) *Technology: Design and Applications*. Chicago: Goodheart-Willcox Company, Inc.

Review 8.4

Harms, H.R., & Swernofsky, N.R. (2003) *Technology Interactions* (2nd Ed.). Woodland Hills, CA: Glencoe/McGraw-Hill.

Review 8.5

Thode, B. & Thode, T. (2002) *Technology in Action* (2nd Ed.). Woodland Hills, CA: Glencoe/McGraw-Hill.

Review 9.1

Hutchinson, P. (in production). *Children Designing and Engineering*. Belmar, NJ: Design and Technology Press.

Review 9.2

Reprinted by permission from *Stuff That Works: Packaging & Other Structures* and *Stuff That Works; Signs, Symbols, & Codes*, by Gary Beneson & James L. Neujahr. Copyright (c) 2002 by Gary Beneson and James L. Neujahr. Published by Heinemann, a division of Reed Elsevier, Inc., Portsmouth, NH. All rights reserved.

Review 9.3

Education Development Center, Inc. (2000). *A World in Motion: The Design Experience, Challenge 1*. Provided by the Society of Automotive Engineers (SAE) Foundation, Warrendale, PA.

Review 9.4

From *BSCS Science T.R.A.C.S.: An Elementary School Science Program*. Copyright (c) 1999 by BSCS. Reprinted with permission.

Review 9.6

From *BSCS Middle School Science and Technology* (2nd Ed.). Copyright (c) 1999 by BSCS. Reprinted with permission.

Review 9.7

Education Development Center, Inc. (1996) *A World In Motion: The Design Experience, Challenges 2 and 3.* Provided by the Society of Automotive Engineers (SAE) Foundation, Warrendale, PA.

Contents

Preface   ix

About the Authors   xiii

1. **What This Book Can Do for You**   **1**
     Helping Everyone Select Appropriate Resources   1
     Overview of the Book   3

Part I: Reviewing Curriculum Materials in Technology Education

2. **The Importance of Technology Education**   **7**
     Why Technology, Technology Education, and
         Technological Literacy?   8
     International Precedents   11
     Overview of *Standards for Technological Literacy* (STL)   12

3. **Encouraging Collaboration Between Science and Technology Educators**   **15**
     A Word to Science Educators   16
     A Word to Technology Educators   19
     Collaboration Between Science and Technology Educators   20

4. **How to Understand and Use the Curriculum Reviews**   **23**
     What Materials Are Reviewed?   23
     How Are Materials Reviewed?   31

Part II: Comparing Curricular Materials: What Matters Most

5. **Content: Standards-Based or Standards-Referenced**   **35**
     Addressing Most Themes   36
     Uneven Standards-Level Coverage   38
     Standards-Based or Standards-Referenced?   42
     Uses of Core Technology and Cross-Curricular Products   43

6. **Quality of Student Activities**   **47**
     Activity Types and Design Approaches   48
     Considering Other Aspects of Activities   51

7. **Teacher Support, Assessment, and Other Pedagogical Features**   **53**
     Teacher Support   54
     Assessment   59
     Other Pedagogical Features   61

Part III: Reviews, Analyses, and Samples of Individual Products

8. **Core Technology Products** **63**
   Late-Breaking Products 63
   Middle Grades
      Technology: Shaping Our World 65
      Technology Education: Learning by Design 87
      Technology: Design and Applications 106
      Technology Interactions 124
      Technology in Action 142

9. **Cross-Curricular Products** **163**
   Elementary Grades
      Children Designing and Engineering 165
      Stuff That Works! 180
      A World in Motion: The Design Experience, Challenge 1 192
      BSCS Science T.R.A.C.S. 203
   Middle Grades
      Integrated Mathematics, Science, and
         Technology (IMaST) 217
      BSCS Science and Technology 233
      A World in Motion: The Design Experience,
         Challenges 2 & 3 249

10. **Supplemental Products** **263**
   Elementary Grades
      Kids Inventing Technology Series (KITS) 265
      Technology Starters 266
      National Educational Technology Standards
         for Students 267
      The Great Technology Adventure 268
      Balancing the World of Technology in the
         Elementary Classroom 269
      All Aboard! 270
      Designing Everyday Things 271
   Middle Grades
      Humans Innovating Technology Series (HITS) 272
      Exploring Technology 273
      Teaching Technology 274
      KidTech 275
      By Design 276
      Design Connections 277

11. **Web Sites and Other Informal Resources** **279**
   Compendiums and Encyclopedias 280
   Inventors and Inventions 282
   Activities 286
   Other Resources 289
   Web Sites 293

Appendix A: More Benchmark-Level Analyses **295**

Appendix B: A Little More About Methods **299**

References **301**

Preface

What can this book do for you? It is the first independent review of curriculum materials for technology education in Grades K–8. The introductory chapter advocates using this book to become familiar with new resources and to examine many technology education products in more detail than has been possible before.

One of our advisors remarked that people often spend more time planning a week's vacation than they do planning for their decades of retirement. He was making an analogy to how the education system selects curriculum materials: Districts often spend only a few days and relatively few dollars selecting materials, in contrast to the years that students will use them and the thousands of dollars that they can cost. This guide can empower teachers and curriculum specialists to take a longer, deeper look at their choices.

In addition to being a guide to curricular resources, this book provides a good understanding of technology education. Chapter 2 defines and explains technology education. Readers glean the scope of technology from the description of the products in our reviews and from the products' own tables of contents and sample pages, reproduced at the end of each review.

What do we mean by technology education? A Gallup poll last year showed wide confusion among the public about the scope of technology and technology education. But after respondents received an explanation of technology, they overwhelmingly believed it should be taught in schools. We find similarly murky perceptions of technology within the U.S. education community. In contrast, modern technology education has already been a required school subject for ten-plus years in a dozen or more nations, including Australia, the Netherlands, New Zealand, and the United Kingdom.

Technology is broadly defined as changing the world to solve human problems. Students need to become technologically literate to enhance their lives in our technology-dependent world and for the well-being of our society. Technology can be understood by contrasting it with other fields. Technology is related to but different from science. Technology is related to but broader than engineering. Technology education does encompass how to use computers, other technological devices, or software in teaching, but it goes beyond such educational technology. The technology education community has its roots in industrial arts, but it has evolved toward something bigger, richer. We discuss all these distinctions.

Chapter 3 argues that it will take both technology and science educators to help students become technologically literate by the end of their schooling. For this reason, we are excited and grateful that both the International Technology Education Association and the National Science Teachers Association are copublishing this book with Corwin.

Leaders in science and engineering education have for some time been trying to increase those communities' attention to technology education. For example, the *National Science Education Standards* explicitly call for some technology education, as do the Benchmarks from Project 2061 at the American Association for the Advancement of Science. The National Academy of Engineering recently made strong calls for more technology education in its report, *Technically Speaking*. Both the National Science Foundation and the National Aeronautic and Space Administration have significantly invested in promoting technology education.

The impetus for this book began in 2000, when the emerging field of technology education dramatically enhanced its credentials for becoming a more prevalent school subject in U.S. schools. By releasing its *Standards for Technological Literacy* (STL) in 2000, the International Technology Education Association provided an explicit vision for this discipline, similar to what the National Science Education Standards and the Benchmarks did for science education.

Now, almost five years after the release of the STL, can nationally available curricular resources help students in Grades K–8 become technologically literate? WestEd's National Center for Improving Science Education obtained a grant from the National Science Foundation to formally analyze curricular resources to investigate this question and questions about many other features of curricular resources. Chapter 4 outlines the kinds of resources we reviewed, how we found them, and why we selected them. As longtime science educators who have been allies of technology education for the last decade, we bring not only expertise but also independence and objectivity to this review. We are aided by Advisory Board members from technology and science education and technology businesses.

We intensively reviewed textbooks and cross-curricular products for technology education—page by page, sentence by sentence. Our results in Part II, Chapter 5 indicate that educators need to choose curricula carefully: Materials are moving toward the STL, but they have a ways to go. Such a result seems reasonable at the moment, because the STL push technology education in directions that build on that field's traditional experience, but also differ significantly from its past. For example, the STL heighten attention to understanding and carrying out the design process and give a contemporary portrayal of the designed world (e.g., increase attention to biotechnologies). It takes years for curriculum materials to evolve toward a new vision, in part due to the time needed to develop and bring major products to market. However, our aim is to help educators know exactly how today's resources can aid them in teaching technology education consistent with the STL.

Also in Part II of the book, we alert readers to contrasts among the student activities found in the products (Chapter 6). Knowledge about the design process and the abilities for carrying out technological design are core ingredients of technological literacy. We formally categorize and describe the structure of the activities (open-ended, guided, or fully directed), as well as the approach to technological design (e.g., using a full-scale design process versus focusing on only particular parts of it).

Chapter 7 helps readers contrast the kinds of student assessment built into products (end-of-chapter tests, student portfolios, performance assessment, etc.) and the kinds of support provided in teacher materials (support for using the curriculum, pedagogical advice and tools, support for promoting technological literacy, and more).

Part III, the largest portion of the book, contains reviews of individual resources:

- Core technology products (Chapter 8, five full reviews). Technology textbooks for the middle grades.
- Cross-curricular products (Chapter 9, seven full reviews). Elementary and middle grades products that integrate technology with other subjects.
- Supplemental products (Chapter 10, thirteen product descriptions). Elementary and middle grades products that focus on technology education but do not constitute an entire grade level or course.
- Informal and other resources (Chapter 11, more than 100 short descriptions). Typically not designed expressly for classroom instruction, but great reference materials, many of which do include student activities. Also includes Web sites and periodicals.

AUDIENCES ■

This book is useful to three main audiences:

- *Curriculum specialists, professional developers, administrators.* People who assist teachers in selecting and/or using curricular resources—curriculum specialists, professional developers, and administrators at the district and school levels;
- *Teachers.* Everyone who might teach technology education at the elementary or middle grades (including science teachers at the middle grades);
- *Curriculum developers.* Authors can gain insights for creating new curricular resources in technology education.

Special Note for the Elementary Grades

More technology education currently is taught in the middle rather than elementary grades. However, we are pleased to find resources that are created expressly for the elementary grades, a little more than half of the cross-curricular products and the supplementary resources reviewed in this book.

We recognize that it is especially difficult for elementary teachers to tackle every school subject and to address shifting recommendations from year to year about what relative balance to strike among them. So it is with great respect that we appeal to elementary educators to take a look at yet another subject area.

We advance four rationales for doing so: Achieving technological literacy by the end of high school will be more attainable if instruction begins from the get-go; early exposure could prompt children to dream of a wider range of possibilities for what they might like to become someday (e.g., engineers in addition to scientists); technology education is great fun for young children (and students of all ages); and it stimulates their creativity, social intelligence, and motor skills, in addition to their overall cognitive development.

We hope this book will prompt and enable U.S. educators to help greater numbers of U.S. students become technologically literate.

■ ACKNOWLEDGMENTS

Most of all, we want to thank educators who use this book to begin or deepen their efforts to help students become technologically literate.

As always, producing and distributing a book requires the inspiration and efforts of many people in addition to the authors. The lead author might never have thought of this project if Senta Raizen had not introduced him to technology education and if she and colleagues had not published a 1995 book that clearly described it. We got wonderful ideas from many authors of technology education materials, such as Franzie Loepp, Ron Todd, and particularly Michael Hacker. Richard Cupp helped review major parts of some products and patiently entered and compiled the data from our analyses.

We are indebted to Kendall Starkweather of the International Technology Education Association (ITEA) and David Beacom at the National Science Teachers Association (NSTA) for making possible the copublication of this book by ITEA and NSTA.

This project would not have been possible without support from the National Science Foundation (NSF). Gerhard Salinger and, especially, Dan Householder at NSF did more than monitor our grant; they provided invaluable advice and assistance over several years.

Finally, we would not have completed this book if our families and colleagues had not put up with odd hours of work. They also overlooked those vacant stares and irritable moods when our minds bogged down in how and what to write. Special thanks go to our partners, husbands, and children: Bill, Phil, Richard, and Chloe.

This work was supported by National Science Foundation grant number ESIE 9911808. All facts and opinions are expressed by the authors and not endorsed by NSF.

Ted Britton,
Bo De Long-Cotty, and
Toby Levenson, San Francisco

About the Authors

Edward (Ted) Britton is associate director of the National Center for Improving Science Education (NCISE), housed within the Mathematics, Science, and Technology program of WestEd. Dr. Britton brings long experience in research and evaluation of curriculum issues and materials to this book. In collaboration with Senta Raizen and others, he developed methods for a cross-national comparison of textbooks in the Third International Mathematics and Science Study (TIMSS). He led a review of curriculum materials that connect science and mathematics to workplace contexts, *Connecting Mathematics and Science to Workplace Contexts*. Britton currently serves on the Technology Education Advisory Council of the ITEA.

His earlier NCISE research includes comparing high-stakes mathematics and science examinations across countries and studying U.S. innovations in mathematics and science education as part of an international study under the auspices of the Paris-based Organization of Economic Co-Operation and Development (OECD). As project director for Mary Budd Rowe of the University of Florida during the 1980s, Ted developed the first CD-ROM in science education and produced videotapes for the professional development of science teachers. During the late 1970s, he taught science courses for Grades 7–12 at a rural junior-senior high school in Florida.

Britton earned an EdD in science education, an MS in analytical chemistry, and a BS in chemistry and education from the University of Florida.

Bo De Long-Cotty is a developmental psychologist and has worked for WestEd since 1991. She currently serves as a project director in the WestEd Math, Science, and Technology program and as director of the Learning and Teaching with Technology initiative for the WestEd Regional Technology Education Consortium (RTEC). Her work at WestEd includes directing pblnet.org, a project-based learning resource, guidance, and collaboration site for teachers; providing information and resources to families and teachers to promote community–home involvement in schools; evaluating educational software and online curricula for Grades K–12; and evaluating and developing teacher professional development programs and projects. She is also Director of Educational Content for Alligator Planet, an animation company whose work includes children's educational television programming.

Dr. De Long-Cotty has served as director of evaluation for several science and math programs at the Lawrence Hall of Science at the University of California, Berkeley, as director of the GALAXY Classroom Science and Language Arts Evaluation for Teacher Universe/Riverdeep Publishing, and as director of evaluation for NASA's online Celestia Solar System activities. Until 1995, she served as coordinator for the WestEd evaluation of the California Statewide Systemic Initiative, focusing on K–5 science and 6–8 mathematics. She has also developed multimedia curricula and products in language arts, math, and science for Disney Ed Studio and Holt, Rinehart, and Winston.

Dr. De Long-Cotty earned an MA in developmental psychology from Teachers' College/Columbia University and a PhD in developmental psychology from the University of California, Berkeley.

Toby Levenson is a senior research associate for WestEd's Mathematics, Science, and Technology program. She has worked in both the nonprofit and for-profit education sectors as an educational designer, producer, and manager. She has developed science software and videodiscs; created math software, video, and curricula; designed literacy software and curricula; developed technology-related ancillaries to textbooks; and produced other educational technology and edutainment products. She has been a primary contributor to more than thirty products from companies such as LeapFrog, The Learning Company, Scholastic Inc., Harcourt, D.C. Heath, Education Development Center (EDC), and CAST, among others.

At WestEd, Levenson continues her interest in technology and curriculum with evaluating the effects of educational technology on student performance and developing interactive Web sites for teachers, curriculum specialists, and other school leaders. Levenson's specialties include using interface, interactive, and information design to increase student learning; applying cutting-edge technologies to increase educational opportunities for students with disabilities; and conceptualizing and developing differentiated curriculum in mathematics, reading, and other subjects to meet the needs of all students.

The daughter of an MIT-trained engineer and an art teacher, Levenson was building and designing inventions from a young age. After earning a BA, with a major in archaeology and a minor in computer science, Levenson was a computer programmer and trainer in industry for seven years while also serving as a curriculum advisor at the Boston Museum of Science. Levenson received an MEd in interactive technology in education from the Harvard Graduate School of Education.

1

What This Book Can Do for You

Which textbook, curriculum series, or other resource is best for teaching technology education in Grades K–8? This is a fair question—and harried educators and curriculum specialists want a quick, bottom-line answer.

It would be unfair, however, to give overly simple answers such as "Textbook 5 is the one for you!" Instead, this book empowers educators to make well-informed choices of curricular resources, ones that can meet their specific classroom needs in the elementary or middle grades.

In addition, we briefly argue for teaching technology in more U.S. classrooms and explain and illustrate its concepts and instructional approaches. In doing so, we exhort those already teaching technology to keep advancing the state of the art. We also help make science educators and educators in other subject areas aware that they may already have put a foot in these waters. Now we urge them to go for a real swim. All these points, as well as the organization and uses of this book, are discussed in the following sections.

HELPING EVERYONE ■
SELECT APPROPRIATE RESOURCES

When one fully considers how much rides on choosing materials, it is amazing how often our educational system is willing to go from the gut. Curriculum materials daily impact what teachers will teach, how they may teach it, the learning experiences that diverse kinds of students can have, and so on. The process of choosing curricular resources should be as deliberative and intensive as it is consequential.

Yet districts typically only support a few days of committee time to select products that must be used for years. Committee members first try to carve out time on their own to look at a few assigned resources. Then they get only a couple of meetings to discuss collectively the weighty decisions of selecting curricula from among many choices. With so little time and so much pressure, no wonder participants inspect candidate resources merely by flipping through the pages, a process sometimes called the "thumb test." Only easily judged features of the products typically get noticed: copyright date, cost, durability, diversity of people in photographs, readability levels, engaging layouts, availability of supporting products, and so on (Chamblis & Calfee, 1998).

Financially, districts will spend enormous sums to purchase the products, while devoting relatively few dollars on deciding how to spend all that money. The situation has changed incrementally in recent years, as organizations are creating more detailed information and methods for reviewing and choosing curricular resources (American Association for the Advancement of Science, 2000; Britton, Huntley, Jacobs, & Shulman-Weinberg, 1999; Goldsmith, Mark, & Kantrov, 2000; Morse et al., 2001; Muther, 1999). Fortunately, school systems and teachers are beginning to see their selection processes as a cornerstone of classroom instruction, an important investment toward a larger expenditure.

This book aims to help technology educators and curriculum specialists overcome four barriers that box local educational systems into using limited selection processes. First, not every person or system interested in choosing products has the time and/or money to obtain copies of all the possibilities. We have done this for you. We collected and describe about twenty-five curriculum materials designed for classroom use, and more than 100 informal resources.

Second, how can one find and pay for the expertise of people who already know these products well, without relying on product developers or distributors? Studies indicate that presentations by publishers' sales representatives can be the most influential factor in districts' selection of curricula—not the healthiest situation (Chamblis & Calfee, 1998; see Chapter 6). This book puts in your hands an extensive analysis done by independent experts of both major and minor features of the products.

In particular, how can one detect whether products are precisely aligned with national content standards? The line-by-line analysis of a resource's topics against specific standards takes weeks or months for a single large product. The third way this book helps one choose resources is by providing just such detailed analyses.

Fourth, how can someone sift through analyses of many curricula and still get the overall essence of the resources? In addition to describing and analyzing the products, we include sample pages from the larger ones, such as textbooks.

This book names names. That is, we contrast and compare the products by name. We formally compare the products in several ways, including how well they empower teachers (or not) to help students

- Attain the technological literacy envisioned by national standards;
- Experience and understand the technology design process;
- Know about the technologies in our lives and communities;
- Have rich opportunities to adequately assess their knowledge and abilities.

We also discuss how well the resources do (or do not)

- Engage *all* students in our increasingly diverse populations;
- Connect to the real world or daily life;
- Relate activities to the goals of the units where they are placed;
- Provide adequate support for teachers to use the product effectively.

We do not include any lemons. All the resources that we describe reviewed well. However, a given resource can be strong in one feature and weaker in another, which brings us back to the matter of why simple answers such as "choose textbook 5" shortchange both educators and students.

We add one more argument: Selection must be local. For us to give overall recommendations or rankings of resources ignores the fact that what is most important in one place may be less important in another. For example, addressing diverse student populations is a paramount consideration in some locales (and more of them all the time). Such districts might choose resources that address diverse student populations particularly well, even if those resources are not the most standards-based. A district elsewhere might be in a state where standards coverage is paramount, and addressing diverse populations is an important but less acute issue at present.

So this book tries to describe resources for everyone. We do not believe one product can meet everyone's needs. Instead, among the many resources we describe, and in the many ways we describe them, everyone should be able to find resources that meet his or her particular needs.

In addition to helping people make judgments about curricular resources in technology education, this book can also help people become more familiar with technology education in general in a couple of ways. Before discussing patterns among resources and giving individual reviews of them, we briefly describe and argue for technology education. In addition, in contrast to entire publications devoted to the definition and importance of technology education, this book has a practical advantage in promoting understanding of technology education. By spending time with the reviews of resources plus their corresponding sample pages, one can get a grounded illustration of the topics and instructional approaches of technology education.

OVERVIEW OF THE BOOK ■

This book is organized into three parts.

Part I briefly defines technology and why science educators as well as technology educators should teach it (Chapters 2–3). Chapter 4 identifies the types of products reviewed and the methods we used to analyze them.

Part II highlights the strengths and weaknesses we found among the curricular resources that we inspected.

The largest portion of the book, Part III, contains reviews of individual curricular resources, grouped into four categories of resources.

Making the Case for Technology Education: Chapters 2–3

Especially because we speak to science educators as well as technology educators, Chapter 2 briefly answers some key questions:

- What are technology, technological literacy, and technology education?

  (Hint: They refer to *more than* computers and technological devices, which they also include.) Why are they important to students, teachers, and society?

- What are the standards for technology education?

  Not everyone is aware that there are bona fide U.S. standards for technology education, just as there are those for mathematics or science education.

In contrast to the United States, about a dozen countries require that technology education be part of the school curriculum in its own right, just like mathematics, science, and so on. However, because technology education has not yet gained similar prevalence in the United States, there currently are not enough formally trained technology teachers.

Therefore, if all students are to become technologically literate today, we argue in Chapter 3 that technology educators must enlist science educators as allies. In fact, in the section A Word to Science Educators, we show that national standards and other seminal documents in U.S. science education already urge science educators to take up some technology education. We also sketch an overview of the technology education community to help pave the way for science and technology educators to collaborate. In A Word to Technology Educators, we make technology educators aware of science educators' perspectives and encourage them to welcome allies to their "territory."

Focusing on Print Materials: Chapter 4

This book focuses on printed curricular resources: textbooks, textbook series, monographs, or monograph series. All these kinds of resources can play an integral role in teachers' lesson planning and instruction for a technology course or a substantial part of a course or grade. By analyzing these products, we aim to help people choose from among the most widely used curricular supports for teaching the subject of technology.

Some prognosticators thought that, by now, the Internet would have made print materials go the way of the dinosaur, and there certainly is a burgeoning world of online resources for technology education. However, many of them currently lend themselves to important but secondary roles in technology courses. They form the basis of individual lessons or units rather than large portions of courses. Further, our educational facilities have not yet reached the point of having enough computer stations and rapid Internet connections to permit most students, or even some teachers, to access the Web on a daily basis.

Obviously, there are exceptions to the previously mentioned points. For example, two Web-based curricula that can provide substantial instruction are Intel Corporation's free *Design and Discovery* program for middle school students (www.intel.com/education/design) and the free Integrated Design Engineering Activity Series (IDEAS) from the American Society of Mechanical Engineers (www.asme.org/education/precollege/ideas), also for the middle grades. We further acknowledge not only that the relative amounts of use of print, online, and other resources are shifting, but also that curriculum developers and teachers often are blending their use. For example, every chapter of the textbook *Technology Education: Learning by Design* (reviewed in Chapter 8) points students to a specific Web site that can help them understand concepts and demonstrates technological systems or processes.

However, given the overall context described earlier, we have chosen to use the limited space available in this book to thoroughly review print materials—the curricular resources still used by the greatest number of teachers as the basis for the largest portion of their technology instruction. In Chapter 11, Informal Resources, we list some Web sites that are resources for teaching technology, even though we do not have space to review the instruction they provide.

In Chapter 4, we provide more detail about the kinds of resources reviewed and how we analyzed them. We also give advice about choosing products from among another class of resources, the "modular" systems that are common in the technology and vocational education communities.

Contrast Among Resources: Part II (Chapters 5–7)

Part II compares several dimensions of the products:

- *Content.* Chapter 5 explains in detail how today's available products are (or are not) able to promote students' technological literacy.
- *Activities.* In Chapter 6, we analyze the student activities contained in the products, describing their purpose, structure, approach to technological design, and more.
- *Teacher support, assessment, and other pedagogical features.* Chapter 7 analyzes the products' teacher support materials. It also discusses the tools and strategies available for assessing student understanding. Finally, this chapter discusses what instructional models the products use.

Reviews of Individual Products: Part III (Chapters 8–11)

Part III contains reviews for the following four types of curricular resources (described in Chapter 4).

- Chapter 8: Core Technology Products (technology textbooks)
- Chapter 9: Cross-Curricular Products (integrated products)
- Chapter 10: Supplemental Products (products intended to supplement courses)
- Chapter 11: Web Sites and Other Informal Resources (topical books, encyclopedias, and more)

In addition to analyses and descriptions, Chapters 8 and 9 contain sample pages, reproduced from the reviewed products. We group the wealth of informal resources of Chapter 11 (more than 100 of them) into categories and provide annotated descriptions of each resource.

2

The Importance of Technology Education

In a recent Gallup poll, researchers learned that the public's perception of technology is murky:

> When hearing the word "technology," approximately two thirds think of only computers and matters related to the Internet while the remaining one third embrace the broader concept of technology as the means of "changing the natural world to satisfy our needs." (Rose & Dugger, 2003, p. 1)

Similarly, the education community at large is *not* familiar with the contemporary technology education that is beginning to be taught in U.S. schools. We begin this chapter by briefly describing technology, technology education, and technological literacy in order to clear up some definitions.

We then point out that some countries are ahead of the game in formally making technology education its own subject in their schools. Fortunately, more U.S. educators are now recognizing its importance. Furthermore, there are national standards for what technology content should be taught, just as there are for science education and other school subjects. Finally, we argue why all this is so important.

■ WHY TECHNOLOGY, TECHNOLOGY EDUCATION, AND TECHNOLOGICAL LITERACY?

In its broadest sense, technology is the process by which humans modify nature to meet their needs and wants. However, most people think of technology only in terms of its artifacts: computers, aircraft, . . . , to name a few. But technology also is the knowledge and processes necessary to create and operate those products, such as engineering know-how and design, manufacturing expertise, various technical skills, and so on. (NAE & NRC, 2002, pp. 2–3)

Technology education equips students with the knowledge and abilities needed to ensure their technological literacy. The International Technology Education Association (ITEA), based in the United States, has issued *Standards for Technological Literacy: Content for the Study of Technology* (ITEA, 2000). We refer to the ITEA document and its standards as the STL throughout this book. The development of these standards was supported by the National Science Foundation (NSF) and the National Aeronautics and Space Administration (NASA). This document paints a vision of technological literacy and education that includes

- Understanding the nature of technology,
- Understanding relationships between technology and society,
- Understanding the process of designing,
- Acquiring the abilities to carry out design activities, and
- Understanding and gaining key abilities in major types of technologies ("the designed world").

The following vignette, which is reproduced from the STL and titled Clean Up an Oil Spill, illustrates technology education in action for a fifth-grade classroom. Undoubtedly, the best way of gaining an understanding of technology education and technological literacy is to read the STL, which we hope every reader has done or will do. We briefly describe the STL later in this chapter.

The ITEA has also released Addenda to the STL: *Teaching Technology for Middle School* (2000) and *Technology Starters* (2002), both of which are described in Chapter 10. These monographs provide guidance for teaching technology in standards-based ways and contain many illustrative student activities.

One also can get a good sense of technology education by perusing the reviews in Part III, in which we compare each curricular resource to the STL. The included sample pages from each product also illustrate some of the knowledge and processes taught in technology education at the elementary and middle grades.

Besides describing them, another way we can explain technology and technology education is to dispel some prevalent misperceptions of them:

- Technology should *not* be regarded merely as the application of science. Technology is different from science, although it has vital connections to science. Technology is complementary to science, not secondary to it. Technology does make use of science, but its scope is much broader than

Vignette of Teaching
Technology: Clean Up an Oil Spill

Ms. G, a fifth-grade teacher, presented her class with a challenge. "On April 5, an oil tanker, *Radical*, sideswiped an iceberg, causing 15 tons of oil to spill into the ocean. You are chosen to join an elite team of scientists to devise a way to clean up the oil spill."

Ms. G then divided the students into groups of four to five members. Each group received a pie pan with one inch of water in it and a small piece of fake fur. Ms. G instructed the students to begin the experiment by placing the fur in the water, and then she used an eyedropper to add a tablespoon of oil to the water in each pan. The students observed what happened and recorded these observations in their journals. The teacher stimulated their thinking by asking questions, such as "Do the oil and water mix? How many layers do you see? What happened to the oil?" The students then estimated the size of the oil spill.

Next, the students received paper towels, cotton balls, toilet tissue, string, coffee filters, and rubber bands. Ms. G challenged them to use these materials to try to contain the oil in a small area and to clean up the oil spill as much as possible. The students worked together as teams to design a method, and they recorded their observations, their successes, and their not-so-successful attempts in their journals.

Ms. G then led the class discussion of the various methods that the students had developed. They discussed the problems that they had encountered in developing a solution and how they had overcome the obstacles. The teacher then asked the students to observe the piece of fur and to describe in their journals how the fake fur had changed and to imagine how oil on an animal's fur might affect its survival. Ms. G then added several drops of detergent to the experimental oil spill, and again she asked the students to write their observations in their journals.

Ms. G concluded the exercise by discussing the importance of petroleum and oil in everyone's life. She also explained the short- and long-term impacts that an oil spill can have on the environment. She shared with them several real-life stories of tanker accidents, the clean-up procedures, the damage to the environment, the community's response to the accident, and the steps taken to design tankers that won't spill oil. As a result of this exercise, the students learned how a technology can have both positive and negative effects on the environment.

Reproduced from *Standards for Technological Literacy* (ITEA, 2000, p. 136)

merely being the application of science. (Actually, because science often is dependent on applying technologies into its pursuits, one could similarly, and incorrectly, perceive science merely as the application of technology.) For more discussion on the relationship between science and technology, and between science education and technology education, see the section A Word to Science Educators in Chapter 3.

- Technology education is related to but *different from* industrial arts or vocational education.

    Vocational education can equip students with skills to work as welders, drafters, plumbers, auto-technicians, and the like in technological fields, such as transportation, agribusiness, and manufacturing. Many vocational education teachers of traditional courses in woodworking, drafting, and so on are changing to become teachers of today's modern technology. However, technology educators go beyond only teaching about knowledge and skills used in "the designed world" technologies of transportation, medical or manufacturing technologies, and the like. They also teach about the design processes and the technological abilities that must be applied in addressing a wider range of human needs.

- Technology education is *not* educational technology.

    Educational technology is about using technologies in the education of students, such as employing the following: computer programs, the Internet, calculators, or heat and temperature probes in science experiments. Although technological knowledge and processes are used in creating such educational technologies, the mere use of them in teaching is far from being technology education. There are separate standards for the appropriate use of technology to further education, which are developed by the International Society for Technology in Education (ISTE, 2000).

- Technology education addresses computer literacy, but also much more.

    Technological literacy certainly includes using computers and gaining some understanding of how they work. The definitional issue is . . . how much? The explosion of knowledge and devices in such fields has spawned specialized, deep areas of expertise—computer scientists, informational technologists, etc. The STL Standard 17 on information technologies prescribes that for today's K–12 graduates to be technologically literate members of society, they must know something about these domains. However, the STL does not advocate that every student delve into these topics exhaustively. If they did, there may not be enough time left for all students to become literate in the many other aspects of technology that impact their lives. In the preface to the STL document, the president of the National Academy of Engineering remarks: ". . . the view of technological literacy spelled out in these standards includes references to computers and the Internet, but it correctly does not focus unduly on these technologies, which would comprise only a small part of our vast human-built world." (ITEA, 2000, p. vii)

Why is it important to teach technology? The previously quoted NRC report, *Technically Speaking*, makes a case for students becoming technologically literate:

"In a world permeated by technology, an individual can function more effectively if he or she is familiar with and has a basic understanding of technology" (NAE & NRC, 2002, p. 25). It outlines ways that adults who graduate from school with a better technology education will improve their lives and our society:

- Making better choices as consumers,
- Enhancing the use of technology in their daily lives,
- Employing better technological abilities in business and industry, and
- Making better citizen choices about technological issues in society.

INTERNATIONAL PRECEDENTS

Returning to the Gallup poll, which was commissioned by the ITEA, once respondents were made aware of contemporary definitions of technology, they had strong opinions about its importance for students: "There is near total consensus among the sampled public that schools should include the study of technology in the curriculum" (Rose & Dugger, 2003, p. 1). The pollsters probably would get a similar or even stronger endorsement from the public in some places abroad.

Several countries have a leg up on the United States in recognizing the importance of technology. The populations of these countries believe that all students should be educated in technology because technologically literate students will lead better lives in today's world and be more able to contribute wisely to technological decisions facing society. We should note, however, that the United States certainly is far from being the lone country whose education system fails to adequately address technology education.

About a dozen countries have officially set technology as a school subject, in addition to and separate from other school subjects such as science, mathematics, and so on. Indicative of this, the STL document has been translated into Chinese, Dutch, Finnish, and Japanese. Other countries that emphasize technology education in their schools include Australia, Israel, New Zealand, and the United Kingdom.

When picking up the national education standards or frameworks for schools in these countries, one finds a section or separate document containing standards for technology education. School schedules list the instructional times required for technology education, broken down by grade levels, and commercial curriculum materials exist for technology teachers to use in these technology courses.

International conferences on technology education occur in several countries. Every year, the annual conference that ITEA holds in the United States draws participants from other countries. From time to time, technology educators in other countries host international conferences. For example, Marc de Vries of the Netherlands and Arley Tamir of Israel convened conferences in Jerusalem, with more than 1,000 technology educators from more than eighty countries attending the most recent one (De Vries & Tamir, 1995). Technology educators in the United Kingdom periodically host international conferences on technology, including ones focused specifically on technology education in the elementary years (Benson & Till, 1999).

■ ## OVERVIEW OF *STANDARDS FOR TECHNOLOGICAL LITERACY* (STL)

The STL document is intended to play the same role in our educational system that the National Science Education Standards play in science education. The STL vision encompasses five broad bodies of technological knowledge and abilities. We call them "themes" throughout this book. Table 2.1 shows which of the STL document's chapters and standards correspond to the themes.

Table 2.1   STL themes and chapters

Standards themes	STL chapter	Standards
Theme 1. Nature of Technology	3	1–3
Theme 2. Technology and Society	4	4–7
Theme 3. Design	5	8–10
Theme 4. Abilities for a Technological World	6	11–13
Theme 5. The Designed World	7	14–20

Table 2.2 lists the twenty standards of STL. Each is broken down into much more detailed "benchmarks," specifically tailored to the grade ranges K–2, 3–5, 6–8, and 9–12. At the elementary grades, the STL calls for instruction for two to four benchmarks per standard. Typically, there are three or four benchmarks for each of the twenty standards at the middle grades, but some standards have many more.

To illustrate the relationship between standards and benchmarks, compare Standard 3 to one of its benchmarks:

Standard 3—Students will develop an understanding of the relationships among technologies and the connections between technology and the other fields of study.

Benchmark, Grades 6–8, 3F—Knowledge gained from other fields of study has a direct effect on the development of technological products and systems.

Note that Benchmark 3F does not merely call for putting random science topics into the technology curricula. It exhorts technology educators to show explicitly how science is involved in technology. Therefore, in the study discussed in this book, a textbook passage that brings in appropriate science—in ways that make it connected to the technology content being explained—is indicated as fulfilling Benchmark 3F. In contrast, some texts have numerous instances where science content is included, but it does *not* relate to the technology content (even though some sections like this have titles such as "science connector").

Leaders in technology education urge the field to truly cover the benchmarks in spirit and depth rather than merely mention or loosely refer to them.

Table 2.2   Overview of ITEA *Standards for Technological Literacy*

Theme 1: Nature of Technology
  S1: characteristics and scope of technology
  S2: core concepts of technology
  S3: relationships among technologies and the connections between technology and other fields of study

Theme 2: Technology and Society
  S4: cultural, social, economic, and political effects of technology
  S5: effects of technology on the environment
  S6: role of society in the development and use of technology
  S7: influence of technology on history

Theme 3: Design *(knowledge/understanding of design processes)*
  S8: attributes of design
  S9: engineering design
  S10: role of troubleshooting, research, and development, invention and innovation, and experimentation in problem solving

Theme 4: Abilities for a Technological World *(doing technological design)*
  S11: apply the design process
  S12: use and maintain technological products and systems
  S13: assess the impact of products and systems

Theme 5: The Designed World *(knowledge in specific technological fields)*
  S14: medical
  S15: agricultural and biotechnology
  S16: energy and power
  S17: information and communication
  S18: transportation
  S19: manufacturing
  S20: construction

Authors have added explanatory phrases following some themes.

Each of the twenty Standards begins with "students will develop an understanding/knowledge of (or abilities to)," as follows:

    themes 1, 2, 3—understanding
    theme 4—abilities
    theme 5—knowledge and abilities

That is, they call for materials to be "standards-based," not merely "standards-referenced." For materials to be considered standards-based, they must capture the specific benchmarks, not just the more general standard. Such a distinction is crucial: "*Benchmarks* . . . provide the *fundamental* content elements for the broadly stated Standards. . . . the *Benchmarks* are *required* for students to meet the Standards" (emphasis added; ITEA, 2000, pp. 14–15).

Consequently, for the major technology textbooks reviewed, we analyzed every line to determine their alignment with the STL benchmarks. We will discuss the extent to which products are standards-based or merely standards-referenced in Chapter 5. Again, having a copy of the STL document handy while using this book would be valuable.

An overview of the STL is incomplete without noting that the ITEA's Technology for All Americans project, which produced the STL, has followed it up with more detailed guidance for implementing STL recommendations. Several addenda have been released, which are included as Supplemental Products in Chapter 10. Most recently, the volumes of the *Advancing Excellence in Technological Literacy* series (ITEA, 2004) provide standards in the key areas of assessment, professional development, and programs.

Further, the ITEA's CATTS project has produced illustrated guides for creating elementary and middle school curricula that can fulfill the vision of the STL. The project also has created sets of lesson plans for elementary (KITS) and middle and high school (HITS), each of which explicitly addresses one or more STL standards and their benchmarks. Because these resources are not extensive enough to form the curriculum for an entire course, descriptions of them are included in Chapter 10.

3

Encouraging Collaboration Between Science and Technology Educators

The masses of today's middle and high school students will become technologically literate only if both science educators and technology educators can be enlisted to get the job done. There are not enough technology teachers yet to go around.

We urge middle-grades educators to consider some particular issues in the sections A Word to Science Educators and A Word to Technology Educators. However, we hope both groups of educators will read both sections. After all, whenever new partners begin collaborating, it helps to understand what issues each one faces.

For current technology educators, this book offers the first opportunity to consider, in one place, the potential uses of so many curricular resources. In particular we hope that technology educators will take this opportunity to compare the extent to which products address the twenty *Standards for Technological Literacy* (STL) and their benchmarks. We also urge technology educators to welcome collaboration with science educators.

For science educators, we document how the science education community has formally recognized the importance of technology education. (As an indicator, consider that the National Science Teachers Association copublishes this book.) As curriculum specialists who have many years' experience in science education and have been working with technology educators for five to twenty years, the authors seek to reach science educators in these ways:

- Make them aware that technology education is part of their purview
- Enrich science educators' conceptions of technology education
- Suggest curricular resources that can help science educators to start including technology education

For elementary teachers, a prime issue is finding the time and means to bring technology into a crowded curriculum, especially because most elementary teachers are both the science and technology teacher. But as elementary teachers know well, integration is the key to covering everything that needs to be taught.

They will find that technology is especially well suited to blending with other subjects, as evidenced by some cross-curricular products in Chapter 9. In fact, technology has vital connections with many subjects besides science: mathematics, social studies, art, and more. Even some of the middle school products in Chapter 9 are specifically designed to integrate technology with multiple subjects.

■ A WORD TO SCIENCE EDUCATORS

Many science educators have unclear conceptions of what technology education is, and they are teaching only small amounts of it. Further, science educators often are unfamiliar with the technology education community, or they have not built relationships with technology educators. This section illuminates these issues and suggests a working relationship between the two communities.

To begin with, we want to acknowledge some challenges that science teachers face when incorporating more material into their courses. First, science teachers already have a lot of science topics to teach. This will only get worse as the scientific knowledge explosion gets ever more powerful. Second, it already is hard for science teachers to cover some science topics that they consider key, such as evolution and inquiry, because of pressures to skip them.

So why should science teachers even consider taking on another challenge? Because technological literacy is crucial to everyday functioning in our world.

Science Education Community Recommends Technology Education

For at least fifteen years, leading science education organizations have urged science educators to address technology education. For example:

AAAS, 1989, *Science for All Americans*. The prominent Project 2061 of the American Association for the Advancement of Science (AAAS) devoted a great deal of attention to technology education in its major reports. Two of twelve chapters in *Science for All Americans* (SFAA) were C3—The Nature of Technology—and C4—The Designed World. Many of the topics that SFAA described as the designed world are similarly treated today in the designed world portion of the International Technology Education Association (ITEA) *Standards for Technological Literacy*. As a follow-up to SFAA, the AAAS produced a separate, companion monograph about technology (1993a).

AAAS, 1993b, *Benchmarks for Science Literacy*. When issuing *Benchmarks*, which gave specific goals for implementing the vision of SFAA, Project 2061 continued a similar amount and type of emphasis on technology education (Chapters 3 and 8). Further, since 1998, Project 2061 has held a series of conferences in which participants from engineering, technology, and science education have deliberated how to foster cross-subject collaboration toward the advancement of technology education in the United States (see, e.g., AAAS, 2000).

NCISE, 1995, *Technology Education in the Classroom*. The National Center for Improving Science Education (NCISE), now at WestEd, continued the discussion about the relationship between science and technology. This book also described how technology education is being taught in some U.S. classrooms, as well as in other countries (Raizen, Sellwood, Todd, & Vickers, 1995).

NRC, 1996, *National Science Education Standards (NSES)*. The National Research Council's (NRC's) NSES included Content Standard E: Science and Technology, which exhorts development of student abilities for technological design as well as understandings about science and technology.

NAE and NRC, 2002, *Technically Speaking*. Continuing an emphasis on technology education, the NRC, in collaboration with the National Academy of Engineering (NAE), recently issued a plea and recommendations for more technology education in U.S. schooling.

So, it's official: Science educators are being asked to teach some technology education. Now, why isn't this happening very often? As acknowledged earlier, science courses are already stuffed full. More reasons follow.

When Science Actually Is Technology

Science educators might be omitting technology education because of misperceptions and lack of awareness. We noted previously a prevalent misperception of technology education—the common view of technology as just computers or other information technologies. However, *Technically Speaking* describes another confusion:

Yet in public discourse, innovations and events that have a significant *technological* component are often described as *science*. Take the building and launching of the Hubble Space Telescope. Although its purpose is scientific, . . . the telescope itself is the product of science and engineering. Similarly, the development of new drugs is often misidentified solely as science. Obviously, a great deal of scientific research underlies the development of a new drug, but that research is put to work toward a technological end. Even in the computer industry, the first thing that comes to many people's minds when they think of technology, cramming more transistors onto a chip or more memory onto a magnetic disk, is a technological advance rather than a scientific one. (emphasis added, NAE & NRC, 2002, pp. 51–52)

Almost 60 percent of the public viewed "science and technology basically as the same thing" (Rose & Dugger, 2003, p. 3).

Science educators often teach material relevant to technology education without calling it that or realizing it. Indeed, some technological content and processes already are common in science education: for example, understanding simple machines, electrical circuits, or manmade systems and conducting some types of problem solving.

A popular phrase warns, however, that "a little bit of knowledge can be a dangerous thing." Because science educators often are teaching a thin slice of technology education but are unfamiliar with the full scope of it, they may understandably think they already are adequately addressing technology education and promoting technological literacy. A good way to more fully absorb the range and details of technological knowledge and abilities is to consult some people who already teach it—technology teachers.

Overview of the Technology Education Community

While technology education is trying to gain a stronger foothold in the nation's education system, its status varies considerably among the states. In May 2004, the U.S. Department of Education convened chief state school officers and relevant state curriculum specialists to discuss ideas for advancing technology education. A number of states have moved their formerly vocational-oriented curriculum specifications toward ITEA's technological literacy. Unfortunately, there also are many states where state-level education leaders and curriculum specialists have little awareness of the STL, except where similar concepts may weakly appear as embedded in science education policies and practices. Few states currently have separate curriculum framework documents that are dedicated to technology education.

In contrast, many states are beefing up their science frameworks to address technology education as well. The state of Massachusetts perhaps has the most forceful and explicit call for teaching technology education. The Museum of Science in Boston is a lead player in helping the state's teachers move into this new curriculum (www.mos.org). Some states are also producing illustrative lessons for technology education. Many of these states have banded together in ITEA's National Science Foundation (NSF)–funded project, the Center to Advance the Teaching of Technology and Science (CATTS). Member states in CATTS are pooling their expertise with ITEA to create technology education guides and student technology activities that are expressly designed to address the STL. Several CATTS products are reviewed in this book.

ITEA is the main organization spearheading the contemporary technology vision discussed in this book (www.iteawww.org). The ITEA annual meeting is held every March or April. We encourage science teachers to join ITEA to receive its monthly magazines of technological activities and discussions: *Technology and Children* for elementary school and *Technology Teacher* for middle and high school. The ITEA hosts a list-serve, the Idea Garden, where participants hold lively discussions on ideas and resources for teaching specific school technology topics.

ITEA also recently created Innovation Curriculum Online Network (ICON), an NSF–funded Web site that reviews hundreds of technology education activities (http://icontechlit.enc.org). Users can select lessons that correspond to particular STL standards and then obtain the lessons themselves. Because ICON only includes lessons in the public domain (i.e., ones that are not copyrighted), this site does *not* describe the commercial products reviewed in this book.

Some technology teachers also belong to the technical education division of the Association for Career and Technical Education (ACTE). This organization was renamed about five years ago from the American Vocational Association (AVA). ACTE members get monthly copies of the magazine *Techniques,* which contains useful information for technology education and related domains such as career education. Independently of ITEA or ACTE, the quarterly *TIES* magazine provides guidance and activities for teaching design, primarily for middle and high school, but with some support for the elementary years as well.

Finally, competitive design events are a popular phenomenon in schools. The competitions most closely aligned with ITEA are run by the Technology Student Association (TSA; www.tsawww.org). Other well-known competitions include Lego League, a competition for elementary and middle school students created with Lego toys by For Inspiration and Recognition of Science and Technology (FIRST; www.usfirst.org/jrobtcs/flego.htm); ThinkQuest, a competition sponsored by the Oracle Education Foundation where students of all ages create educational Web sites (www.thinkquest.org); and Toshiba Exploravision, a contest administered by the National Science Teachers Association (NSTA) where students at any grade level may design technologies for the future (www.exploravision.org).

A WORD TO TECHNOLOGY EDUCATORS ■

This book is intended to help the technology education community accelerate its metamorphosis from its historical roots in industrial arts into classrooms that empower students to achieve the full technological literacy that STL describes and society needs.

By focusing on the elementary and middle grades, this book promotes the inclusion of technology education from the start of schooling. Having more students experience technology at early school levels will enable the more prevalent high school technology courses to teach prepared students, ones who can achieve the full literacy advocated for our high school graduates.

The book can also help those educators who have been teaching traditional technology to take the next steps. Setting aside whether it's good or bad, the fact is that policymakers are increasingly pressuring schools to make industrial arts and vocational courses "more academic." In response, instructors of those courses have been able to validate their "technology" courses by pointing to the existence of national standards for technology education. It is a challenge for any teacher, however, to make substantial, effective changes in the scope and style of his or her instruction without help from some appropriate curricular resources.

That time has come. All of the technology textbooks and most of the other kinds of resources reviewed in this book, many of them created since the release of the STL, address the standards. The products vary in the extent to which they address different standards, but the reviews spell out those contrasts to help readers make informed choices.

■ COLLABORATION BETWEEN SCIENCE AND TECHNOLOGY EDUCATORS

There are not enough bona fide technology teachers to help all of today's students be technologically literate by the time they graduate. Teachers who taught traditional technology but are broadening their knowledge and skills to encompass the STL are a significant source of technology teachers. And some of these teachers are less inclined than others toward these changes. As a result, some current "technology" courses are not necessarily realizing the potential of the STL.

Science teachers could help bridge the gap between demand and supply to the extent that they become familiar with technology education and are willing to infuse some of it into their science courses. However, in doing so, we encourage science teachers to actively consult and collaborate with technology teachers in their schools or districts. These colleagues will have invaluable information and expertise in technology education that will complement the knowledge of science teachers.

We also strongly encourage science educators to take advantage of some of the professional development that is available. It would be very challenging to use some of the reviewed technology education curricula without help. The Materials section of each review gives cues about classroom resources needed, and the Special Preparation section indicates whether teachers would need to plan on making extra preparation, including learning more themselves beyond what is needed when first using any new product. The Special Preparation section also mentions any availability of professional development by the product's authors.

National sources of professional development are also available. Both the CATTS Consortium and the Technology for All Americans projects of the ITEA have staff around the country that regularly provide workshops and the like. Teachers should also consider attending the advance workshops and regular sessions of an annual ITEA conference, both for professional development and as an opportunity to forge collaboration with technology teachers.

Once science teachers better understand technology education, they will be pleased to discover that it strongly engages all students. Almost everyone can be intrigued to find a technological solution to a real human problem of interest to them. Science educators and their students already like the hands-on aspect of science, and they will like hands-on technology as a complementary way of looking at the world. While science investigates why phenomena happen in the natural world, technology finds solutions to the problems and needs that people face.

What considerations should technology educators make regarding the collaboration we urge with teachers of science or of other subjects? First, such collaboration will not lead to supplanting technology teachers. Even if large numbers of science teachers become involved in technology education, there still will be a need for technology teachers. Because science teachers still have to teach science, they cannot make time to cover the full scope of technology education, nor are they fully equipped to do so, in terms of both knowledge and classroom resources. The best way to scale-up contemporary technology education in order to reach all students is for still more technology teachers to transform traditional courses into ones that promote the technological literacy of the STL.

We hope that technology teachers will welcome collaboration with science and other teachers. After all, STL Standard 3 calls for making explicit connections between technology and other subjects. For example, health teachers can collaborate with technology teachers on medical technologies (Standard 14), and agriculture teachers can help with Standard 15 (agricultural and related biotechnologies). Finally, there are STL standards where technology teachers could benefit from the aid of science teachers. For example, the science teacher is typically better trained in research experimentation, called for by Standard 13, and at incorporating it into the fair testing or evaluation of products as part of the technology design cycle.

We recognize that cross-subject collaboration is outside the typical experience of U.S. educators: A science teacher or technology teacher is lucky to have moments to speak with other science or technology teachers, let alone with teachers of other subjects. However, in these times of tight resources and policy emphasis on reading and mathematical literacy, science and technology could benefit from such an alliance to bolster attention to their subjects. And, more importantly, students and communities will be shortchanged if teachers of different subjects fail to collaborate in developing technologically literate citizens.

4

How to Understand and Use the Curriculum Reviews

This chapter answers some basic questions about the book: What resources do we review? How did we find and choose them? How did we analyze them? How do we describe them?

WHAT MATERIALS ARE REVIEWED? ■

This book describes, analyzes, and illustrates curricular resources that are available in hard copy. In Chapter 1, we elaborated our rationale for focusing on such resources rather than Web-based curricula and other forms of curricular resources. In brief, we want to empower educators to make informed choices among resources by providing thorough descriptions and critiques of resources. Because such reviews require more room than do brief descriptions, we felt an obligation to devote the limited space available in one book to the class of resources that are most prevalent, accessible to all, and influential in the classroom—print resources. Here are some specifics:

- All of the reviewed products promote technology education and support the broad, contemporary STL definition of technological literacy.
- None of the resources mostly or solely focus on computer, educational, or any other specific technology.
- Many resources do, however, include attention to computer and educational technology, just as the STL includes principles of those technology topics.
- All resources are designed for elementary or middle grades, or both.
- All products are recent and readily available in the United States.

Recent, Readily Available Print Materials

The print-based curricular resources discussed in the following chapters are recent and accessible:

- Most are U.S. products copyrighted 2000–2004, although a few were printed before the STL.
- They are readily available to individual teachers.

We considered reviewing some technology curricula from the countries mentioned earlier in which technology education is a required course. Unfortunately, they presented challenges for U.S. educators. Many of the foreign publishers do not distribute the products to the United States, and many lessons include elements particular to the source country's communities or classrooms. U.S. teachers would have to make significant adaptations before using such curricula.

Most of the products we describe for K–8 technology education have come to market since the release of the International Technology Education Association's (ITEA's) *Standards for Technological Literacy;* however, some preceded the STL. Since 2000, we continually searched for relevant products being published and analyzed them as they became available. We searched for products in several ways, especially consulting with our advisory board, program officers at the National Science Foundation (NSF), and leaders in ITEA and the National Science Teachers Association (NSTA); scouring the exhibit halls and presentations at those organizations' annual conferences; and scanning their periodicals and Web sites. We also include some pre-STL products that still are useful for promoting technological literacy, especially if the authors of these products have not yet produced an updated or alternative version.

Because every book is a snapshot in time, some technology resources could not be included here. Some NSF-funded developers or commercial publishers are creating products that are not yet ready. It was tempting to review the trial versions of these. However, final versions can be structurally different, having been revised on a basis of feedback gained from the trials. Still other products are now available, but were not released by late 2003 when we had to discontinue our analysis and turn to writing this book. At the beginnings of Chapters 8–10, we mention some of these products in a section titled Late-Breaking Products.

Finally, we describe products of varying cost, but all are readily available. By readily available, we mean the distributor is well prepared to send the materials. As already noted, this criterion caused us to forgo reviewing foreign products. It also made us exclude products that are difficult to obtain, for example, ones that are no longer actively marketed by the publisher in its catalogs or Web site and instead are sold only on demand. As for cost, a few products are free, whereas others require from tens to hundreds or even thousands of dollars. Each review includes a list of costs for the product's components.

Four Categories of Technology Curricula

Table 4.1 identifies the specific products reviewed for the three categories of materials that are created expressly for teachers to use with their students: Core Technology Products, Cross-Curricular Products, and Supplemental Resources. Within each category, newer products are provided before older ones. If more than one product is published the same year, reviews are ordered alphabetically by the last name of the lead author. The following brief discussion describes and contrasts these categories of materials, plus a fourth category, Informal and Other Resources.

Core Technology Products

Chapter 8 provides comprehensive reviews of five technology textbooks for the middle grades. Between four and six sample pages are included from each product.

These curriculum materials are intended for use in the classroom or in a formal educational setting. They include a teacher instructional component of some sort, in addition to the student materials and information. Core materials can be used as a technology curriculum for a substantial period of the school year (e.g., a semester, a nine-week wheel, the entire year). They are also comprehensive in their standards coverage. That is, they address a significant amount of the content found in the STL (they must have breadth of coverage, not just depth) and are intended to promote technological literacy for a certain grade level(s).

Cross-Curricular Products

Chapter 9 provides extensive reviews of seven products that integrate technology with other subjects: four are for the elementary grades and three are for the middle grades. Between two and four sample pages are reproduced from each product.

Like Core Technology products, these curriculum materials also are intended for classroom use, but they address technology *and* some other subject area(s). Most often, technology receives a treatment in these products that is comparable or less than the treatment given to the other subjects. Some cross-curricular materials present multiple content areas in such a way that they "get at" one area through focusing first on one of the other disciplines (e.g., students learn technology content during the course of science inquiry activities, social studies investigations, mathematical problem solving). Some others of these integrated products blend the subjects so seamlessly or holistically that they do not explicitly indicate when various subjects are being taught. A few cross-curricular products cover much of the STL. Most of these products differ from

Table 4.1   List of curriculum materials reviewed

CORE TECHNOLOGY PRODUCTS (CHAPTER 8)			
Author	*Title*	*Publisher/Distributor*	*Publication date*
John B. Gradwell, Malcolm Welch, and Eugene Martin	Technology: Shaping Our World	Goodheart-Willcox	2004
Michael Hacker and David Burghardt	Technology Education: Learning by Design	Pearson Prentice Hall	2004
R. Thomas Wright and Ryan A. Brown	Technology: Design and Applications	Goodheart-Willcox	2004
Henry R. Harms and Neal R. Swernofsky	Technology Interactions	Glencoe/McGraw-Hill	2003
Brad and Terry Thode	Technology in Action	Glencoe/McGraw-Hill	2002

CROSS-CURRICULAR PRODUCTS—ELEMENTARY (CHAPTER 9)			
Author	*Title*	*Publisher/Distributor*	*Publication date*
Pat Hutchinson et al.	Children Designing and Engineering	Design and Technology Press	2004
Gary Benenson and James Neujahr	Stuff That Works! A Technology Curriculum for the Elementary Grades	Heinemann	2002
Education Development Center, Inc.	A World in Motion: The Design Experience, Challenge 1	Society of Automotive Engineers (SAE) Foundation	2000
Rodger Bybee, Nancy Landes, Harold Pratt, et al.	BSCS Science Teaching Relevant Activities for Concepts and Skills (T.R.A.C.S.)	Kendall/Hunt	1999

CROSS-CURRICULAR PRODUCTS—MIDDLE SCHOOL (CHAPTER 9)			
Author	*Title*	*Publisher/Distributor*	*Publication date*
Franzie Loepp, Richard Satchwell, et al.	Integrated Mathematics, Science, and Technology (IMaST)	RonJon Publishing, Inc.	2002–2004
Rodger Bybee, Janet Carlson Powell, Pamela Van Scotter, et al.	BSCS Middle School Science and Technology, 2/E	Kendall/Hunt	1999
Education Development Center, Inc.	A World in Motion: The Design Experience, Challenges 2 and 3	Society of Automotive Engineers (SAE) Foundation	1998 & 1996

SUPPLEMENTAL PRODUCTS—ELEMENTARY (CHAPTER 10)			
Author	*Title*	*Publisher/Distributor*	*Publication date*
ITEA	Kids Inventing Technology Series (KITS)	ITEA	2001–2003
ITEA	Technology Starters: A Standards-Based Guide	ITEA	2002
Larry Hannah, Ed.	National Educational Technology Standards for Students: Multi-disciplinary Units for Grades 3–5	ISTE	2002
Technology Student Association	The Great Technology Adventure: Technology Learning Activities Guide	Scarecrow Education	2001
Kim Weaver	Balancing the World of Technology in the Elementary Classroom	Kim Weaver	1996–1997
Toronto School Board Teachers	All Aboard! Cross-Curricular Design and Technology Strategies and Activities. Springboards for Teaching Series	Trifolium Books	1996
Helen Clayfield and Robin Hyatt	Designing Everyday Things: Integrated Projects for the Elementary Classroom	Heinemann	1994

SUPPLEMENTAL PRODUCTS—MIDDLE SCHOOL (CHAPTER 10)			
Author	*Title*	*Publisher/Distributor*	*Publication date*
ITEA	Humans Innovating Technology Series (HITS)	ITEA	2001–2003
ITEA	Exploring Technology: A Standards-Based Middle School Model Course Guide	ITEA	2001
ITEA	Teaching Technology: Middle School Strategies for Standards-Based Instruction	ITEA	2000
Lucy Miller	KidTech: Hands On Problem Solving with Design Technology for Grades 5–8	Dale Seymour Publications	1998
Metropolitan Toronto School Board Teachers	By Design: Technology Exploration and Integration	Trifolium Books	1996
National Science and Technology Week	Design Connections Through Science and Technology: National Science and Technology Week 1996	National Science Foundation	1996

the Core Technology products in that they are not intended to provide the same comprehensive, in-depth coverage of the STL.

While all five Core Technology Products are textbooks, the product structures or components of the Cross-Curricular Products vary. The product components range from an elementary series having one volume per grade level over K–5 (*T.R.A.C.S.*), or a set of modules, each of which can span several elementary grades (*Children Designing and Engineering, Stuff That Works!*), to a single large module that contains long-term projects (*A World in Motion*). Because these curricula integrate at least three subjects, technology is not their sole or even primary focus. The three reviewed products for the middle grades also have quite different structures.

Supplemental Products

Chapter 10 provides brief descriptions of thirteen supplemental products. Unfortunately, space considerations preclude us from including sample pages. These materials often are intended for the formal educational setting; however, they do not necessarily include a teacher component or package. Supplemental materials are often a collection of activities, design challenges, projects, and so on that give students practice and experience with only a limited range of technology content, covering only a few standards, and not necessarily in depth.

Informal and Other Resources

Chapter 11 gives annotated descriptions of more than 100 publications and other resources that can be used to augment classroom instruction. No sample pages are included.

These include reference books, how-to books, activity books, and so on that may be useful in the classroom, but were not necessarily written to be formal classroom materials. For example, they do not necessarily specify a target grade, include information about how to use them in a classroom, or include instructional support materials. Examples of trade books include *The Way Things Work, The Incredible Invention Book, Why Zippers Have Teeth*, and *How Things Work*. In addition to these kinds of books, this chapter notes some journals, magazines, and Web sites.

A Word About Modular Curricula

"Modular" systems are a popular means of delivering technology education courses. They are "learning systems," "labs," and the like, designed for a course, an entire year, or several years. Developers provide a physical environment that supports the instruction (even furniture). Modulars include in-depth curricula (usually delivered in multiweek units) that promote teamwork and collaboration. The learning units are often integrated across several subject areas. These self-contained systems provide everything required to teach and learn the curriculum. Some of them also have turnkey designs, where all major instructional decisions are laid out for the instructor. The flip side is that often little room remains for tailoring instruction within such modules.

We were not able to obtain or review this expensive category of curricular resources. A modular system from just one company offers the option of

Table 4.2   Vendors for modular curricula

1. AMATROL Integrated Learning Modules, 714-978-9452

2. Applied Educational Systems (AES), www.aeseducation.com/tc21group.htm

3. Chec Systems, Inc., 800-283-2432, www.checsystems.com

4. Crystal Creations, 800-575-5321, www.crystalmodules.com

5. Depco, 800-767-1062, www.depcoinc.com/

6. Hearlihy Modules, 866-622-1003, www.hearlihy.com

7. Intelos Technology, 800-825-9343

8. Lab-Volt Systems, 800-LAB-VOLT, www.labvolt.com/index.asp

9. Paxton Labs, 800-323-8484, www.paxtonpatterson.com/

10. PTC 3-D Design, 781-370-5000, www.ptc.com/for/education/index.htm

11. Spectrum Systems and Synergistic Systems (division of Pitsco), Introduction to Technology Module for 5th–8th grades, 800-828-5787, www.synergistic systems.com

12. Tech-Design (Tech-Core, Tech-Design) by Lab-Volt, 800-877-6720, www.oliver labs.com

13. T.R.A.C.S., Project-Based Learning Systems, 800-334-4943, www.applied technologies.com

14. Unilab Systems for Technology Education, 800-391-3695

purchasing as many as thirty or more units, each unit requiring hundreds or thousands of dollars. About a dozen companies listed in Table 4.2 currently sell such modular systems, although several vendors' systems offer more limited numbers of modules. Most modular systems target high school, but some specifically address the middle grades, and a few address the elementary grades.

We did conduct a brief inspection of each of the modular systems for sale in the exhibit hall at the ITEA and Association for Career and Technical Education (ACTE) conferences. The systems differ considerably in many ways, including cost, range and number of modules available, curricular design, training available, vendor service for replacing stock or making repairs, and more.

We paid special attention to their alignment with the STL. Given that these products constitute the entirety of one or more technology courses, it seems very important that they adequately address the technology standards. We asked the vendors how their products could be used to help students meet the technology standards. The answers they provided in 2002, two years after the release of the STL, gave us pause.

- One company had such information in a database. Prospective purchasers could search for modules by any configuration of standards.
- A couple of companies had documents showing how the products aligned in specific ways with the standards. Their analyses permitted someone interested in particular standards to determine which modules or module sets would best correspond to them.

- Four companies could indicate the standards addressed by their modules. They had tables to indicate which of the twenty standards were addressed by each of their modules. However, one could not readily proceed in reverse, specifying a standard and finding out which modules best teach it.
- Three companies claimed their products were standards-based. However, they did not have documentation to illustrate any analyses.
- Three companies had no idea. They were familiar with the STL, but had not done any analyses to determine their alignment with it.

Given the cost of modular systems, plus the fact that teachers rely on them for entire courses and course sequences, it is important to know the extent to which a modular product can promote technological literacy. When we did the same exploration at more recent conferences, the situation improved somewhat. However, only a few companies had invested in a third-party analysis of their products' alignment with the STL.

Further, none of the vendors' self-analyses had progressed to examining their products' alignment with the STL at the more detailed *benchmark level* versus the broader standards level. The STL document stipulates that addressing the standards level of the STL is just a beginning. A curriculum is not standards-based unless it addresses the more specific benchmarks of the STL.

None of this is to say that modular systems cannot be useful for achieving technological literacy. Some modules of some vendors undoubtedly competently address some STL standards and benchmarks. Perhaps some of these "somes" should actually be "many." One cannot know, however, based on current information.

The Idea Garden, discussed in Chapter 3, is a good source of information about features of modular products, other than their standards alignment. However, this list-serve is only open to ITEA members. Following is an illustrative recent exchange. Participants have many similar discussions about curricular resources other than modular systems:

I would like to hear some opinions about the W system. Is it user friendly? Does it keep the students' attention? Is there a lot of software and equipment to keep track of? Is it adaptable? Is it durable? Our current system has given us problems over the years. We have worked with the vendor and they worked with us, but some of our teachers have a bad taste in the relationship and want something different. I noticed a few weeks ago that W was getting good reviews from the list-serve, and I would like to hear the opinion of some of the teachers who are using these modules. [questions from a technology teacher]

I have twelve modules of W and have been to a training. I had a combination of systems from W, X, and Y when I first got to my school. The past three years I have upgraded everything to W. These guys are my top pick for service, variety, and equipment. I do teach without the modules, but the majority of the semester is spent on them. The W management software leaves others years behind, and I can edit any part of the module I want. I've even used the shell software to write my own module for some equipment I had lying around. [response from another technology teacher]

HOW ARE MATERIALS REVIEWED?   ■

We examined some categories of products more deeply than others, as shown in the following table. Core technology products received the most extensive treatment. We used similar methods for examining the cross-curricular products:

Product Type	Depth of Analysis	Analysis Time
5 Core technology products	every page, every word	4–6 weeks each
8 Cross-curricular products	every page, every word	1–2 weeks each
18 Supplemental products	many pages, skim read	1–3 days each
100+ Informal resources	flip pages, inspect	1–2 hours each

Table 4.3 shows the features of the curricular resources that we inspected. These features and the methods used to examine them are discussed in the sections that follow.

Table 4.3   Annotated outline of reviews

Developer/Author	Name of developer and/or author
Distributor/Publisher	Name of distributor/publisher
Publication date	Year of publications
Funders	(Cross-curricular only) Name of funder
Ordering information	Name phone number, Website
Target audience	Elementary or middle school (or grades)

BRIEF DESCRIPTION

Brief synopsis of product, plus introduction to particular strengths or weaknesses

CURRICULUM COMPONENTS

Components for sale, number of pages, cost, etc.

Materials/Equipment

Types of materials, equipment and facilities needed to implement the product

Special preparations

Any extra teacher preparation required beyond routine product familiarization; availability of professional development

CURRICULUM OVERVIEW

Topic Overview (for Cross-Curricular, limited to technology topics)

(Continued)

Table 4.3 (Continued)

Integration review (Cross-Curricular Products only)

Blended versus segmented integration; subjects included

Instructional model

Any formal model used as basis for student learning experiences; articulation of activities with related text; description of the elements of the product; readability of text; uses and quality of graphics and photographs

Duration

The estimated time span for individual activities and/or for the entire program

Activities (Core, all activities; Cross-Curricular, only technology activities)

Description, purpose, and count of activities; types (structure) of activities; types of design approaches used

Assessment

Types of assessments recommended and assessment instruments or tools included

---

STL STANDARDS AND BENCHMARK-LEVEL ANALYSES (CORE)

Standards coverage in the overall curriculum

Five most and least frequent standards, in the overall curriculum

Standards Coverage in the Text; Standards Coverage in the Activities

Analyses of STL coverage in the text; separate analysis of coverage in activities; analyses at both standards and benchmarks levels of the STL

STL STANDARDS-LEVEL ANALYSES (CROSS-CURRICULAR)

Analyses of STL coverage in the overall curriculum, at standards level of the STL

TEACHER MATERIALS REVIEW

Support for teaching the curriculum, pedagogy, student assessment, teaching technology standards, and teaching 21st-century knowledge and skills
(See Table 7.1 for details). Core Technology products—separate sections for each of five types of support; Cross-Curricular products—single section briefly discusses all five.

TABLE OF CONTENTS

Table of contents reproduced, with added count of pages that are devoted to each portion of product

SAMPLE PAGES

Core Technology products, 4–6 pages reproduced from product
Cross-Curricular products, 1–2 pages reproduced from product

We performed two formal analyses. First, we include a very detailed analysis of how well technology education curricula are aligned with ITEA's standards. It is the only such extensive analysis to be done independently of product developers, ITEA, or other groups with a stake in the results. Second, we thoroughly analyzed the nature of the student activities found in the products.

In addition to these formal analyses, we systematically, qualitatively reviewed many other product features. In particular, we examined how the curricula incorporate opportunities for student assessment and what kinds of support the teacher materials provide.

In Table 4.3, under Curriculum Components, we give information about durable and consumable materials required (Materials/Equipment) and any special training or other preparation that teachers would need to undertake before first use of the product (Special preparations). Under Curriculum Overview, we give information about the instructional model upon which the product is based, the instructional features of the product and how they are organized, and the instructional time suggested by the publisher (Duration).

We created review procedures by drawing upon our experiences in such endeavors as analyzing and/or evaluating curricular resources, developing curricula, and providing professional development to teachers on the selection and use of materials (Britton et al., 1999; Britton & Raizen, 1996; McKnight & Britton, 1992). We also learned from similar projects at other leading organizations in mathematics, science, and technology education (e.g., AAAS, 2000; Goldsmith, Mark, & Kantrov, 2000; Morse and the AIBS Review Team, 2001; Muther, 1999).

Details of how we analyzed each of the review elements are provided, sparingly, in the corresponding chapters of Part II, where we discuss patterns among the resources for various elements. In Chapter 5, in discussing the ways in which products did and did not align with the STL, we briefly explain how that exhaustive analysis was done. Similarly, Chapter 6 includes an explanation of how we analyzed the products' student activities. Chapter 7 discusses how we reviewed the products' tools and strategies for assessing students' understanding and the amount and kinds of teacher support materials provided. Appendix B provides a few further details about the analysis methods used in this book.

5

Content

Standards-Based or Standards-Referenced

What topics are found in the products reviewed in this book? Some insights can be gleaned from the reviews in Chapters 8 and 9, which give an overview of the products' topics and reproduce the tables of contents from the products. But will the products' treatments of these topics promote students' technological literacy? Because most educators care a great deal about these questions when choosing curriculum materials, this chapter is dedicated to giving in-depth answers, and our answers are far from casual. See the section "How Are Materials Reviewed?" in Chapter 4 to learn how we inspected every line on every page of the products.

As this chapter proceeds, we delve into the products' topics in progressively more detail by using the levels of organization in the *Standards for Technological Literacy* (STL): themes, standards, and benchmarks. For an introduction to the STL's organization, see Chapter 2.

First, we give an overview of the topics by using the five general STL themes. Then, topics are mapped against the STL's twenty standards. These themes and standards are discussed for both the core technology products of Chapter 8 (five textbooks for technology at the middle grades) and cross-curricular products of Chapter 9 (seven textbooks, sets of monographs, or other large products for the elementary or middle grades).

Finally, for the core technology products of Chapter 8, we further examine their treatment of topics, because these are primarily technology textbooks and can serve as the basis for a year or more of technology courses. We check these products for alignment with the many benchmarks found within each of the twenty STL standards.

This most detailed kind of comparison relates to this chapter's organizing question: What do we mean by "standards-based" versus "standards-referenced" content? We explain this distinction, which is a crucial one, because product developers and educators at large often inappropriately use the term "standards-based." For example, it is common to hear that a product's treatment of topics is standards-based even though the treatment is only related superficially to the STL.

The chapter concludes with a discussion of how the different kinds of products (core technology and cross-curricular) might be useful to different teachers (elementary teachers and teachers of technology or science at the middle grades).

■ ADDRESSING MOST THEMES

Both the core technology and cross-curricular products have substantial material related to the first four of the five STL themes:

Theme 1: Nature of Technology

Theme 2: Technology and Society

Theme 3: Design

Theme 4: Abilities for a Technological World

In addition, all of the core technology products extensively cover Theme 5: the designed world. However, only one cross-curricular product includes a substantial treatment of it.

Most supplemental products (Chapter 10) are useful primarily for engaging students in technology activities. The activities of some of the supplemental resources can help develop technological abilities and promote literacy in Themes 3 and 4. There are also some supplemental resources, particularly those produced by the International Technology Education Association (ITEA) since the STL were published, that promote literacy in the nondesign themes as well (Themes 1, 2, and 5). The rest of this chapter focuses on the core technology and cross-curricular products.

Core Technology Products

While every one of the five textbooks we reviewed addresses all five themes of the STL, these products do not necessarily give them equivalent emphasis as recommended by the STL (Britton, DeLong-Cotty, & Levenson, 2004). All the textbooks should give more attention to the standards of Theme 2: the effects of technology on society (Standard 4), the effects of technology on the environment (Standard 5), the influence of society on technology development (Standard 6), and the influence of technology on history (Standard 7).

Using Table 5.1, notice the following characteristics of the *text* portion of the products:

- The text of the books dominantly or substantially covers the nature of technology and the designed world (Themes 1 and 5).
- *Technology: Design and Applications* stands out for the instruction its text provides on knowledge of design (Theme 3).

Table 5.1   Master data table for five core technology products

Resource & publication date	Percent of middle school benchmarks treated	Percent of STL content that is standards-based	Text — *Amount of codeable, STL content in text devoted to each STL theme*					Activities — *Amount of codeable, STL content in activities devoted to each STL theme*				
			T-1	T-2	T-3	T-4	T-5	T-1	T-2	T-3	T-4	T-5
Technology: Shaping Our World 2004	82%	81%	◆◆◆◆	◆◆◆	◆◆◆	◆◆	◆◆◆◆	◆◆	◆	◆	◆◆◆◆	◆◆
Technology Education: Learning by Design 2004	86%	79%	◆◆◆	◆◆◆	◆	◆	◆◆◆◆	◆◆	◆	◆◆◆	◆◆◆◆	◆
Technology: Design & Application 2004	98%	81%	◆◆	◆◆◆	◆◆◆◆	◆◆◆	◆◆◆◆	◆	◆	◆◆	◆◆◆◆	◆◆
Technology Interactions 2E 2003	80%	61%	◆◆◆◆	◆◆◆	◆	◆◆	◆◆◆◆	◆	◆	◆◆	◆◆◆◆	◆
Technology in Action 2002	76%	53%	◆◆◆	◆◆◆	◆	◆	◆◆◆◆	◆	◆	◆	◆◆◆◆	◆◆

◆◆◆◆   Dominant amount

◆◆◆   Substantial amount

◆◆   Moderate/Some amount

◆   Marginal amount or missing

As for the books' activities, notice the following particulars in Table 5.1.

- Every book's activities emphasize its first purpose, helping students develop technological abilities (Theme 4).
- While students conduct activities in *Technology Education: Learning by Design,* or to a lesser extent the activities in *Technology Interactions,* they also will gain substantial or moderate formal knowledge about design (Theme 3).
- While students conduct activities in *Technology: Shaping Our World* or *Technology Education: Learning by Design,* they also will gain some knowledge about the nature of technology (Theme 1).

Although the obvious purpose of activities is to develop students' technological abilities, such as design and problem-solving processes (Theme 4), are the activities also designed to do double duty? That is, while doing activities, will students learn some other things? A parallel discussion has been going on in science education for decades. Advocates of learning scientific process emphasize activities that require students to predict, observe, hypothesize, and so on. However, if such activities focus only on developing these process skills, critics contend that the activities are "content free."

Cross-Curricular Products

Using any of these products, students will become acquainted with the nature of technology, gain some knowledge of design, and engage in technology activities (Themes 1, 3, and 4; see Table 5.2). With most products, students will not learn enough about the designed world or technology and society (Themes 2 and 5). Following are some additional details:

- Most products give substantial attention to the nature of technology (Theme 1), with *BSCS Science and Technology* placing a dominant emphasis on it.
- Only three products give moderate attention to technology and society (Theme 2).
- All the products give at least moderate attention to design (Theme 3). *A World in Motion* gives the deepest understanding of design in both grade ranges.
- Every product except one places a dominant emphasis on technological abilities (Theme 4).
- Only *IMaST* provides substantial emphasis on the designed world (Theme 5).

■ UNEVEN STANDARDS-LEVEL COVERAGE

We previously noted the STL themes that the products address, but do the products thoroughly cover these themes? A theme is covered when *all* of the standards within it are included. The STL document "is meant to be used in its *entirety. All* standards should be met for a student to obtain the optimal level of technological literacy" (emphasis added; ITEA, 2000, p. 18).

Table 5.2   Theme-level coverage in cross-curricular products

	Theme 1: *Nature of Technology*	Theme 2: *Technology & Society*	Theme 3: *Design*	Theme 4: *Abilities for the Technological World*	Theme 5: *The Designed World*
Elementary					
T.R.A.C.S.	◆◆◆	◆◆	◆◆◆	◆◆◆◆	◆
AWIM, Challenge 1	◆◆◆	◆	◆◆◆◆	◆◆◆◆	◆
Stuff That Works!	◆◆◆	◆	◆◆	◆◆◆◆	◆◆
Children D&E	◆◆	◆	◆◆◆	◆◆◆◆	◆◆
Middle School					
AWIM, Challenges 2 & 3	◆◆	◆	◆◆◆	◆◆◆◆	◆◆
BSCS Science Technology	◆◆◆◆	◆◆	◆◆	◆◆	◆◆
IMaST	◆◆	◆◆◆	◆◆	◆◆◆	◆◆◆

◆◆◆◆   Dominant amount

◆◆◆   Substantial amount

◆◆   Moderate/Some amount

◆   Marginal amount or missing

In Chapters 8 and 9, the individual reviews of products discuss their specific coverage of the twenty standards. In this chapter, we discuss patterns among the products' standards coverage.

Core Technology Products

Table 5.3 shows that the technology textbooks address a good range of standards, but some standards are particularly emphasized, and some weaknesses need to be pointed out.

• Within the lightly addressed Theme 2 (Standards 4–7), three books have especially weak treatments of Standards 6 and 7, understanding the role of society in the development and use of technology and the influence of technology on history, respectively. The other two books weakly treat Standard 5, effects of technology on the environment.

• Within Theme 3 (design), only *Technology: Design and Applications* and *Technology Interactions* emphasize Standard 9, knowledge about engineering design. Only *Technology Education: Learning by Design* emphasizes understanding the attributes of design (Standard 8). No products emphasize understanding Standard 10, the role of troubleshooting, research and development, invention and innovation, and experimentation in problem solving.

• Within Theme 4 (technological abilities), the textbooks' very strong emphases on Standards 11 and 12 overshadow attention to Standard 13, abilities to assess the impact of products and systems.

• Within the designed world (Theme 5), four of the five books place some of their greatest emphasis on information and communication technologies (Standard 17). *Technology: Shaping Our World* especially emphasizes Standards 16 and 19, energy and power technologies and manufacturing technologies, respectively.

• Only *Technology Interactions* and *Technology Education: Learning by Design* give moderate attention to biotechnologies (Standard 15). All five books pay small attention to agricultural and related biotechnologies (Standard 14).

The last finding is a bit disheartening. Medical and biological technologies are rapidly growing fields, and ones that increasingly impact our daily lives. Science education is grappling with the science of these fields but is hard-pressed to teach the technological aspects as well. The incorporation of these technologies into the STL is an attempt to broaden the traditional domain of technology education to embrace emerging issues.

Within the Nature of Technology (Theme 1), most books emphasized Standards 2 or 3 over Standard 1. However, this seeming imbalance makes sense to us. Because Standard 1 is an overview of the characteristics of technology, it does not require as much treatment as the core concepts of technology (Standard 2), or the relationships among technologies, and connections between technology and other fields of study (Standard 3).

Table 5.3   Standards-level coverage in core technology products

Standard	Technology: Shaping Our World (2004)	Technology Education: Learning by Design (2004)	Technology: Design & Application (2004)	Technology Interactions 2E (2003)	Technology Action (2002)
		Strongest 5 and weakest 5 standards			
1		○	○	○	○
2	●	●	●		●
3			○	●	●
4					
5		○	○		
6	○	○		○	○
7	○			○	○
8		●			
9		○	●	●	
10	○				
11	●	●	●	●	●
12	●	●	●	●	●
13					
14	○	○	○	○	○
15	○		○		○
16	●				
17		●	●	●	●
18				○	
19	●				
20					

Top 5: ●
Bottom 5: ○

Between approximately 10 to 20 percent of each textbook is not specifically related to the STL.

- The textbooks contain technology topics that are not expressly raised in STL, such as space science or detailed explanations of simple machines such as levers.
- Most textbooks devote considerable space to technology careers.
- Several textbooks also include detailed, discrete technological knowledge, such as understanding different kinds of gears, or very specific skills (versus broader technological abilities) such as working with different materials (e.g., woodworking or metalworking or drawing architectural plans).

We do not suggest that non-STL content is inappropriate; in fact, such content often is quite valuable. However, because these already large products are not addressing some standards, we urge that developers' inclusion of non-STL material be intentional rather than an inadvertent use of precious space.

Cross-Curricular Products

While Chapter 9 reviews give details of these products' standards coverage, here are a few noteworthy patterns:

- Within Theme 1 (nature of technology), the cross-curricular products strongly emphasize Standard 3, connecting technology to other subjects.
- Within Theme 2 (technology and society), *no* products significantly discuss the influence of technology on history (Standard 7).
- Within Theme 4 (abilities for technological design), the two *BSCS* products and two *A World in Motion* products give significant treatments of Standard 13, which includes using scientific research and experimentation in the design process.
- Among the few products that significantly address Theme 5 (the designed world), the most commonly emphasized standard is Standard 17, information and communication technologies.

■ STANDARDS-BASED OR STANDARDS-REFERENCED?

So far we have looked at whether the textbooks cover the STL themes by addressing a range of their standards. Now, getting even more specific, how well do the books address the range of the 101 benchmarks for the middle grades, or the 86 for the elementary years? The core technology products received this deepest level of analysis.

As first introduced in the Chapter 2 overview of the STL, there are vital distinctions in answering whether the products' treatments of a topic are consistent with the benchmarks of the STL.

For example, STL Standard 2 is about core concepts of technology. If a product includes a discussion about some core concept of technology, is that a match? Product developers typically will say that this situation is indeed a match and that their products are standards-based. Such claims are overstatements. We use the term "standards-referenced" for such superficial matches.

Standard 2 more specifically calls for particular concepts and knowledge, not just whatever a product wishes to discuss as core concepts. Standard 2 and every one of the twenty STL standards include multiple, explicit benchmark statements of the knowledge or abilities required for students to be technologically literate.

If a product's topic is only vaguely related to a benchmark, we again use the term "standards-referenced" to describe such limited matches. But when a product's discussion clearly elaborates upon the concepts described in a benchmark, we use the term "standards-based" to describe such explicit matches with the STL. (In other words, we only call something "standards-based" if it is actually benchmark-based.)

Our previously discussed schema for distinguishing standards-based from standards-referenced stems from the STL's own charge to the field, which we first provided in Chapter 1 but repeat now for emphasis: "*Benchmarks* . . . provide the *fundamental* content elements for the broadly stated Standards; The Benchmarks are *required* for students to meet the Standards" (emphasis added; ITEA, 2000, pp. 14–15).

Previously, Chapter 2 used Standard 3 and one of its benchmarks to illustrate the difference between standards-referenced and standards-based. Table 5.4 further illustrates the two situations using benchmarks from Standards 2, 5, 7, and 18.

Table 5.5 indicates that at least half of every book is standards-based. In three books, an impressive 80 percent of the STL-related portions of the textbook address at least one of a standard's benchmarks. (As noted earlier, 10 to 20 percent of each book is devoted to material that is not directly related to the STL, such as career information.) We were somewhat generous: Although many benchmarks include multiple concepts, we counted a benchmark as met even if only one concept of such a compound benchmark is addressed.

All core technology textbooks address at least three-quarters of the middle-grades benchmarks, if both standards-referenced and standards-based treatments are counted. *Technology: Design and Applications* (Wright & Brown) addresses 98 percent of them. On the other hand, a textbook may fail to address up to one-fourth of the STL benchmarks.

In these middle-grades products, we found a considerable amount of material that is more relevant to elementary or high school benchmarks. There are rationales for both situations, for example: Middle school texts might incorporate some elementary-level benchmarks because technology education is more absent than present in elementary classrooms at this point in time; select high school material could be useful for advanced middle-grades students. Further, a well-designed K–12 curriculum includes intentional spiraling, progressive treatments of similar topics over the school years. However, we encourage developers to look carefully at these already extensive products to be sure instances of going outside of the products' grade ranges are intentional rather than inadvertent divergence from the STL.

See the individual reviews in Chapter 8 and Appendix A for these and additional details of how the core technology products addressed the STL benchmarks. Each review in Chapter 8 identifies, for each of the twenty standards, which benchmark(s) are most addressed. Appendix A goes further: For each of the twenty standards and in each product, this appendix reports the percentage of concepts that are treated in a standards-based manner.

USES OF CORE TECHNOLOGY AND CROSS-CURRICULAR PRODUCTS ■

We advocate that any middle-grades teacher interested in technology should make use of some combination of core technology and cross-curricular products, and add supplemental products for particular purposes. For elementary teachers, cross-curricular and supplemental products are the only types available for getting started on technology.

Table 5.4 Examples of standards-referenced versus standards-based

STL standards Students will develop:	Benchmark under consideration	Example of standards-referenced passage	Example of standards-based passage
Std. 2. An understanding of the core concepts of technology	C (Grades K–2) Tools are simple objects that help humans complete tasks.	A hammer and nails are types of tools we use to build.	A tool is anything you use to help you do or make something. Think about what tools you would need to hold two pieces of wood together—hammer, nails, glue, screws, rope. Now think about how you might hold two pieces of wood together if you had no tools.
Std. 5. An understanding of the effects of technology on the environment	F (Grades 6–8) Decisions to develop and use technologies often put environmental and economic concerns in direct competition with one another.	Electric- and hydrogen-powered automobiles are becoming more and more popular because they reduce pollution and save natural resources. Some auto companies are working to come up with better and better designs for these cars.	Once automobiles were mass-produced, they became cheaper and more available. However, with the mass production and increased sales of automobiles in the U.S., serious problems arose with air pollution from car exhaust and a drain on oil resources that is unequaled in all the world. Are the benefits of owning a car worth the drawbacks of pollution?
Std. 7. An understanding of the influence of technology on history	I (Grades 9–12) Throughout history, technology has been a powerful force in reshaping the social, cultural, political, and economic landscape.	Sextants helped sailors like Magellan navigate the oceans. Sextants work by	The invention of the sextant enabled explorers and traders to more safely and successfully discover new lands and expand trade to new cultures. This changed the nature of both European culture and the course of people that the explorers and traders visited. For example, . . .
Std. 18. An understanding of and ability to select and use transportation technologies	F (Grades 6–8) Transporting people and goods involves a combination of individuals and vehicles.	Design a transportation system that will keep a raw egg safe (unbroken) as it moves it from the top of your desk, down to the floor, and over to the classroom door.	Work in your group to come up with a list of the different transportation systems that work together to transport eggs from the chicken to the grocery store.

Table 5.5   Coverage of STL benchmarks by technology textbooks

	Technology: Shaping Our World	Technology Education: Learning by Design	Technology: Design and Applications	Technology Interactions	Technology in Action
Percent of STL coverage that is standards-based (clearly relates to a benchmark)	81%	79%	81%	61%	53%
Percent of all middle-grades STL benchmarks that are treated (standard-referenced or standards-based)	82%	86%	98%	80%	76%

Educators love to hate textbooks. For example, they often view textbooks as mere encyclopedias, containing mountains of information. Media reports have even highlighted the backpack phenomenon, where these tomes may injure students' backs if they regularly tote several around. Some technology teachers also have a particular concern: They feel that textbooks do not address well the designing and making aspects of technology, an essential component of technology education. However, we will discuss how textbooks can play an important role at this historic moment in the technology education movement.

Cross-curricular products that contain technology are crucial for acquainting teachers of other subjects with technology. However, they can be useful to technology teachers as well. For example, these products generally do a better job than some of the technology textbooks of making vital connections to other subjects (Standard 3).

Core Technology Products

A hallmark of technology education today is its exceptional ability to engage students by having them design and make things to address real-world, human problems (Theme 4). But to be technologically literate, students also need to gain formal knowledge about the nature of technology, technology and society, the design process, and the designed world (Themes 1–3 and 5). Understanding these themes will help students refine their technological abilities and apply them to a variety of problems.

The STL description of the concepts in Themes 1–3 and 5 helps authenticate technology education as a discipline, as do the formal bodies of knowledge in science and mathematics education. Some policymakers and scientists have criticized hands-on science curricula that do not also incorporate sufficient scientific knowledge. They characterize such curricula as activity for activity's sake, which deprive students of the opportunity to learn facts. As the field of technology education seeks to grow brighter on policymakers' radar, it should keep this hazard in mind.

Textbooks can be a useful curricular medium for balancing hands-on design activity with formal concepts about technology education. The major textbooks that have been released since the STL head in this direction. Educators should consider the complementary role that textbooks can play in technology education along with other curricular resources. For example, there are many other collections of technological activities available, such as some of the supplemental resources in Chapter 10. With these, students typically conduct design and make activities, but seldom have the opportunity to address STL Themes 1–3 and 5. At the very least, technology teachers might consider adding several textbooks to their own resource library to draw upon when crafting lessons.

While the five new textbooks we review can play an influential role in helping students attain technological literacy, it would be depressing if textbook authors and publishers react to this by thinking, "We've arrived—we've met the standards!" After all, our results can be viewed as the half-empty glass as well as the half-full glass. There are a few standards that the textbooks mostly ignore, and numerous holes appear in coverage at the benchmark level of the STL. The goal of advancing technology literacy is too crucial to students' and to the nation's future to pause for long in the quest for more progress.

Cross-Curricular Products

To get started in technology, elementary teachers and middle school science teachers can readily use the seven cross-curricular products reviewed in Chapter 9. Middle school technology teachers also should consider using cross-curricular products to augment their core technology textbooks.

For both elementary teachers and science teachers at middle grades, the included nontechnology subjects (science, mathematics, etc.) are a base of familiarity for expanding into technology. Some conceptual treatments of technological knowledge and developments of technological abilities are first-rate. However, only *IMaST* adequately addresses the designed world (Theme 5). Teachers at the middle grades would benefit from having on hand copies of some core technology textbooks, which they could use as references to address any content gaps in the cross-curricular products.

Teachers should consider how much technology content a product contains, because the range of subjects that a product integrates and its emphasis on technology is hazy. Most of the curricula claim to integrate many subjects: science, mathematics, technology, language arts, social studies, and possibly more. In reality, some of these products would be more useful for teaching some subjects than others.

Middle school technology teachers may also benefit from using cross-curricular products. Because technology teachers are better prepared to address a full technology scope and sequence, they probably should first take advantage of the core technology textbooks. Several technology textbooks already provide ample opportunity to integrate technology with other subjects. However, teachers using other reviewed core textbooks will need to find additional and better examples of how technology relates to science and other subjects.

6

Quality of Student Activities

Technology instruction is a hands-on experience, similar to science instruction, but also different. In science activities, students conduct experiments to understand how and why a phenomenon is happening. In technology activities, students create and build, within design constraints, solutions to human problems or needs. However, one can argue that, in the science education community at large, more time is spent learning science concepts and facts than participating in science activities. The mirror image is perhaps more typical in technology education: Teachers emphasize technology activities (Theme 4), but give less attention to developing students' understanding of technological knowledge and concepts (Themes 1–3 and 5).

Among the core technology textbooks, *Technology Interactions* and *Technology in Action* lean toward lots of activities but fewer concepts. *Technology: Design and Applications* leans toward more concepts than activities, having more than 200 pages of explanation and illustration of knowledge about the design process, for example. The relative roles of activities and concepts in the other two products lie somewhere in between.

Putting aside the issue of how strong a role activities should play in technology education, there is no doubt that technology activities are central to it. Unfortunately, people outside of technology education generally are unclear about the particulars of design activities or have misconceptions about it, as illustrated by this finding from a recent Gallup poll:

> When asked about "design" in relation to technology, over half of the public (59%) viewed it in more of a traditional perspective of blueprints and drawings, rather than in the contemporary perspective of being a creative process for solving problems. (Rose & Dugger, 2003, p. 4)

Ideally, according to the *Standards for Technological Literacy* (STL), technology activities are experiences where students can design something, beyond just building according to directions or learning drafting techniques. See the vignette in Chapter 2 for an illustration of a design activity in Grade 5.

■ ACTIVITY TYPES AND DESIGN APPROACHES

We formally analyzed the products' activities in several ways that shed light on how they make use of the design process. First, in each review of Chapters 8 and 9, we examine whether activities address the STL standards relevant to them (Theme 4, Standards 11–13). Second, for core technology products, we further analyze whether activities fulfill the benchmarks within these standards (Chapter 8 and Appendix A).

Third, this chapter explains how we categorized activities in two other ways—by activity type, or structure, and by its approach to the design process, as defined in Table 6.1.

Activity types and design approaches have different levels of complexity and require different levels of student skill, becoming less complex as the reader goes down the lists. Because they offer less structure and "hand-holding" in their instructions or setup, open-ended and guided activity types typically require more independent thinking and working from students than do directed activities. Likewise, a full-scale design approach usually demands that the student follow all the design steps and end up with a product or service. This approach requires a fair amount of knowledge about the design process, working in teams, and selecting resources (to name a few). In contrast, these skills are not usually required for activities that use the investigate/disassemble/evaluate design approach.

Before discussing more and less desirable uses of the activity types and design approaches, we provide brief examples of each.

Examples of Activity Types

Open-ended. "With your partner, design an ergonomic desk chair."

Guided. The sample activity pages in the review of *Technology: Shaping Our World* (Chapter 8)

Directed. "Make a paper airplane following the seven steps outlined below."

Supporting. Experimenting with the slope of a ramp to see how it is related to the speed of a rolling ball

Examples of Design Approaches

Full-scale design. The sample activity pages in the review of *Technology: Learning by Design* (Chapter 8)

Scaffolded. The sample activity page in the review of *Technology Interactions* (Chapter 8)

Table 6.1   Activity types and design approaches

Activity types	
Open-ended explorations	Outline a challenge or brief for the student, but then leave her to figure out what materials to gather, what steps to take to plan and implement the process, etc.
Guided explorations	Walk the student through a design challenge or activity while still providing plenty of opportunity for him to make choices along the way and end up with a product that is personalized.
Directed activities	Give the student steps to follow that determine all of his activities. Sometimes they include a choice between, for example, baking a chocolate chip cookie or an oatmeal cookie, but a directed activity is still lockstep in nature.
Supporting exercises or tasks	Those activities that are really math or science in technology's clothing or are small technology exercises, for example, changing the amounts on a recipe to feed more people or making an electric circuit for no other purpose than to see how electricity works.
Design approaches	
Full-scale design and make	Represent the most student-centered format. Usually this approach has students respond to a design brief or challenge that involves them in all the design steps, plus revisions, and results in a product (not just a prototype).
Scaffolded	Provide or suggest substantial parts of the design or design process, but still leave some design up to student. Usually this approach involves students in all the design steps, plus revisions, and results in a product or prototype.
Redesign/modify/improve	Call for students to take an object and improve its design in some way, use it for a novel purpose, or examine it and redesign it (also usually to improve it).
Investigate/disassemble/ evaluate	Involve carrying out basic research or taking an object or system apart to examine how it works or was built.
Short/focused/practical warm-up	Usually involve making observations or performing small, simple experiments to investigate properties of materials, see how technology works, etc.

Redesign/modify/improve. "Take a set of measuring cups from your kitchen and think about how you might make them easier for a sight-impaired person to use."

Investigate/disassemble/evaluate. "Read about how a radio works, and then take an old radio apart and label its parts."

Short/focused/practical. "Ask the other students in your class what their favorite subject is."

Balancing and Scaffolding the Activity Types and Design Approaches

Every review in Chapters 8 and 9 provides breakdowns of the products' activities by activity type and design approach. How can one recognize a "good" profile from a "bad" one? The only "bad" profile is a product that has an overwhelming preponderance of one type or approach. For example, although the lists of types and activities are progressively more complex or sophisticated as one goes from the bottom to the top, this does not imply that it is desirable for all a product's activities to be open-ended or to use the full-scale design approach.

Fortunately, all of the products in Chapters 8 and 9 strike some kind of balance among the varied activity types and design approaches.

Whether a product's balance of activity types and design approaches is "good" depends on how well it matches the pedagogical needs of the particular students in the educational setting. The differences in complexity among the various types and approaches make them suitable for different instructional purposes. Less demanding types and approaches can be used more frequently with younger students, with students who are new to design-based learning, or with students who are just beginning to learn about technology. The same is true for teachers. Those who are comfortable with student-centered instruction might be more comfortable with open-ended activities or full-scale design approaches than those who are new to using design as a pedagogy.

Determining a good balance is also influenced by the range of abilities and learning styles among students being served: Some students thrive in more structured learning experiences, whereas a steady diet of defined activities can seem confining to other students. Some students have the creativity, motivation, and skill to be inventive in activities that are open-ended or have full-scale design approaches, whereas students who seek structure can get frustrated. We are not advocating that the range of activities used should exclusively cater to students' styles without ever challenging them to grow. However, educators will want the right balance of activity types and design approaches available for both accommodating and challenging their students' abilities and preferences.

In addition to considering the distribution of different activity types and design approaches in each product, the reviews in Chapters 8 and 9 pay attention to the order and relationship of different kinds of activities.

Some products have a more sound progression, or scaffolding, of activity types and design approaches. Scaffolding occurs when the activity types and design approaches progress from less complex and demanding (as in supporting-type exercises and short/focused/practical warm-up approaches) to more complex and demanding (open-ended types and full-scale design approaches). This progression can occur within each individual chapter or across an entire curriculum.

CONSIDERING OTHER ASPECTS OF ACTIVITIES ■

Finally, each review addresses some other characteristics of the products' activities. Consider the following questions when reading the reviews.

- Do the activities extend the major learning goals of the chapters or sections? How well articulated or aligned are the activities with the content of the text?
- For cross-curricular products, are the activities integrated across more than one subject area, or do they mostly focus on one subject at a time?
- Do the activities teach a design or engineering design loop? Is the design process directly taught, implicitly taught through example, or not consistently applied in the activities?
- What is the proportion of individual to group work in the activities? Do they involve students in teams and also allow them to grapple with problems individually?
- Which STL do the activities focus on?

Most products hold up fairly well when examined using these questions. However, we reiterate that it is disheartening that the activities in some products too often had little relationship to the concepts being taught in the text.

7

Teacher Support, Assessment, and Other Pedagogical Features

Until this chapter, we have focused on the learning experiences of students: What topics will students encounter? Do these topics and the products' treatments of them promote technological literacy (Chapter 5)? What kinds of technological activities will students carry out (Chapter 6)?

We now turn to whether products provide support for the teacher, and we discuss some of the products' pedagogical features.

- Teacher support. How much and what kinds of support do products include for helping teachers carry out instruction?
- Assessment. How many and what kinds of opportunities do products include for assessing students' technological knowledge and abilities?
- Other pedagogical features. The chapter closes by discussing a few more pedagogical issues: whether products use an explicit instructional model, how much preparation a teacher would need to make before using products for the first time, and what kinds of materials and equipment teachers need to acquire beforehand.

■ TEACHER SUPPORT

What if a product contains a desirable learning experience for students, but does not equip teachers to teach it? Table 7.1 lists the many questions we investigated for analyzing how products provide five categories of teacher support: support for teaching the curriculum, pedagogy, assessment, teaching technology standards, and teaching twenty-first-century knowledge and abilities.

Table 7.1   Questions for analyzing teacher support materials

---

Support for Teaching the Curriculum

Do teacher support materials help the teacher teach the curriculum by

- Providing background knowledge for the teacher?
- Providing grade-level content knowledge to use in teaching?
- Providing extension activities/additional lesson or activity ideas for the teacher?
- Providing handouts, blackline masters, workbook pages, etc.?
- Providing specific, embedded supports for differentiated teaching and learning of all students, including English learners and those with special needs?
- Providing vignettes and specific classroom examples?
- Providing teacher's guides that are user friendly?
- (Core only) providing suggestions for integrating technology with other areas of the curriculum?

Support for Pedagogy

Do teacher support materials provide pedagogical direction for teachers to

- Help students become independent, self-directed learners?
- Tailor learning opportunities to student needs? (embedded supports)
- Facilitate inquiry?
- Encourage collaboration, respect for diverse ideas, and other values that are consistent with technological problem solving?
- Facilitate learning by all students? (general supports)
- Provide a balance of student-directed and teacher-facilitated activities as well as discussions?
- Encourage students to grapple with significant technology concepts and problems?
- Focus on students and their learning: student generated knowledge, inquiry, reasoning, and design and problem-solving processes to produce logical, effective designs and engineered solutions?

Support for Assessment

Do teacher materials address and support student assessment that

- Is integrated into the instructional program?
- Includes multiple means of assessment?

- Incorporates technological problem solving?
- Incorporates students' data collection?
- Facilitates critical thinking and decision making?
- Provides ongoing assessment instruments and/or support (pre-, post-/formative, summative)?
- Provides embedded assessment instruments and/or support?
- Provides guidance to create rubrics that students have helped design and/or are familiar with?
- Includes opportunities to assess children's prior knowledge and experience?

Support for Teaching Technology Standards

Do teacher support materials enable the teacher to teach the *Standards for Technological Literacy* by

- Creating an environment that provides resources and the atmosphere needed for technology learning?
- Explicitly addressing the STL and making the main ideas clear?
- Including background content knowledge for the teacher that helps him or her explain and apply the STL with students?
- Providing a justification of the importance of specific benchmarks or STL topics to the teacher as they relate to technological literacy?
- Providing a justification for technology education and/or technological literacy?
- Promoting exemplary practices to stimulate student interest and confidence in technological studies, develop technological literacy, and enhance student achievement?
- Engaging students in creating design plans, engaging in design and problem-solving processes, and systematically evaluating the effectiveness of design and solutions to practical problems?
- Providing a framework for planned student experiences for achieving content standards for technology education at respective grade levels?
- (Core only) suggesting ways to integrate technology purposefully with other school subjects?
- Focusing on concrete experiences with technology phenomena?
- Ensuring that aspects of technological knowledge and how they are interrelated are assessed?

Support for Teaching Twenty-First-Century Workplace Skills

Do the teacher support materials help the teacher teach twenty-first-century work skills such as (adapted from SCANS)

- Technological/digital age literacy?
- Effective communication and collaboration skills?
- Inventive thinking/focus on design and problem solving?
- High productivity?

In the discussion that follows, we provide ratings for each product, for each of the five categories. Notice from Table 7.1, however, that each category covers quite a range of product features. A high rating for a category seldom means that a product receives a high rating for every feature listed within it. More often, a product thoroughly incorporates several features of the category, while missing or giving only marginal treatment to a few others. The reviews of individual products in Chapters 8 and 9 discuss such details. In this section, we summarize what products have in common, as well as important contrasts among them.

Overview of Teacher Support Materials

All of the major products discussed in Chapters 8 and 9 provide a lot of teacher support, in varying formats. All five core technology products have teachers' editions of the textbooks. Among the cross-curricular products, similarly, some have separate teachers' editions or manuals, while other products combine teacher and student materials into one document.

Overall, we have good news and two cautions:

- All of the products in Chapters 8 and 9 provide enough support for current technology teachers to use them effectively.
- However, none of the products thoroughly represent every category of support. Prospective users should check to see whether products contain the particular kinds of support that they need.
- Some of these products may not provide enough support for teachers who are new to technology education.

Regarding the last point, those teachers who are new to technology education will need more and more explicit support. Because it is important for more students to become technologically literate than has been the case, more teachers will have to be enlisted to teach technology. Therefore, adequate support for new teachers in technology education is an important consideration.

Table 7.2 compares the five categories of teacher support among the twelve products reviewed in Chapters 8 and 9. Generally, both core technology products (five middle-grades technology textbooks in Chapter 8) and the cross-curricular products (seven elementary or middle-grades multisubject products in Chapter 9) had similarly good levels of support for teaching three of the five types of support: curriculum, pedagogy, and assessment.

Technology (Gradwell, Welch, & Martin), *Technology Education* (Hacker & Burghardt), and *Children Designing and Engineering* (Hutchinson) provide the strongest, most wide-ranging support for teachers. Again, most other products contained good amounts of support. However, teachers new to technology education may need more support than is provided by *Technology Interactions* (Harms & Swernofsky) and *Technology in Action* (Thode & Thode).

As a group, cross-curricular products include slightly more support on how to teach the curriculum to all students than the core technology products. In addition, these products provide considerably more support for how to assess student learning. Most products of both types have room for improvement in supporting the teaching of technology standards and twenty-first-century knowledge and abilities.

Table 7.2 Kinds of teacher support available

Category of support	Core technology products *					Cross-curricular products *						
						Elementary grades			Middle grades			
	Gradwell, Welch, & Martin	Hacker & Burghardt	Wright Brown	Harms & Swernofsky	Thode & Thode	Children D&E	Stuff That Works!	AWIM 4–6	T.R.A.C.S.	IMaST	BSCS	AWIM 7–8
Teaching the curriculum	◆◆◆	◆◆	◆◆	◆◆	◆◆◆	◆◆◆	◆◆◆	◆◆	◆◆	◆◆	◆◆	◆◆
Pedagogy	◆◆	◆◆◆	◆◆	◆	◆	◆	◆◆◆	◆◆	◆◆	◆◆	◆◆	◆◆◆
Assessment	◆◆	◆◆	◆	◆	◆	◆◆	◆◆	◆	◆◆	◆◆	◆◆◆	◆◆◆
Teaching technology standards	◆	◆◆	◆	◆	◆	◆	◆	◆	◆	◆	◆	◆
Teaching 21st-century knowledge and abilities	◆	◆	◆	◆◆◆	◆◆	◆◆	◆	◆	◆	◆◆	◆	◆

* Core technology products listed by author. Cross-curricular products listed by product name.

◆◆◆◆ Extensive support available

◆◆◆ Substantial support available

◆◆ Moderate/some support available

◆ Marginal or missing support

In the following section we discuss particularly strong, weak, or interesting instances of teacher support. For further discussion, consult the reviews in Chapters 8 and 9, each of which contains two to four pages of analysis about the product's teacher support materials. One thing to look for in the Chapters 8 and 9 reviews is how and where the products handled background information for the teacher. For example, while *Technology Interactions* (Harms & Swernofsky) and *Technology in Action* (Thode & Thode) provide interesting background information at the front of the products, little of this is linked explicitly to where teachers would need it during the course.

Support for Teaching the Curriculum

Following are a variety of characteristics of support for teaching the curriculum, which illustrate the kinds of information provided in the reviews. Only *Technology Education* (Hacker & Burghardt) provides any significant amount of information about diversifying instruction for less or more advanced students. The *World in Motion* products (SAE) uniquely use industry volunteers as an important part of the curriculum, and their teacher materials include explicit support for doing this. *Technology Interactions* (Harms & Swernofsky) and *Technology in Action* (Thode & Thode) explain how they can be used in conjunction with modular technology systems. The *IMaST* product (Loepp) gives excellent advice on teaching this constructivist curriculum, but teachers who are not already experienced in using a constructivist model may need even further assistance.

Support for Pedagogy

Both *Technology* (Gradwell, Welch, & Martin) and *Technology Education* (Hacker & Burghardt) immerse students in the design process and provide teachers with the requisite higher levels of support that are needed for teaching this way. *Children Designing and Engineering* (Hutchinson) currently is a little short on support for pedagogy, but authors are developing ancillary support materials.

Stuff That Works! (Benenson & Neujahr) has the most creative and extensive support for pedagogy of any product. It teaches technology to teachers in a way that models the instruction intended for students. Further, it includes engaging and helpful teacher stories, which are implementation challenges actually experienced by teachers during the field testing of the product.

Support for Assessment

This is a related but separate consideration from the degree to which the student editions include strategies and tools for student assessment, which is discussed in the next part of this chapter. Here we refer to whether teacher support materials help teachers know *how* to use these strategies and tools.

Especially *Technology Education* (Hacker & Burghardt), but also *Children Designing and Engineering* (Hutchinson), best support teacher assessment of students' knowledge and abilities. *Technology* (Wright & Brown) includes the least support for assessment.

In general, the cross-curricular products do a better job of helping teachers know how to use student work for assessment purposes, but two core technology products also give substantial or dominant support. In contrast, several other core technology products only briefly suggest that teachers use particular assessment strategies and do not explain how to go about doing so. A small but noteworthy feature is found in the student questions included in *Technology Education* (Hacker & Burghardt) product: Teachers are aided by having student questions grouped and labeled explicitly as "recall and comprehension" and "critical thinking" (analyzing, comparing and contrasting, evaluating, summarizing, etc.).

Support for Teaching Technology Standards

Most products indicate which STL standards they address overall; further, many products provide tables or margin notes that indicate which standards particular lessons or chapters address. However, only *Technology Education* (Hacker & Burghardt) and *Children Designing and Engineering* (Hutchinson) explain *how* particular lessons, sections, or chapters are relevant to the standards indicated.

At the beginning of their teacher support materials, *Technology Interactions* (Harms & Swernofsky) and *Technology in Action* (Thode & Thode) give rich descriptions of technological literacy and why they are important. However, neither of these second-edition products infuses this information throughout the product in ways that would enable teachers to make use of it in a timely manner as students progress through particular aspects of literacy.

Support for Teaching Twenty-First-Century Knowledge and Abilities

Most products strongly support teachers in having students collaborate on work in small groups, particularly the two products from BSCS. *Children Designing and Engineering* (Hutchinson) and *IMaST* (Loepp) also give clear attention to other workplace skills. The former was created in collaboration with science and technology businesses in New Jersey, where state education policy emphasizes workplace skills. *Technology Interactions* (Harms & Swernofsky) has the most extensive and inventive presentation of information about technology careers, while *Technology Education* (Hacker & Burghardt) pays little attention to them.

ASSESSMENT ■

Every product in Chapters 8 and 9 has a good range of opportunities to assess student understanding. Because the kinds of assessment available vary among products, however, prospective users should closely examine the assessment section of each review (from one to three pages) found in Chapters 8 and 9. These discussions will inform decisions about whether the particulars of assessment in the products match users' preferences and needs.

Table 7.3   Explicit and embedded assessment opportunities

Assessment Tools (always explicit)

    Paper-and-pencil tests (limited responses such as multiple-choice, short answer)
    Open-ended questioning (critical thinking and essay questions)
    Computerized assessment banks (ancillary CD-ROMs)
    Rubrics/checklists (for evaluating student work)

Other Assessment Opportunities (usually embedded)

    Projects/products/media (individual and group activities, projects, media)
    Portfolios of student work (reports, work samples, research notes)
    Student work (lab journal pages, handouts, graphs, charts)
    Informal observations/discussions (teacher observations)
    Performance-based activities (demonstrations, presentations, multimedia)
    Student self-evaluation (peer assessment, self-reflections, self-evaluations)

    Overall, products have comparable amounts of assessment tools, but cross-curricular products tend to have more of the embedded opportunities for assessment as well.

We cast a wide net in looking for assessment opportunities. By "opportunities," we refer to two main forms of assessment possibilities: tools provided in the student or teacher materials with the express purpose of assessing students' understanding or work and features of the product that are part of the students' learning experience, but also lend themselves to being used for assessment purposes. These embedded assessment opportunities may or may not be identified or encouraged as such by the teacher support materials. Table 7.3 lists the types of assessment opportunities that we find.

All of the technology textbooks that comprise our core technology products have the bells and whistles typically provided by major publishers. They contain each of the listed explicit assessment tools, particularly end-of-section or end-of-chapters questions and tests, and optional CD-ROM discs that contain more test items.

Similarly, the cross-curricular products have the same explicit assessment tools, except for the extra CD-ROMs. However, the cross-curricular products generally have fewer of the limited response items (paper-and-pencil tests) and more of the open-ended questions. These products also provide more rubrics/checklists for teachers' use in appraising student work.

Every core technology and cross-curricular product has a combination of some embedded assessment opportunities. Not surprisingly, every product is full of student project/products/media and other student work that teachers can use to assess students' learning.

The other embedded assessment opportunities are more prevalent among the cross-curricular products: performance-based assessments (student demonstrations, presentations), the encouragement of student portfolios, the use of student self-evaluations, and informal observations by teachers. In some instances, these assessment opportunities can take the form of explicit tools rather than embedded strategies, for example, the provision of rubrics for students to use in self-evaluation or a performance-based task, which students complete specifically for assessment purposes.

OTHER PEDAGOGICAL FEATURES   ■

The following sections of the reviews in Chapters 8 and 9 also discuss pedagogical features of the products.

Instructional Model

All of the cross-curricular products explain and explicitly use an instructional model to organize students' learning experiences. For example, the *World in Motion* products organize instruction around a modified version of the Engineering Design Experience (EDE), a model used by engineers: Set goals, build knowledge, design, build and test, finalize the model, and present.

Among the core technology products, only *Technology Education* (Hacker & Burghardt) makes use of an instructional model as explicitly as the cross-curricular products. The other core products may implicitly have instructional models, for example, by presenting lessons in the same format and flow. However, such embedded instructional models do not guide students' learning as clearly as explicit ones.

What roles do the products' graphics or photographs play in students' learning? All of the products contain them, but only some products use these elements to explicitly deliver the instruction. In other products, they seem to contribute to form rather than function. The topic matter of graphics or photographs in a few products is mostly unrelated to their adjacent text passages, and the nontext elements in some products are "pretty pictures" that are not accompanied by meaningful captions.

Graphics or photographs can make material accessible to diverse learners or connect subject matter to contemporary, real-world examples. In contrast, the photographs of several products lean toward particular people or things: for example, the use of mostly Caucasian people, more men than women, lots of adults but few students, industries rather than everyday settings around students, or somewhat dated versus recently developed technologies. No single product contains all or most of these representations, but many products have one or more of these inadequacies. Every review in Chapters 8 and 9 carefully examines the product's uses of nontextual elements.

Materials and Special Preparations

All of the products are good at listing the materials that teachers will need to acquire for teaching the products. However, the amount, types, and costs of these required materials and equipment vary quite a bit. Most of the core technology products include activities that involve computer-assisted drawing (CAD) or other uses of computers, such as accessing the Internet. Every major section of *Technology Education* (Hacker & Burghardt) refers to a particular Web site that helps students understand the specific concepts being covered. Prospective users of a product should carefully consider the Materials section of each review in Chapters 8 and 9 to be sure the requirements are acceptable for their local situation and budgets.

When first using any product, a teacher will have to make time to become thoroughly familiar with it. However, the Special Preparations section of each review notes whether prospective users may need to make extra efforts beyond such routine familiarization and whether professional development opportunities or teacher support materials exist to help them do so. For example, most middle school teachers who use *IMaST* (Loepp) as intended will need to make special preparations; this product is designed for teams of mathematics, science, and technology teachers (and, to a lesser extent, teachers of other subjects) to jointly plan and coordinate their lessons. The teacher support materials provide extensive assistance for forging such collaboration.

8

Core Technology Products

This chapter provides comprehensive reviews of five technology textbooks for the middle grades. All of them have been published since the International Technology Education Association (ITEA) released the *Standards for Technological Literacy*. Between four and six sample pages are included from each product, as well as their tables of contents. Newer products are provided before older ones. If more than one product is published the same year, reviews are ordered alphabetically by the last name of the lead author.

These curriculum materials are intended for use in the classroom or in formal educational settings. They include a teacher instructional component of some sort, in addition to the student materials and information. Core products have enough material to be used as a technology curriculum for a substantial period of the school year (e.g., a semester, a nine-week wheel, the entire year). They are also comprehensive in their standards coverage.

Before providing the reviews, we briefly describe a couple of late-breaking products that we could not analyze.

LATE-BREAKING PRODUCTS ■

Invention-Innovation-Inquiry units are currently in development for Grades 5 and 6 by the ITEA (www.iteawww.org). Through support from the National Science Foundation, faculty at the California University of Pennsylvania are developing such units as Invention (design a new household gadget), Innovation (design a device that applies ergonomics), Manufacturing (design, market, and package a new candy), Transportation (understanding different transportation systems and environments), and Technological Systems (creating mechanical toys).

ugh listed as a core technology product, these curriculum materials will
trong connections to mathematics and science.

er we completed our intensive analyses of the core technology prod-
lencoe/McGraw-Hill pre-released a middle-grades technology text-
..ith a 2005 publication date: *Introduction to Technology*, by Pierce and
Karwatka. According to the table of contents and promotional literature, this
textbook will have entire chapters or multiple chapters devoted to each of
the designed world standards (Theme 5), as well as some chapters for the
nature of technology (Theme 1) and design (Theme 3), especially engineering
design (Standard 9). Treatment of technology and society (Theme 2) appears
mostly to be embedded within other chapters. The textbook package contains
all typical components (student edition, teacher edition, etc.) and features (e.g.,
chapter tests, connections to other subjects).

Technology: Shaping Our World

Developer/Author:	John B. Gradwell, Malcolm Welch, and Eugene Martin
Publisher:	The Goodheart-Willcox Company, Inc.
Publication date:	2004
Ordering information:	Goodheart-Willcox, 1-800-323-0440; www.goodheart-willcox.com
Target audience:	Middle school

BRIEF DESCRIPTION

Based on the criteria described earlier, *Technology: Shaping Our World* (*SOW*) is one of the highest-rated curricula of the five core technology products. It seamlessly integrates text and activities and keys both text and activities to specific *Standards for Technical Literacy* (STL) standards and benchmarks. Activities are carefully scaffolded so that students experience less complex activities at the beginning of the text and move on to increasingly sophisticated activities as the text progresses. The activities are relevant to students' lives and involve them in authentic, real-world experiences.

This product strongly promotes technological literacy. Eighty-one percent of the curriculum is standards-based, and all twenty of the STL are covered. Eighty-four percent of the middle school benchmarks are also addressed. In particular, the book gives excellent coverage of the STL Themes 1 (core concepts of technology), 4 (abilities for a technological world), and 5 (the designed world).

SOW has especially strong student assessment and teacher instructional support materials. The *Teacher's Manual* and *Wraparound Edition* offer a wide array of hints, extensions, and methods for dealing with diverse learners in the classroom, in addition to pedagogical guidance and information. More than 300 additional activities are provided to supplement the activities found in the student text and the *Student Activity Manual*.

CURRICULUM COMPONENTS

- *Student Edition*, hardcover, 463 pp., $35.25
- *Student Activity Manual*, softcover, 314 pp., $9.96
- *Teacher's Wraparound Edition*, hardcover, 464 pp., $45.00
- *Teacher's Manual*, softcover, 394 pp., $28.50
- *Teacher's Resource Binder*, softcover, $88.50
- *Teacher's Resource CD*, $141.00

Materials/Equipment

The beginning of every activity includes a list of student materials, tools, consumables, and equipment. In general, the materials and equipment are readily available and/or found in most middle school classrooms. Some activities require special software (such as CADD) that could be more difficult to obtain.

Special Preparations

Because there are more activities than can be completed in a school year, teachers will have to plan ahead and preselect those activities that they feel best suit their learning goals and students. Activities that involve computer software, applications, or Internet work could require significant preparation, depending on teacher experience. No specific professional development is required to use this product.

CURRICULUM OVERVIEW

Topic Overview

The curriculum addresses the technology information, design process, and "making" skills that the authors feel are essential to achieving technological literacy. See the Table of Contents at the end of this review for chapter titles and topics. In addition to covering topics from all twenty of the STL, the curriculum also deals with technology-related topics that are not directly covered by the STL, such as electricity and magnetism, ergonomics, careers, understanding simple machines, space, drawing techniques, and principles of graphic design.

Instructional Model

The authors promote design as the ideal pedagogical model for teaching technological literacy. The text includes embedded design experiences for students, and the activities are closely linked to the content and subject matter presented in the chapters. Text and activities are carefully articulated to give students opportunities to both apply conceptual knowledge about technology and gain design skills.

Each chapter contains the following elements:

- Key Terms: 3–30 vocabulary and concept words
- Objectives: 3–10 skills students will have mastered after they finish a chapter
- Chapter Summary: .5–1.5 page recap of the essential information and skills covered
- Modular Connections: 15–40 related modular technology topics and labs
- Test Your Knowledge: 5–20 multiple-choice, true/false, completion, and essay questions
- Apply Your Knowledge: 3–12 activities and questions for students to apply concepts from the chapters to everyday, real-world situations

Information about technology-based careers is found primarily in Chapter 15, where careers in the primary, secondary, and tertiary work sectors are described in detail. Other technology careers are addressed sporadically throughout the text.

Easily identifiable headings and subheadings aid student comprehension and support common learning strategies. The text should be understandable to most middle school students, based on a Lexile score of 850L and a grade-level rating of 5.8. English language learners or students from lower reading levels might have trouble with some of the vocabulary and sentence structure. The charts, tables, and diagrams are clean, uncluttered, and easy to read. The drawings and pictures present multicultural people in a variety of life settings. Middle school children are often featured participating in common activities that are authentic to students' lives and the real world.

The graphics generally underscore the content in the text and help to move the lessons along. Captions and labels are interesting and clearly written so that students with limited reading abilities can still learn basic concepts. Finally, the graphics are modern and feature contemporary technology and twenty-first-century life. The sample pages at the end of this review show the use of graphics in the student text.

Because of the unusual number of activities and time requirements for completing them (see Duration, in the following section), the *Teacher's Manual* and the *Teacher's Wraparound Edition* offer help in selecting and sequencing the text and activities to fit the school calendar.

Duration

The curriculum is designed to be completed in one school year. The sixteen chapters average twenty-five to thirty pages in length and include activities embedded in the text and end-of-chapter activities in the Apply Your Knowledge sections. The *Student Activity Manual* is a separate, softcover book that contains the major, large-scale activities called Design and Make Activities (DMA), plus smaller Supporting Tasks (ST) that accompany them. The *Teacher's Manual* and the *Teacher's Wraparound Edition* contain hundreds of supplemental activities to support the text and DMAs. Because there are so many activities, teachers will have to make careful choices about which ones to use. A program addendum in the *Teacher's Manual* and *Teacher's Wraparound Edition* helps teachers develop an articulated program model for sixth through eighth grades using a subset of the activities for each grade. See Table 8.1.1 for details.

Nature of Activities

SOW offers an array of articulated activities, exercises, and tasks that support student knowledge and skill building. All three types of activities offer students opportunities to use a wide range of media and materials, across several different real-world contexts. The *Teacher's Manual,* the *Teacher's Wraparound Edition,* and the embedded activities in the student text provide more than 300 ancillary exercises and tasks that supplement the text, STs, and DMAs. (See Table 8.1.1 for time requirements.)

The Apply Your Knowledge sections require students to apply higher-order thinking skills through answering thought-provoking questions, engaging in debate, carrying out simple research exercises, and completing 40 design activities that result in some sort of product or service. These design experiences expand students' general knowledge while also encouraging the application of concepts from the chapters to real-life situations and problems. The activities are of varying difficulty, include about 25 percent group work and 75 percent individual work, and take from one to two class periods to complete.

The 96 ST exercises differ from the other activities presented in the curriculum. They generally do not involve a design process, and they focus on how to carry out a

Table 8.1.1   Kinds, numbers, and durations of activities in *Technology: Shaping Our World*

Kinds of activities (and locations)	How many offered per chapter (and product total)	Approximate time required for each
Text reading (in student text)	16 chapters	2 weeks
Embedded and Apply Your Knowledge activities (in student text)	5–10 (100 total)	.75–2.5 hours
Design and Make Activities (DMA; in Student Activity Manual)	1–2 (28 total)	20–35 hours
Supporting Tasks (ST; in Student Activity Manual)	10–15 for each DMA (96 total)	.75–2.5 hours
Supplemental activities (in Teacher Wraparound Edition)	10–20 (218 total)	15–30 minutes
Supplemental activities (in Teacher's Manual)	3–7 (84 total)	15–45 minutes

particular design step or how to learn a design skill (e.g., how to draw straight lines freehand, how to read a scale drawing in conventional measure). The ST worksheets tell students what they will learn, what materials they will need, and the steps to any applicable procedure. The STs are aligned to specific book chapters and help students build the prerequisite skills they will need before moving on to the DMA. Each ST takes from one to two class periods. The following concepts are emphasized in the STs:

- Designing
- Structures
- Information & communication technology
- Learning from the past, Predicting the future
- Communicating ideas
- Machines & transportation
- Biotechnology
- Evaluation
- Materials
- Electricity & electronics
- World of work

In the 28 DMAs, students practice all steps of the design process:

- Writing a design specification based on teacher-generated, open design briefs
- Conducting appropriate research
- Generating ideas
- Developing ideas

- Communicating ideas through 2- and 3-D models
- Working with resistant materials to produce high-quality products
- Evaluating products
- Evaluating student learning
- Identifying ways to improve student capabilities

The DMA worksheets are design briefs that take three to thirty hours each to complete. Each one contains the following sections:

- Related Chapters
- The Context—the story or problem the design brief will address
- The Design Brief itself
- Design Decisions—a list of decisions students will need to make in order to plan their designs (i.e., criteria and constraints)
- The Support Tasks—a list of the STs that relate to the activity and provide needed skills to complete it

Most students will first need to work through all or most of the recommended 10–15 STs that accompany each DMA. Teachers can assign individual STs as stand-alone exercises to underscore textbook content or skill-building.

We analyzed the activity type and design approach of 64 DMAs and Apply Your Knowledge activities. The STs were *not* analyzed because they are primarily how-to exercises and do not generally involve students in an actual design process. Because they are presented as optional, the ancillary activities in the *Teacher's Manual* and *Teacher's Wraparound Edition* also were not analyzed for activity type and design approach.

We found that the analyzed activities provide a broad range of experiences with in-depth, major design projects that give students ample opportunities to gain knowledge, skill, and facility with the design process.

As Figure 8.1.1 shows, half of the activities are guided explorations, and one-third are open-ended explorations. Guided explorations walk students through the design process but still allow them to make major decisions about the specifics of their designs and projects. Open-ended explorations require the most independent and higher-order thinking from students and generally involve them in large-scale design activities. The remaining activities are mostly supporting exercises. Note the relative lack of directed activities.

The types of activities presented in the curriculum become increasingly complex as students progress through the chapters. By purposefully exposing students to a progression of increasingly difficult activities, the curriculum guides the development of students' design and problem-solving skills and scaffolds their learning.

Three-quarters of the analyzed activities use full-scale design (see Figure 8.1.2). In this product, the full-scale design approach applies the entire design loop (including revisions and evaluations) to multifaceted projects that result in products or services. Like the activity types, the design approaches become more sophisticated (from short/focused/practical warm-up through full-scale design) as the curriculum progresses. Again, this provides stepwise support for students to develop increasingly sophisticated design and problem-solving skills.

Teachers and students receive the guidance, information, and practice necessary to become seasoned designers who can apply conceptual knowledge in a wide variety of design contexts.

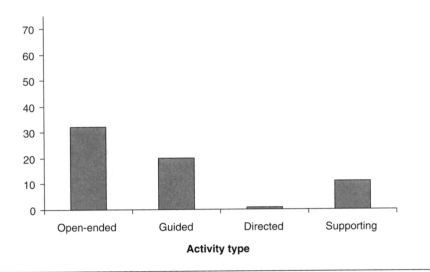

Figure 8.1.1 Number of activities by type in *Technology: Shaping Our World*, N = 64

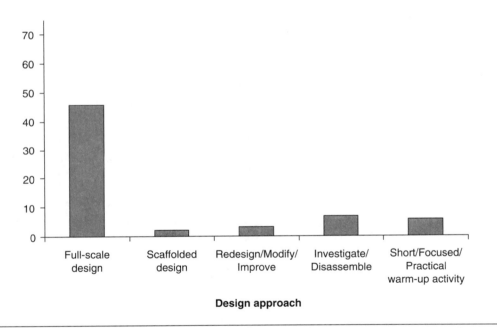

Figure 8.1.2 Number of activities by design approach in *Technology: Shaping Our World*, N = 64

Assessment

The *Student Edition, Teacher's Manual,* and the *Student Activity Manual* contain a very broad array of assessments.

The *Student Edition* features three main sources of assessment. At the end of each chapter, Test Your Knowledge provides 15–20 review questions, and Apply Your Knowledge features 5–8 activities and short exercises that teachers can use as assessments. The Objectives section at the beginning of each chapter is an additional source of assessment and lists 10–15 skills that can be used as a student self-assessment checklist.

The *Teacher's Manual* contains sixteen chapter tests with answers and a total of 218 ancillary activities (with answers as applicable). The ancillary activities, designed to be used as skill-builders and assessment tools, range from completing simple worksheets to multisession design briefs that end in a product, service, or prototype. The *Teacher's Manual* also includes a small section in the front matter called "Assessing Capability" that provides background and strategies for assessing student progress in an activity-based curriculum.

The *Student Activity Manual* includes two evaluation activities (EV1, Evaluating the Final Product; and EV2, Unit Review) to be completed following each DMA. Finally, the DMAs from the *Student Activity Manual* are intended to become part of a Designer's Portfolio where students keep evidence of their progress in achieving technological literacy. This focus on individual and peer evaluation of both the process and products of design is unusual and helps *SOW* stand out among the core technology products.

Table 8.1.2 shows the kinds and amounts of student assessment tools provided in the curriculum. The ratings in the right-hand column reflect how prominent each type

Table 8.1.2   Student assessment tools and their presence in *Technology: Shaping Our World*

Assessment approach	Presence in the curriculum
Paper-and-pencil tests—multiple-choice, short answer, true/false, vocabulary, completion	◆ ◆ ◆ ◆
Projects/Products/Media—individual and group activities, projects, products, media	◆ ◆ ◆ ◆
Performance-based assessments—demonstrations, presentations, multimedia, performances	◆ ◆ ◆
Portfolios—student papers, notes, project reports, research, work samples	◆ ◆ ◆
Student work—workbook or lab journal pages, handouts, graphs, charts, etc.	◆ ◆ ◆ ◆
Open-ended questioning—essays, extended writing exercises, critical thinking questions, etc.	◆ ◆ ◆
Computerized assessment—online simulations, tests, etc.	◆
Evaluations—peer assessments, self-reflections, self-evaluations	◆ ◆
Rubrics/Checklists	◆
Informal observations/Discussions—teacher observations	◆

◆ ◆ ◆ ◆   Dominant—There are a large number of assessments of this type in the curriculum.

◆ ◆ ◆   Substantial—There are a substantial number of assessments of this type in the curriculum.

◆ ◆   Some/Moderate—There are a moderate number of assessments of this type in the curriculum.

◆   Marginal/Missing—There are very few or no assessments of this type in the curriculum.

of assessment tool is in the curriculum but do not reflect the quality of the individual tools provided.

Although we did not analyze the quality of the individual assessment tools, the focus, variety, and number of assessments in this curriculum place it among the top two core technology products for assessment coverage.

STL STANDARDS AND BENCHMARK-LEVEL ANALYSES

SOW, which was written after the STL was published, addresses all of the STL and 82 percent of the middle school benchmarks. Eighty-one percent of the curriculum is standards-based, meaning it accurately and thoroughly teaches a large proportion of the STL.

Referring to Table 5.1 and Appendix A will provide detailed information about the standard- and benchmark-level analyses.

Standards Coverage in the Overall Curriculum

The overall curriculum (meaning the text and activities combined) addresses all twenty of the STL. The five most frequently addressed standards and the five least frequently addressed standards are presented in Table 8.1.3. Standards 11, 12, and 2 combined account for 46 percent of the overall curriculum. They reflect the authors' beliefs that design (as presented in Standards 11–13) is the appropriate pedagogy for teaching technology education and achieving technological literacy. Understanding the core concepts behind technology (Standard 2) is also presented as crucial to technological literacy, and this standard is woven throughout the text. For more details about the specific benchmarks covered in the text and activities, see Appendix A.

The five least addressed standards, combined, make up only about 5 percent of the total standards coverage.

Table 8.1.3   Five most frequent and five least frequent standards in the overall curriculum

5 most frequent standards	5 least frequent standards
Standard 12 (16%)—using and maintaining technological products and systems	Standard 10 (<1%)—problem solving
Standard 2 (15%)—the core concepts of technology	Standard 6 (1%)—the role of society in the development and use of technology
Standard 11 (15%)—applying the design process	Standard 7 (1%)—the influence of technology on history
Standard 16 (11%)—energy and power technologies	Standard 14 (1%)—medical technologies
Standard 19 (6%)—manufacturing technologies	Standard 15 (1%)—agriculture and related biotechnologies

Standards Coverage in the Text

The student text for *SOW* addresses 18 of the 20 STL, and 81 percent of that overall coverage is standards-based. Although Standards 10 (problem solving) and 11 (applying the design process) do not get much attention in the text, they are covered in the activities. Table 8.1.4 presents a more detailed description of the analysis.

Following is a discussion of the most and least frequently addressed standards:

Standards 12 (using and maintaining technological systems), 2 (understanding the core concepts of technology), and 16 (energy and power technologies) receive the most text treatment and are at least 78 percent standards-based. For the most part, the Standard 12 benchmark coverage focuses on developing students' abilities to use information to understand how things work. This is particularly true for the text, where there are many sections and displays that provide students with detailed information about how different technologies and processes operate. The Grades 9–12 benchmark K, concerning the rate of technological development and diffusion, is also stressed for this standard. Fifty percent of the middle school benchmarks are addressed.

The Standard 2 (core concepts of technology) coverage focuses primarily on the Grades 3–5 benchmarks that address properties of materials, the seven technology resources, and the various processes that comprise different kinds of technologies. This standard is the most frequently covered standard in the curriculum and is 78 percent standards-based. Ninety percent of the middle school benchmarks are addressed.

For Standard 16 (energy and power technologies), the benchmark coverage predominantly addresses explanations and examples of how energy is the capacity to do work, discussions and information about renewable versus nonrenewable sources of energy, and a general treatment of electronics and electricity that is standards-referenced rather than standards-based. Eighty percent of the middle school benchmarks are treated, and that treatment is 84 percent standards-based.

Standards 10 (problem solving), 11 (applying the design process), and 13 (assessing the impacts of products and services) receive the weakest treatment. In fact, Standards 10 and 11 are not covered at all, and Standard 13 is addressed only once in the text. The lack of attention given to these standards may not be as strong a deficit as it appears. Two of these standards, 13 and 11, are actually part of the Abilities for a Technological World theme. This means they are skill-based standards and can be expected to concentrate in the activities rather than in the text. In fact, all three of these standards do receive treatment in the activities.

Standard 3 (the connections between technology and other fields) receives only moderate emphasis in the text, and its benchmark treatment is only 33 percent standards-based. Although there are numerous presentations of science facts and concepts in the text, particularly in Chapters 10, 11, and 12, these very rarely leave the realm of science teaching to address the intent of the Standard 3 benchmarks.

It is worth noting that the text treatment of Standards 14 (medical technologies) and 15 (agricultural and related biotechnologies) invokes only Grades 9–12 benchmarks. Eighty-one percent of the middle school benchmarks receive some kind of treatment, either standards-based or standards-referenced. Nine of the standards treated in the text address all the middle school benchmarks associated with them.

Table 8.1.4   Results of analyses of STL coverage in the text for *Technology: Shaping Our World*

STL covered	Percent of text devoted to each STL	Percent of coverage that is standards-based for each STL	Primary benchmarks covered for each STL			
			K–2	3–5	6–8	9–12
Standard 1	2%	73%			FG	K
Standard 2	18%	78%	J			
Standard 3	4%	33%			F	
Standard 4	6%	79%			D	
Standard 5	4%	85%			D	J
Standard 6	1%	86%			E	
Standard 7	1%	60%			D	
Standard 8	2%	38%			E G	
Standard 9	3%	100%			F	I
Standard 10	0%	—	—	—	—	—
Standard 11	0%	—	—	—	—	—
Standard 12	16%	99%			H	
Standard 13	<0.5%	—	—	—	—	—
Standard 14	2%	73%				K
Standard 15	2%	36%				M
Standard 16	16%	84%			F	M
Standard 17	4%	68%			H K	
Standard 18	3%	88%			G	
Standard 19	9%	95%			F H	
Standard 20	5%	70%			F G	

Primary benchmark coverage = 21% or more of total benchmarks for the standard

Benchmarks are not listed for standards that are covered in less than 0.5% of the text.

The highlighted standards are represented most often in the text.

Standards Coverage in the Activities

The activities are completely articulated with the text and with each other. Each major topic is supported by a full set of exercises, tasks, and activities that help underscore the teachings of the text. Each of these tasks and activities is directly related to a specific STL benchmark and to a more general technology topic. The STs were included as part of the coding and review of each of the DMA, based on the authors' intent that the ST be treated as essential, readiness-building components of the specific DMA they support. Table 8.1.5 gives the results of the standards analysis for the activities. Once again, referring to Appendix A will provide further details.

All twenty of the STL are treated in the activities. It is worth noting that *SOW* is one of two curricula evaluated for this book that does address all twenty standards in the activities. Fifty percent of the middle school benchmarks are treated in the activities.

Standard 11 (applying the design process) is the most prominent standard in the activities. All of the middle school benchmarks for that standard, plus two high school benchmarks are addressed. Benchmarks H (apply a design process to solve problems), L (make a product and document the solution), and N (identify criteria and constraints) are the most heavily covered benchmarks for this standard. Only one other product in our review covers the Standard 11 benchmarks so thoroughly.

Standard 12 (using and maintaining technological products and systems) is the second most cited standard. Its emphasis is primarily on using tools and materials safely (3–5 Benchmark E) and on using information to understand how things work (6–8 Benchmark H).

Standard 2 (understanding the core concepts of technology) is represented in 10 percent of the activities. Its benchmark coverage gives the most attention to the seven technology resources and the various attributes and properties of materials, as presented in the 3–5 benchmarks.

Standard 17 (information and communication technologies) is also well covered in the activities. The most common benchmarks for this standard focus on using signs and symbols in communication and on the design of messages.

The results of the standard- and benchmark-level analyses of the activities are evidence that the authors fulfilled their goal of providing an integrated, broad-based learning experience that is sufficiently deep to encourage technological literacy. The strong emphasis on activities and the careful alignment between them and the text also contribute to meeting this goal. The fact that a few of the more heavily covered benchmarks come from Grades 3–5 or 9–12 should not be too troubling. The inclusion of both lower and higher level benchmarks could help students revisit previously acquired knowledge and/or challenge them with higher level learning.

TEACHER MATERIALS REVIEW

The teacher materials for *SOW* give strong support for novice and veteran teachers to understand, implement, and complete the curriculum with most middle school students. Teachers who do not normally use design-based learning in their classrooms are given sufficient guidance to begin doing so with this product. Longtime design and technology teachers will find the text and activities novel and interesting. However, it could be difficult for teachers new to the STL to teach some of the standards because the teacher materials do not provide background content knowledge about the standards.

Table 8.1.5   Results of analyses of STL coverage in the activities for *Technology: Shaping Our World*

STL covered	Percent of activities devoted to each STL	Primary benchmarks covered for each STL			
		K–2	3–5	6–8	9–12
Standard 1	3%			G	
Standard 2	10%		H J		
Standard 3	1%			F	
Standard 4	1%			D	
Standard 5	1%			*D	
Standard 6	1%				J
Standard 7	< 0.5%	—	—	—	—
Standard 8	5%			G	
Standard 9	2%			G	
Standard 10	3%				I
Standard 11	36%			H L	N
Standard 12	16%		E	H	
Standard 13	4%		C	F G	
Standard 14	1%	C			
Standard 15	1%		D	I J	L
Standard 16	4%			*F	
Standard 17	8%			J K	
Standard 18	< 0.5%	—	—	—	—
Standard 19	2%			F	
Standard 20	2%		C	F	

Primary benchmark coverage = 21% or more of total benchmarks for the standard

An asterisk (*) in front of a benchmark indicates that, while the topic of the STL is addressed, no specific benchmarks are covered.

Benchmarks are not listed for standards that are covered in less than 0.5% of the text.

The highlighted standards are represented most often in the text.

Overview of Teacher Materials Components

The *Teacher's Manual* and *Teacher's Wraparound Edition* contain the primary instructional support materials. These same materials, plus forty-eight transparencies, can also be purchased as a three-ring *Teacher's Resource Binder*. A *Teacher's Resource CD* contains all these materials, plus a test-generation program.

The introductions to the *Teacher's Manual* and *Teacher's Wraparound Edition* provide information and support in the following areas:

- The Material for Learning and Teaching
- Teaching Students to Design and Make
- Types of Support Tasks
- Using the Support Tasks
- Using the Design and Make Activities
- Using the Textbook
- Achieving Breadth and Balance
- Progression and Differentiation
- Assessing Capability
- Evidence from the DMA—The Designer's Portfolio
- Using the G-W Test Creation Software
- Safety
- References
- Using Other Resources
- Planning Your Program
- Teaching Techniques
- Teaching Students of Varying Abilities
- Effective Communication Skills
- Classroom Management
- Promoting Your Program

There are also three charts in the front of the *Teacher's Manual* and *Teacher's Wraparound Edition*: (1) Standards for Technological Literacy Correlations, (2) Basic Interdisciplinary Skills, and (3) Scope and Sequence.

The second half of the *Teacher's Manual* contains chapter resources: chapter objectives and learning goals; a list of corresponding text and activities; instructional strategies and student learning experiences; answers to questions in the textbook; sets of supplementary activities with handouts, student worksheets, and answers; and end-of-chapter tests.

The *Teacher's Wraparound Edition* has margin notes on each page that offer suggestions and comments in nineteen instructional areas:

- Links to other subjects
- Student Activity Manual
- Resources
- Technology and Society
- Chapter discussion starters
- Standards correlations
- Chapter outlines
- Safety
- Vocabulary
- Useful Web sites
- Career connections
- Designing and making
- Enrichment
- Examples
- Test answers
- Reflection
- Discussion
- Activities
- Community resources and services

Table 8.1.6 shows how strongly *SOW* treats each major category of teacher support. (Refer to Chapter 7 for a breakout of the specific criteria that constitute each category.)

Table 8.1.6   Categories of teacher support materials and adequacy ratings for *Technology: Shaping Our World*

Categories of support found in teacher support materials	Adequacy of teacher support
Support for teaching the curriculum	◆ ◆ ◆ ◆
Support for pedagogy	◆ ◆ ◆ ◆
Support for assessment	◆ ◆ ◆
Support for teaching technology standards	◆ ◆
Support for teaching twenty-first-century knowledge and abilities	◆ ◆

◆◆◆◆   Dominant—Almost all of the criteria for support in this category are present.

◆◆◆   Substantial—Most of the criteria for support in this category are present.

◆◆   Some/Moderate—Some of the criteria for support in this category are present.

◆   Marginal/Missing—Very few or none of the criteria for support in this category are present.

Support for Teaching the Curriculum

The *Teacher's Manual* and the *Teacher's Wraparound Edition* offer support for teachers in several key areas of learning, as shown by the lists in the preceding section. The *Teacher's Manual* begins with a discussion of what "technology education" means to the authors and how that meaning is reflected in the curriculum. The next section walks teachers through the textbook and ST, EV, and DMA activities. It explains in detail how to use the various components and how they relate to the curriculum.

Following this are nine pages of detailed information and resources aimed at helping teachers plan their technology education programs and improve their teaching in a design-based learning context.

The Planning Your Program section includes theoretical and pedagogical information about best practices in design- and activity-based learning. Specific areas include:

- Aims and goals
- Role of the teacher
- Assessment and evaluation

- General principles of instruction
- The relationship between theory and practical work

The *Teacher's Manual* also includes three comprehensive charts. One correlates the chapters and activities with the STL. The other shows the essential basic interdisciplinary skills (reading, writing, verbal, math, science, analytical) that are taught in the text and activities. The third chart presents the scope and sequence, demonstrating how each chapter is aligned with a set of major concepts in technology education. Teachers are encouraged to consider and select major concepts and topics that best suit their curricular needs

Support for Pedagogy

The Teaching Techniques section provides specific strategies for teachers to use with their students in the activity-based context of the curriculum. These include the following:

- Teaching styles
- Helping students gain basic information
- Helping students question and evaluate
- Helping students participate in discussion

- Helping students apply learning
- Helping students develop creativity
- Helping students review information

The section called Teaching Students of Varying Abilities offers guidance for differentiating instruction and making adjustments for students with special needs. There is also an extensive list of resources in the *Teacher's Manual* that provides additional help in this area. Only one other core technology resource provides similar support for differentiating instruction for all learners.

Support for Assessment

The curriculum gives extensive attention to providing teachers and students with a variety of assessments and offers support in helping teachers understand the theory and practice of assessing student progress and knowledge. The curriculum features more than 160 activities specifically designed to be used as assessments of student skill and understanding. Teachers and students are instructed to conclude each activity with two evaluation exercises: a peer evaluation of student projects and a student self-evaluation. In addition to the many questions, tests, tasks, and activities provided in the curriculum, teachers are given instruction in helping students to build a DMA portfolio to evaluate student performance.

Support for Teaching the Technology Standards

Although the technology education content of *SOW* promotes strong, standards-based learning in the student text and activities, there is less support for teachers who may be unfamiliar with the STL. No direct discussion or information is provided in the teacher materials to help them master the content of the STL. The STL-alignment chart notes that the standards present the essential knowledge and skills students need to be technologically literate, but nothing else expands on this notion from a teaching perspective. Likewise, the margin notes in the *Teacher's Wraparound Edition* announce the STL being taught in each text section but do not offer additional guidance to understanding them. Only a few resources in the resource section focus on the STL.

Support for Teaching Twenty-First-Century Knowledge and Abilities

The introductions of the *Teacher's Manual* and the *Teacher's Wraparound Edition* discuss how technology education and a focus on design activities foster workplace skills development. Workplace skills such as critical thinking and creativity, communication and collaboration, business and economic skills, and some leadership skills are developed through the activities and supporting tasks. However, there is no direct teaching on this topic. Chapter 15 is devoted to showcasing and examining different technology-related careers.

Table of Contents—*Technology: Shaping Our World*, Student Edition
(Number of pages indicated in parentheses)

Chapter 1 Technology and You—An Introduction (12)

Chapter 2 Generating and Developing Ideas (32)

Chapter 3 Communicating Ideas (26)

Chapter 4 Materials (30)

Chapter 5 Processing Materials (36)

Chapter 6 Structures (18)

Chapter 7 Construction (26)

Chapter 8 Machines (36)

Chapter 9 Transportation (24)

Chapter 10 Energy (26)

Chapter 11 Electricity and Magnetism (26)

Chapter 12 Using Electricity and Electronics (24)

Chapter 13 Information and Communication Technology (18)

Chapter 14 Agriculture, Biotechnology, and Medical Technology (28)

Chapter 15 The World of Work (32)

Chapter 16 Learning From the Past: Predicting the Future (33)

SAMPLE PAGES

The sample pages from the student edition of *SOW* show the general reading level, format, layout, kinds of activities, and how graphics, pictures, and text boxes are used. The graphics are a typical example of how the diagrams and drawings help explain the content of the lessons and how they can support lower-level readers to understand the text.

The selected activity shows a large-scale DMA. Note how all the STs that are related to the DMA are listed, as well as explicitly stated learning goals and required materials.

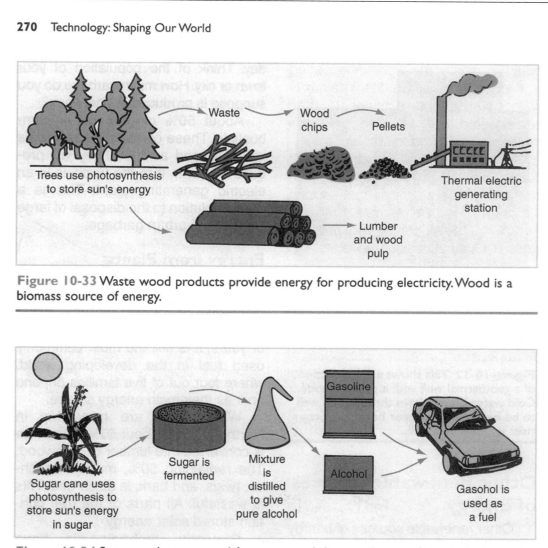

Figure 10-33 Waste wood products provide energy for producing electricity. Wood is a biomass source of energy.

Figure 10-34 Sugar can be processed from cane and then used to produce alcohol. Blends of alcohol and gasoline are used to fuel automobiles.

Energy from Decomposing Matter

On farms, manure can be collected. Farms also have plant wastes. There are pasture plants that have not been eaten, leftover feedstock, fruits, vegetables, and grains that are damaged or unsold.

When manure and organic wastes are put into closed tanks, bacteria will digest them. This produces methane gas, which scientists call "biogas." This can be used for cooking, lighting, and running engines. It is a common method of producing energy in many parts of the world. In China, there are over 7 million biogas digesters supplying energy for 35 million people.

Digesters are designed to be batch load or continuous load. In a batch load type, the digester is loaded with a soupy mix of wastes. The mix is called slurry. The digester is then sealed and not emptied until the materials stop producing gas.

A continuous load digester accepts a small amount of fresh slurry continuously. This type produces gas as long as slurry is being fed into it. Figure 10-35 diagrams two different kinds of continuous load digesters.

Hydrogen

The name *hydrogen* comes from the Greek word meaning "water generator," as water is produced when hydrogen burns in the presence of oxygen. One of the first successful uses of this fuel was in the Saturn V rocket that took men to the moon. The Space Shuttle has a huge external tank filled with liquid hydrogen and

liquid oxygen. This fuel not only lifts the shuttle into orbit but also produces the electricity needed during a mission. The power to make the two elements combine comes from a fuel cell. A fuel cell is a device that allows hydrogen and oxygen to combine without a combustion process. Reaction occurs when electrons are released from the hydrogen and travel to the oxygen through an external circuit. As electrons travel through the circuit, they generate a current that can power any electrical device. The reaction benefits the astronauts in another way. The only by-product is water, which is the water that astronauts drink.

If fuel cells produce energy without any toxic by-products, why don't we use them in other vehicles? The main reason is cost. Fuel cells use

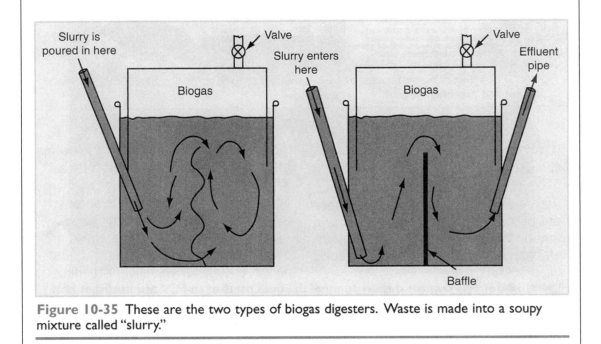

Figure 10-35 These are the two types of biogas digesters. Waste is made into a soupy mixture called "slurry."

Support Tasks   Designing

ST-14
Designing for People—
Anthropometric Data

Name:_____ Date: _____

What You Will Learn
◆ How to collect anthropometric data.

Materials
◆ ST-14 worksheet
◆ Pencil

One of the major tasks of the industrial designer is to ensure that objects will be comfortable, safe, and easy to use. To achieve this, the designer must know and use average dimensions of the human body. Measurements of the human body are known as anthropometrical data.

Procedure
One of the most commonly used objects is a chair. To produce a well-designed chair, the designer must know the size of the persons who will be using it. This information is quite easy to get. The dimensions you need to find are shown in the diagram below. Fill out the chart, using measurements from family members. NOTE: You should only measure people over the age of 15 years.

Support Tasks   Designing

Use the chart for recording your measurements.

Name of Family Member	Dimensions							
	A	B	C	D	E	F	G	H
Total								
Average								

Design and Make Activities

Machines and Transportation

DMA-16
Pneumatic Ergonome

Related Chapter: Chapter 10, Energy

The Context

How many times have you sat on a chair and, after a very short time, found yourself moving your body trying to get comfortable? How often have you bought a product that was difficult or uncomfortable to use? Ergonomics (the study of humans in relation to their environment) and anthropometrics (the science of human measurement) help designers ensure that products are comfortable and convenient for people to use. Ergonomes are models of the human figure that can be used to help the designer produce items that are the correct size for the consumer.

The Design Brief

Design and make a pneumatic ergonome that will assist with the design of a consumer product.

The Design Decisions

You can decide on the following:

The Need
◆ What product requires the use of an ergonome in its design stage?
◆ Who is the average consumer of the product ?
◆ Where do consumers use the product?
◆ When do consumers use the product?

The Ergonome
◆ What size ergonome is required?
◆ What shape ergonome is required?
◆ Which parts of the ergonome must move?

The Mechanism
◆ Which parts of the ergonome will be pneumatically-controlled?
◆ What pneumatic system is required?
◆ What linkages are required?

The Construction
◆ Of what material will it be made?
◆ What type and size mediums will be used to transmit force?

The Appearance
◆ Will the color matter?

Design and Make Activities   Machines and Transportation

The Support Tasks

ST-15	Making an Ergonome
ST-16	Modeling Ideas with Cardboard, Wood Strip, and Dowel
ST-30	Scaling Up—Drawing Things Bigger
ST-67	Investigating Pneumatics and Hydraulics
ST-14	Designing for People— Anthropometrical Data
ST-68	Understanding Systems
ST-5	Writing a Design Specification
EV-1	Evaluating the Final Product
EV-2	Unit Review

What You Will Learn

- About the importance of human factors in design.
- How an ergonome can assist with the design of an everyday product.
- About pneumatically and hydraulically controlled products.
- How air pressure is used in pneumatic systems.
- To use anthropometrical data in the design of a product.
- To generate, develop, and communicate design ideas using 2-D and 3-D models.
- To write a design specification.
- To design and make a pneumatic system.
- To mark, cut, and join materials with a high degree of accuracy.
- To evaluate a product against a design specification.
- To evaluate your designing and making.

What You Will Need

Stimulus Materials
- Anthropometric data tables

Tools
- Junior hacksaw
- Cutting mat
- Utility knife
- Scissors
- Bench hook

Consumables
- 3/8" × 3/8" (10 mm × 10 mm) wood strip
- Thin cardboard
- PVA glue
- 1/4" wood dowel
- Syringes
- Plastic tubing

Technology Education: Learning by Design

Developer/Author:	Michael Hacker and David Burghardt, Hofstra University, Center for Technological Literacy
Distributor/Publisher:	Pearson Prentice Hall
Publication date:	2004
Ordering information:	Pearson Prentice Hall, http://vig.prenhall.com
Target audience:	Middle school (Grades 6–8)

BRIEF DESCRIPTION

This product's Informed Design Approach gives students hands-on, interactive instruction to work on authentic design challenges and projects. Each chapter begins with brief, simple activities and exercises that become increasingly complex and sophisticated as they lead up to the chapter's two major design activities.

Written after the *Standards for Technological Literacy* (STL) were published, this curriculum strongly promotes technological literacy through a balance of text and activities. The text is strongest in its presentation of Standard 2 (part of the STL Nature of Technology theme) and Standards 16, 17, and 19 (STL Designed World theme). The activities focus most on Standard 2 and Standards 8, 9, 11, and 12 (from the Design and the Abilities for a Technological World themes). The different foci of the text and activities serve to round out the standards offering for this product and complement one another. All twenty of the STL are addressed, and 79 percent of the text was rated as standards-based. Eighty-six percent of the middle school benchmarks are covered, including all of the Standard 3 middle school benchmarks (connecting technology to other subject areas). Connections are made between math, science, technology, history, social studies, and art throughout the text.

The teacher support materials are especially comprehensive and offer new and veteran teachers the kind of help they need to understand the STL, techno ogical literacy and design as the central technology education pedagogy. *Technology Education: Learning by Design* was rated among the highest of the five core curricula reviewed for this book.

CURRICULUM COMPONENTS

- *Student Edition*, hardcover, 558 pp., $45.97
- *Student Activity Guide*, softcover, 256 pp., $9.97

- *Annotated Teacher's Edition*, hardcover, 558 pp., $69.97
- *Teacher's Resource Binder*, softcover, $74.97
- Test Bank with *ExamView* CD-ROM, $99.97
- Time-Line Poster, $14.97
- Online support activities—www.PHSchool.com (register for online access)

Materials/Equipment

Each activity includes a list of required materials and equipment. For the most part, the materials are readily available and the equipment is commonly found in most middle schools. Some of the activities and lessons call for computer and Internet use, and some applications or software could be difficult or expensive to obtain.

Special Preparations

Generally, no special preparations are required. Activities that involve computer software, applications, or Internet work could require significant preparation, depending on teacher experience. No special professional development is needed to use this curriculum.

CURRICULUM OVERVIEW

Topic Overview

The eighteen chapters in this textbook are divided into seven units, each covering a major area of technology:

- The Nature of Technology
- Design for a Technological World
- Materials, Manufacturing, and Construction
- The Future of Technology in Society
- Communication and Information Technology
- Energy, Power, and Transportation
- Biological and Chemical Technology

All twenty of the STL are addressed in the curriculum, plus a variety of technology topics not explicitly found in the STL—understanding simple machines and engines, ergonomics, space, electricity, careers, and people in technology.

Instructional Model

This product uses a model called FOCUS as its pedagogical basis. The FOCUS model provides the essential framework from which all the student content and activities hang, and it is used to articulate the various components of the curriculum:

Focus students on the problem context

Organize for informed design

Coordinate student progress

Unite the class in thinking about accomplishments

Sum up progress on the learning goals

Each activity addressed in the *Teacher's Resource Binder* is accompanied by an implementation plan. This plan includes a time line for integrating the FOCUS approach with the activities, the Informed Design loop, and suggested instructional strategies. The major end-of-chapter design activities teach the eight-step Informed Design loop to guide students through the problem-solving process. The FOCUS model is further supported by shorter activities that are embedded in the text or featured in the chapter reviews. These activities reflect and support the content taught in the text and give students the opportunity to build the knowledge and abilities promoted in the STL, particularly Themes 3 and 4.

The chapter sections begin by specifically stating the benchmarks they cover as well as vocabulary to look for and reading strategies to help students organize and study the materials.

The chapters contain the following features:

- Benchmarks for Learning
- Section Assessments (Recall & Comprehension, Critical Thinking questions, and Quick Activities)
- People in Technology
- How Technology Works (web-based activities and explorations)
- Activities
- Connecting to Math, Science, and Technology
- Technology in the Real World
- Chapter Review
- Design Activities

Chapter Reviews include

- Chapter Summary
- Building Vocabulary
- Applying Your Knowledge
- Reviewing Content
- Critical Thinking
- Connecting to Math-Science-Technology (questions and activities)

Following the chapter review are two major design activities that support and extend the themes of the chapters.

The text is written at a 6.5 grade level and has a Lexile score of 970L. However, some of the passages may be difficult for lower level middle school readers. The text layout in the *Student Edition* includes easy-to-read and easy-to-identify heads and subheads, and, along with the Reading Strategy sections at the beginning of each chapter, they help students organize and focus their learning. The figures, graphs, tables, and charts are very important to understanding the text and activities and often add essential information to the lesson. The drawings and pictures also relate directly to the text and help move the lessons along. The photographs sometimes feature middle school children, but mostly show (primarily Caucasian) adults in the process of using technology.

The captions under the graphics are also tightly articulated with the lesson content. Below most of these graphics are questions for students to answer that are labeled according to the type of higher order thinking skill they require:

- Inferring
- Summarizing
- Comparing
- Contrasting
- Extending
- Interpreting
- Applying
- Evaluating

Finally, the text does a good job of making connections between technology education and other subject areas. Connecting to Math, Science, and Technology provides questions and activities that integrate the technology content with these subjects. All the Standard 3 middle school benchmarks (connecting technology to other subject areas) are addressed in the text and activities. Numerous connections between technology, history, social studies, and art, in addition to math and science, are made throughout the text (see the Standards and Benchmark-Level Analyses section for details).

Duration

The authors recommend that students read the text at a rate of about 15 pages per week. Because most of the chapters are from 25 to 30 pages long, students would cover one of the eighteen chapters every two weeks, using an entire school year to complete the text.

Most of the 36 Design Activities can be done in four or five fifty-minute sessions. These activities could easily be expanded to become large-scale, multiweek projects, if desired. Activities that are embedded in the text or that come at the end of the chapter vary in duration, but most are short, single-session activities.

Nature of Activities

Learning by Design offers many different kinds of activities and projects, and all of them relate directly to the topics covered in the text. There are two major, end-of-chapter Design Activities for each of the eighteen chapters and at least three shorter activities per chapter as part of the section assessments. Brief activities and exercises are sometimes embedded in the text as well.

Web-based, interactive activities are featured in each chapter in a boxed text section called How Technology Works. These activities are part of www.PHschool.com, an online repository of simulation-based activities published by Prentice Hall. In addition to online activities, many of the text activities require students to do Internet research.

All the activities underscore key learning and extend and challenge student thinking and skills. Because design is the primary instructional strategy, the role of the activities takes on additional importance. An eight-step process, called the Informed Design process, is used to structure the 36 Design Activities:

1. Clarify the design specifications and constraints

2. Research and investigate

3. Generate alternative designs

4. Choose and justify the optimal solution

5. Develop a prototype

6. Test and evaluate

7. Redesign the solution

8. Communicate your achievements

Of the 106 activities in this book, 12 are classified as open-ended explorations and 27 are classified as guided explorations. These types of activities are most often seen in the end-of-chapter Design Activities and require more skill in applying the design process than do the directed or supporting activity types. The 23 directed activities and the 44 supporting science, math, or technology exercises generally are found in the section assessments or are embedded in the text itself (see Figure 8.2.1).

Figure 8.2.2 shows that the most commonly used design approaches are short/focused/practical, followed by investigate/disassemble/evaluate. These two

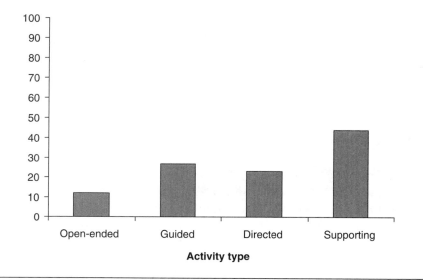

Figure 8.2.1   Number of activities by type in *Technology Education: Learning by Design*, N = 106

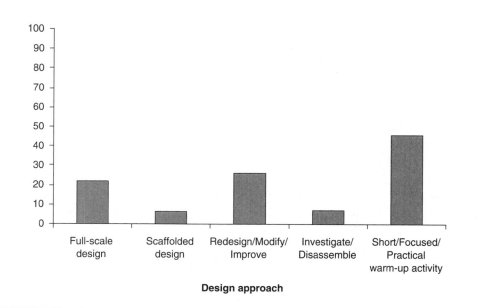

Figure 8.2.2   Number of activities by design approach in *Technology Education: Learning by Design*, N = 106

approaches are generally used to give students basic practice in selected aspects of the design process or to supply them with background or content information that enriches the learning goals of the lessons. Full-scale design is the next most-used approach. This approach requires that students employ all parts of the design process and produce a product (not just a prototype) or service of some sort. A full-scale design activity requires higher levels of student mastery of the design process and generally takes the most classroom time to complete.

The early activities in each chapter are used to scaffold student learning and design abilities. The abundance of supporting exercises and directed activities that follow the short/focused/practical approach, and the fact that these are most often seen in the section assessments, indicates that students have the opportunity to practice skills on a less complex scale as they proceed through the text.

Once students work through the chapter and the scaffolded design challenges, they are given the chance at the end of each chapter to tackle more complex challenges, with less hand-holding from the text. The majority of the larger, more challenging design activities are classified as either guided exploration/full-scale design or open-ended exploration/full-scale design. The rollout of activity types and approaches across the entire text follows this same pattern of increasing complexity, leading students to greater and greater facility with the design process.

Assessment

Although analyzing the quality of individual assessments was not part of the review of this product, the variety and number of assessments place it among the top two core technology products for assessment coverage.

Assessments can be found in four locations in the *Student Edition:* in the section assessments, in the chapter reviews, in the thirty-six major design activities, and embedded in the text. The *Annotated Teacher's Edition* and *Teacher's Resource Binder* also include ideas for assessing student learning. Table 8.2.1 shows how the curriculum uses several kinds of assessment strategies.

Each section assessment includes three basic Recall and Comprehension questions and two Critical Thinking questions. The questions are labeled by the higher order thinking skills they require: analyze, predict, make judgments, hypothesize, summarize, and extend. They are also intended as ongoing assessments of student understanding and skills. The section assessments also include Quick Activities. These short exercises and projects enhance and underscore the lesson goals and content and are also meant to be used as assessments.

The chapter reviews include five Reviewing Content questions, five exercises or activities called Applying Your Knowledge, and four or five Critical Thinking questions. As is the case for the section assessments, the questions are labeled according to the type of higher order thinking skills they invoke: predicting, applying concepts, making judgments, and the like. Each chapter review ends with a math-science-technology connection exercise that integrates the learning in the chapter across these subject areas.

In addition to those mentioned earlier, numerous other assessment activities are offered. The major design activities can be used as performance assessments, and each chapter includes a section called How Technology Works, which directs students to online multimedia simulations and activities that can be used as assessments. A computerized test bank CD-ROM is also available.

The *Teacher's Resource Binder* and the *Annotated Teacher's Edition* provide answers to all the questions and assessments found in the student text. These teacher resources

Table 8.2.1   Student assessment tools and their presence in *Technology Education: Learning by Design*

Assessment approach	Presence in the curriculum
Paper-and-pencil tests—multiple-choice, short answer, true/false, vocabulary, completion	◆ ◆ ◆ ◆
Projects/Products/Media—individual and group activities, projects, products, media	◆ ◆ ◆ ◆
Performance-based assessments—demonstrations, presentations, multimedia, performances	◆ ◆ ◆
Portfolios—student papers, notes, project reports, research, work samples	◆ ◆ ◆
Student work—workbook or lab journal pages, handouts, graphs, charts, etc.	◆ ◆ ◆ ◆
Open-ended questioning—essays, extended writing exercises, critical thinking questions, etc.	◆ ◆ ◆ ◆
Computerized assessment—online simulations, tests, etc.	◆ ◆
Self-evaluations—peer assessments, self-reflections, self-evaluations	◆ ◆
Rubrics/Checklists	◆
Informal observations/Discussions—teacher observations	◆

◆◆◆◆   Dominant—There are a large number of assessments of this type in the curriculum.

◆◆◆   Substantial—There are a substantial number of assessments of this type in the curriculum.

◆◆   Some/Moderate—There are a moderate number of assessments of this type in the curriculum.

◆   Marginal/Missing—There are very few or no assessments of this type in the curriculum.

also include additional assessments and strategies for evaluating student progress, such as a safety test, more activities to be used as performance assessments, crossword puzzles, and a regular chapter feature called Assess/Close.

STL STANDARDS AND BENCHMARK-LEVEL ANALYSES

Written after the STL were published, *Technology Education: Learning by Design* offers thorough, standards-based coverage of the STL and supports student attainment of technological literacy. All twenty of the STL are covered in the curriculum. Each chapter in the *Student Edition, Annotated Teacher's Edition,* and the *Teacher's Resource Binder* gives the specific STL benchmarks addressed in the chapter, and teachers are encouraged to go over these benchmarks with the students on a regular basis.

Table 8.2.2   Five most frequent and five least frequent standards in the overall
curriculum for *Technology Education: Learning by Design*

5 most frequent standards	*5 least frequent standards*
Standard 11 (20%)—applying the design process	Standard 10 (< 1%)—problem solving
Standard 2 (17%)—the core concepts of technology	Standard 6 (< 1%)—the role of society in the development and use of technology
Standard 12 (13%)—using and maintaining technological products and systems	Standard 5 (< 1%)—the effects of technology on the environment
Standard 8 (9%)—the attributes of design	Standard 14 (1%)—medical technologies
Standard 17 (7%)—information and communication technologies	Standard 1 (1%)—the characteristics and scope of technology

Standards Coverage in the Overall Curriculum

Table 8.2.2 shows the standards that appear most and least frequently in the curriculum overall. For more details about the specific benchmarks covered in the text and activities, see Appendix A.

More than 54 percent of the standards coverage in the overall curriculum is accounted for by the five most frequently addressed standards. This is consistent with the use of the Informed Design Process and the FOCUS model as the pedagogical basis for the curriculum. Standard 17 rounds out the top five with its focus on information and communication. The five least frequent standards total less than 4 percent of the standards coverage in the overall curriculum.

Standards Coverage in the Text

The *Learning by Design* text treats all twenty of the STL, and the coverage, overall, is 79 percent standards-based. Eighty-six percent of the middle school benchmarks are addressed in the text. See Table 8.2.3 for details.

Following is a discussion of the standards that comprise the highest and lowest percentages of the text. Appendix A will provide further details.

Standard 2 (the core concepts of technology) is by far the best covered standard in the text. Twenty of the 32 K–12 benchmarks are covered and are 83 percent standards-based. The most addressed benchmark is the 3–5 Benchmark H (resources are the things needed to get a job done).

Standard 17 (information and communication technologies) represents 13 percent of the text, and just over half of its benchmark treatment is standards-based. The primary benchmarks for this standard deal mostly with the definition of information systems, the parts of that system, and the use of symbols in information systems. All of the middle school benchmarks for this standard are covered.

Standard 19 (manufacturing technologies) also comprises 13 percent of the text, and its benchmarks are 62 percent standards-based. Fourteen of the 18 K–12 benchmarks

Table 8.2.3 Results of analyses of STL coverage in the text for *Technology Education: Learning by Design*

STL covered	Percent of text devoted to each STL	Percent of coverage that is standards-based for each STL	Primary benchmarks covered for each STL			
			K–2	3–5	6–8	9–12
Standard 1	2%	73%				K
Standard 2	24%	83%		H		
Standard 3	4%	47%			F	
Standard 4	4%	79%			D	
Standard 5	1%	88%			D E	
Standard 6	1%	88%			G	
Standard 7	4%	81%				G H I
Standard 8	< 1%	80%			G	H
Standard 9	< 1%	100%			G	
Standard 10	< 1%	100%			H	I
Standard 11	< 1%	100%			K	
Standard 12	7%	87%			H	
Standard 13	< 1%	86%				L
Standard 14	2%	75%		E	J	
Standard 15	3%	67%		D		L
Standard 16	10%	54%			*	M
Standard 17	13%	54%			H I K	
Standard 18	3%	92%			G	
Standard 19	13%	62%			F H	M
Standard 20	4%	69%			*	

Primary benchmark coverage = 21% or more of total benchmarks for the standard

An asterisk (*) in front of a benchmark indicates that, while the topic of the STL is addressed, no specific benchmarks are covered.

Benchmarks are not listed for standards that are covered in less than 0.5% of the text.

The highlighted standards are represented most often in the text.

are represented, and all of the middle school benchmarks are covered. The definition of a manufacturing system, the manufacturing process, and the classification of different types of materials comprise the focus of the primary benchmarks.

Standard 16 (energy and power technologies) accounts for 10 percent of the text, with benchmark coverage that is 54 percent standards-based. All of this Standard 16's middle school benchmarks are covered, along with four of five Grades 9–12 benchmarks. The primary benchmark coverage for Standard 16 focuses on renewable and nonrenewable resources or on more general, standards-referenced content, such as electricity and electronics, types of circuits, and so on.

Standards 8, 9, 10 (understanding design standards) and Standards 11 and 13 (abilities for a technological world) receive the least coverage in the student text. However, the benchmark treatment of all five of these standards is strongly standards-based (from 80 to 100 percent) and can provide opportunities to achieve technological literacy for the benchmarks covered.

One of the stated goals of this curriculum is to present technology education as an integrating discipline that cuts across all subject areas. It is worth noting that all the Standard 3 benchmarks are covered in the text, and there are numerous instances where connections are made between technology education and mathematics, science, social studies, history, and so on. In many cases, students are called on to apply their knowledge of mathematics, science, and the like in the process of solving technology problems. Just less than half of the instances of Standard 3 benchmarks are standards-based.

Although this curriculum was developed for middle school students, many of the standards it addresses are presented at the 9–12 grade level, using Grades 9–12 benchmarks. This is particularly true for information given about how various electronic technologies work. While this would probably not be problematic for many middle school students (particularly with good teaching intervention), some of the text could be too challenging for less advanced middle school students. The number of Grades 3–5 benchmarks addressed may help to offset this problem, and the inclusion of both lower and higher level benchmarks could go far toward giving students opportunities to revisit previously acquired knowledge and challenge themselves with higher level learning.

Standards Coverage in the Activities

All of the activities relate directly to the topics covered in the text, with no instances of "floating activities" that do not relate to the lesson content. The activities support the STL in such a way that completing the activities as presented should underscore the benchmarks they address and provide opportunities for mastery of those benchmarks. The combination of ability, skill, and informational standards in the activities also contributes to the high quality of this curriculum.

As Table 8.2.4 demonstrates, 19 of the 20 STL are addressed in the activities. This means that the activities, as well as the text, provide students with opportunities to gain knowledge and skills from many different standards. It is also further evidence that the activities and text support one another. Referring to Appendix A will provide further details.

Standard 11 (abilities to apply the design process) comprises 34 percent of the activities and is evenly distributed throughout them. Its most frequently addressed benchmarks focus on applying the design process and evaluating requirements, criteria, and constraints. The abundance of benchmark coverage for Standard 11 in the activities serves to balance out the relative lack of coverage of that standard in the text. All of the middle school benchmarks are treated for this standard.

Standard 12 (abilities to use and maintain technological products and systems) makes up 17 percent of the standards' focus in the activities. Its primary benchmark coverage looks at following directions to assemble products (3–5 benchmark), using information to understand how things work, using various computer and

Table 8.2.4   Results of analyses of STL coverage in the activities for *Technology Education: Learning by Design*

STL covered	Percent of activities devoted to each STL	Primary benchmarks covered for each STL			
		K–2	3–5	6–8	9–12
Standard 1	< 1%			G H	
Standard 2	12%		H		Z
Standard 3	2%			F	
Standard 4	< 1%			D E	
Standard 5	< 1%			F	
Standard 6	< 1%			E	
Standard 7	—	—	—	—	—
Standard 8	14%			E G	H J
Standard 9	11%			F G H	
Standard 10	< 1%			H	
Standard 11	34%			H K	
Standard 12	17%		D	H J	L
Standard 13	2%			F G H	
Standard 14	< 1%		E F	G	
Standard 15	< 1%		D	H I J	
Standard 16	1%			H	K
Standard 17	2%			J K	
Standard 18	<1%			G H I	
Standard 19	1%			H	
Standard 20	1%			F	L

Primary benchmark coverage = 21% or more of total benchmarks for the standard

Benchmarks are not listed for standards that are covered in less than 0.5% of the text.

The highlighted standards are represented most often in the text.

calculator applications, and communicating documented processes and procedures to various audiences.

Standard 8 (the attributes of design) accounts for 14 percent of the standards' content in the activities. Its primary benchmarks address two middle school benchmarks (design is a creative planning process that leads to useful products and systems, and requirements are made-up criteria and constraints) and two high school benchmarks (the steps of the design process, and critiquing, redefining, and improving design).

Standard 2 (core concepts of technology) makes up 12 percent of the activity content, with primary benchmark coverage coming from the 3–5 standards (resources are things needed to get a job done) and the 9–12 standards (trade-offs in selecting resources).

Standard 9 (engineering design) deals with 100 percent of its middle school benchmarks and accounts for 11 percent of the content presented in the activities. Its primary benchmark focus is on the steps of the engineering design process; brainstorming; and modeling, testing, evaluating, and modifying designs.

The remaining fifteen standards comprise a total of about 11 percent of the activity content. Standards 3, 13, and 17 tie for least-treated standard (2 percent of the activity content each).

The analysis of the activities shows that they provide students with ample, broad-based practice in applying the design process. Although the activities are not strong in using the nondesign standards, the fact that the text presents highly standards-based treatment of all twenty standards helps balance the overall treatment of the STL, giving students a very good chance at attaining technological literacy.

TEACHER MATERIALS REVIEW

The teacher materials in *Technology Education: Learning by Design* provide both novice and veteran teachers with more than sufficient support for teaching the Informed Design Process using the FOCUS pedagogy. The materials offer clear, concise explanations of the STL and why they are important to attaining technological literacy, and they show step-by-step how to teach the standards using design as pedagogy.

The teacher materials are a critical, enriching part of this product. Although the *Student Edition* is of very high quality, using it without the aid of the *Annotated Teacher's Edition* and the *Teacher's Resource Binder* would greatly reduce the student experience and lessen students' chances to attain technological literacy. This is particularly true because the *Teacher's Resource Binder* is the sole source of information about the STL and technological literacy, beyond the STL alignment chart found in the *Annotated Teacher's Edition*.

Table 8.2.5 shows five kinds, or categories, of teacher support and rates how strongly those categories are represented in the teacher support materials for this product.

Overview of Teacher Materials Components

The instructional support materials for this curriculum are located in the *Annotated Teacher's Edition* and the *Teacher's Resource Binder*. The *Annotated Teacher's Edition* was designed to work in tandem with the *Teacher's Resource Binder*, and each chapter refers the teacher to additional materials and strategies in the *Binder*. A time-line poster and computerized test bank CD-ROM are also available.

The *Annotated Teacher's Edition* is an expanded, wraparound version of the *Student Edition*. The front matter offers STL and benchmarks alignment for the text, brief chapter outlines, and answers to the assessment questions raised in the text, section assessments, and chapter reviews. Brief notes and guidelines for teaching the materials, assessing student understanding, and approaching and completing the activities are provided in the margin notes.

The introduction to the *Teacher's Resource Binder* explains the Informed Design Approach, which is the central, underlying pedagogical approach for the curriculum. Background information about technological literacy, technology education, and the

Table 8.2.5 Categories of teacher support materials and adequacy ratings for
Technology Education: Learning by Design

Categories of support found in teacher support materials	Adequacy of teacher support
Support for teaching the curriculum	◆ ◆ ◆
Support for pedagogy	◆ ◆ ◆ ◆
Support for assessment	◆ ◆ ◆ ◆
Support for teaching technology standards	◆ ◆ ◆ ◆
Support for teaching twenty-first-century knowledge and abilities	◆

◆◆◆◆   Dominant—Almost all of the criteria for support in this category are present.

◆◆◆   Substantial—Most of the criteria for support in this category are present.

◆◆   Some/Moderate—Some of the criteria for support in this category are present.

◆   Marginal/Missing—Very few or none of the criteria for support in this category are present.

STL are also featured. The student chapters reproduced in the *Teacher's Resource Binder* have additional aids for teachers such as chapter summaries and outlines, key ideas in technology, benchmarks for learning, teaching hints, additional student content, answers to assessments, and blackline masters and handouts.

Support for Teaching the Curriculum

Although they are not extensive, the teaching notes in the *Annotated Teacher's Edition* offer helpful suggestions that support and extend instruction. These margin annotations are grouped into six types and occur on almost every page:

- Teacher Resources—materials required for teaching the chapter
- Chapter Objectives—learning goals for each chapter
- Engage—suggestions to further student engagement through using interesting, authentic activities across the curriculum
- Customize for Less Advanced Students and Customize for More Advanced Students—suggestions for individualizing lessons and addressing differentiated instruction and students with special needs
- Teach—a section that provides additional activities and suggestions for supplementing and integrating the lessons across the curriculum
- Assess or Assess/Close—additional assessment ideas and various methods for closing each section

The Customize for Less/More Advanced Students annotations contain useful information about altering or extending the lessons to accommodate differentiated learning. However, this type of annotation does not appear very frequently in the margin notes. With growing class sizes and the movement to reduce pull-outs, it would be beneficial to teachers and students to have more customized annotations. Assess/Close also offers teachers ideas for embedded assessment of student learning or end-of-chapter assessments.

Support for Pedagogy

The *Teacher's Resource Binder* includes 28 introductory pages that address the following topics and issues:

- Learning Standards
- Using This Text
- Length of Reading Assignments
- Integrating Readings With Hands-On Activities
- Optimizing the Benefits of the Text
- Understanding Technology Education
- Uniqueness of Technology
- Technology in Common Parlance
- Design as an Instructional Strategy
- Design as the Core Process in Technology

- Pedagogical Rationale for Design
- Problems With Design in Classrooms
- Informed Design
- Knowledge and Skill Builders
- An Example in a Familiar Context
- The FOCUS on Design: A Pedagogical Strategy for Teachers
- Using the FOCUS Model to Guide Instruction
- General Safety Unit

The sections from Design as an Instructional Strategy to Using the FOCUS Model to Guide Instruction deal specifically with pedagogy. These nine pages offer practical, in-depth guidance and information about essential pedagogical issues promoted in the curriculum.

The remainder of the *Teacher's Resource Binder* walks teachers through the student lessons, providing additional important information and resources. Implementation plans that show how to integrate the FOCUS model components with the Informed Design loop and the Design Activities are a major focus of each *Teacher's Resource Binder* chapter. Answers to all assessments, questions, and exercises are included. Blackline masters, handouts, and additional assessments, activities, and exercises are also provided.

Support for Assessment

As discussed earlier in the Assessment section, this product showcases multiple approaches and instruments for assessing student learning. The *Teacher's Resource Binder* and the *Annotated Teacher's Edition* offer detailed answers to the assessments in the *Student Edition*, as well as additional ideas for performance-based and written assessments. The two teacher support resources do not provide much information about the purpose or execution of the various assessments. Teachers new to performance-based or portfolio assessments, for example, may have difficulty knowing how to convert these activities into actual assessments.

Support for Teaching the Technology Standards

The *Annotated Teacher's Edition* features a six-page section in the introduction that presents the STL addressed in the student material. Specific benchmarks are noted, and an indication of whether the authors consider the benchmark coverage to be "primary" or "additional" is included. These indicators are roughly equivalent to this review's standards-based and standards-referenced analyses. The *Teacher's Resource Binder* offers a description and explanation of the standards and a discussion of their significance in the text. It also offers an in-depth treatment of the role and importance of technology education and how the relatively new STL can be used to promote technological literacy for students. Particular emphasis is put on Standards 8–13, understanding and doing design, because they form the pedagogical underpinnings of the curriculum.

Support for Teaching Twenty-First-Century Knowledge and Abilities

The teacher materials do not directly address the development of workplace skills as a category of learning; however, the suggestions and guidelines in the *Annotated Teacher's Edition* and *Teacher's Resource Binder* address such skills as critical thinking and creativity, communication and collaboration, business and economic skills, and some leadership skills. Technology-related careers are not directly addressed in this product; however, some information about careers in technology can be found in the nine People in Technology text boxes. These sections focus on innovators whose technological inventions and products had major impacts on society.

Table of Contents—*Technology Education: Learning by Design*
(Number of pages indicated in parentheses)

Unit 1: The Nature of Technology (2)

Chapter 1—The Nature of Technology (20)

Chapter 2—Technology and Society (26)

Unit 2: Design for a Technological World (2)

Chapter 3—Design and Problem Solving (26)

Chapter 4—Communicating Design Solutions (24)

Chapter 5—Resources for Technology (24)

Chapter 6—Technological Systems (26)

Unit 3: Materials, Manufacturing, and Construction

Chapter 7—Processing Materials (38)

Chapter 8—Manufacturing (32)

Chapter 9—Construction (38)

Unit 4: Communication and Information Technology (2)

Chapter 10—Communication Systems (22)

Chapter 11—Electronics and the Computer (34)

Chapter 12—Information Technology (36)

Chapter 13—Graphic Communication (30)

Unit 5: Energy, Power, and Transportation (2)

Chapter 14—Energy and Power (32)

Chapter 15—Transportation (30)

Unit 6: Biological and Chemical Technology (2)

Chapter 16—Biotechnical Systems (28)

Chapter 17—Chemical Technology (28)

Unit 7: The Future of Technology in Society (2)

Chapter 18—The Future of Technology (24)

SAMPLE PAGES

The sample pages from *Technology Education: Learning by Design* were selected to provide readers with an overall impression of how the text is written and the content presented. The opening page from a chapter section is included to show how the Benchmarks for Learning and Reading Strategy guides are handled. An example of the regular feature How Technology Works (an online activity supplement) is also showcased. Sample pages from Design Activity 1 demonstrate how the 36 major design activities are structured and how they follow the steps of the Informed Design Process.

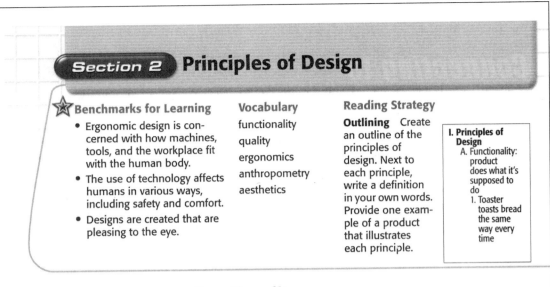

Section 2   Principles of Design

⭐ Benchmarks for Learning

- Ergonomic design is concerned with how machines, tools, and the workplace fit with the human body.
- The use of technology affects humans in various ways, including safety and comfort.
- Designs are created that are pleasing to the eye.

Vocabulary

functionality
quality
ergonomics
anthropometry
aesthetics

Reading Strategy

Outlining Create an outline of the principles of design. Next to each principle, write a definition in your own words. Provide one example of a product that illustrates each principle.

> **I. Principles of Design**
> A. Functionality: product does what it's supposed to do
> 1. Toaster toasts bread the same way every time

Functionality

Functionality refers to the capability of a product, system, or process to fulfill its intended purpose over the course of its desired life span. For example, a light bulb designed to give 1,000 hours of service is not expected to burn out before that amount of time, and a software program should complete all the tasks it was designed to perform.

The form of an object is often determined by its function. Dining tables hold plates of food, so they are made to be flat. Because drinking glasses are usually held in one hand, they are designed to be higher than they are wide. It would make no sense to design dining tables with slanted tops or drinking glasses too wide to grasp.

Figure 3.11 These kitchen products were designed for use by many different people.

Interpreting *What makes these products ergonomic?*

Quality

The product, system, or process must be designed to meet certain minimum standards of quality. **Quality** is the degree of excellence with which a product is made. For example, it is essential that medicines use the same formulation in every batch produced. Products made in different locations all need to meet the same standard for quality.

Ergonomics

Ergonomics is the science of adapting the work environment to people. Also called human factors engineering, it deals with designing products so they can be used easily and comfortably (Figure 3.11). Ergonomics combines an understanding of the human body with the techniques of design and engineering. A good design fits the user's size and capabilities. A desk chair, for example, must be designed for human comfort. The design solution would differ depending on the specifications—whether it's for a teenager, a man, a woman, a child, or all four. Another example of ergonomic design is an automobile's dashboard. All the information is displayed so that the driver can read it in a glance.

When designing for people, the designer must keep in mind that people come in many sizes and shapes. There really is no average person. To determine appropriate sizes, designers depend on data from the field of anthropometry. **Anthropometry** is the science of measuring people. It provides information about the average size and shape of people's bodies. Most often, designers accommodate the middle range of body sizes. They ignore the bottom 5 percent and the top 5 percent of dimensions. For this reason, a pocket calculator may have buttons too small for people with very large fingers.

Safety

A product, system, or process must be designed so it is safe for consumers to use. For example, cooking utensils that are made of heat-conducting materials should have handles

How Technology Works...

Design a Space Travel Chair Online

Ergonomics is the study of people in their working environment. It determines how new technologies are applied to everyday products. When combined with advances in technology, ergonomics allows us to improve products. Go online to see how it is used to develop a chair for space travel.

3D VIEW

SEE IT LIVE ON THE WEB
VISIT **PHSchool**.com

For: Ergonomics Activity
Visit: phschool.com
Web Code: GAI-0203

Supports forearms

Supports lower back

Principles of Design **63**

Design ACTIVITY 1

Innovation

Problem Situation

Changes and improvements are often made to a product to satisfy a need. People may ask that a device be made better. Awareness of the needs of others can challenge us to improve products so more people can use them. For example, opening the screw top of a bottle is difficult for people who cannot grip objects tightly. Twist-off jar openers do exist, but they function primarily on jars and larger bottle tops. The tops on soda bottles and other beverage bottles are smaller. Your task is to improve on an existing jar opener so that it will work on beverage bottles.

Your Challenge

You and your teammates are to design and construct a bottle opener.

> Go to your **Student Activity Guide, Design Activity 1.** Complete the activity in the Guide, and state the design challenge in your own words.

❶ Clarify the Design Specifications and Constraints

To solve the problem, your design must meet the following specifications and constraints:
- The bottle opener should accommodate a variety of top sizes.
- It should be easy for most people to use.
- It needs to have enough force to open most bottles.

> In your Guide, state the design specifications and constraints. Add any others that your team or your teacher included.

❷ Research and Investigate

To better complete the design challenge, you need to first gather information to help you build a knowledge base.

> In your Guide, complete Knowledge and Skill Builder 1: Investigate Existing Products.

Materials

You will need:
- bolts and nuts
- glue gun
- locking pliers
- metal strips
- rubber bands
- spring scale
- Velcro®
- wooden strips

In your Guide, complete Knowledge and Skill Builder 2: Size Requirements.

In your Guide, complete Knowledge and Skill Builder 3: Force Requirements.

③ Generate Alternative Designs

In your Guide, describe two possible solutions that your team has created for the problem. Your solutions should be based on the knowledge you have gathered so far.

④ Choose and Justify the Optimal Solution

Refer to your Guide. Explain why you selected the solution you did, and why it was the better choice.

⑤ Develop a Prototype

Construct your bottle opener. Include a drawing or a photograph of your final design in your Guide.

In any technological activity, you will use seven resources: people, capital, time, information, energy, materials, and tools & machines. In your Guide, indicate which resources were the most important in this activity, and how you made trade-offs between them.

⑥ Test and Evaluate

How will you test and evaluate your design? In your Guide, describe your testing procedure. Explain how the results will show that the design solves the problem and meets the specifications and constraints.

⑦ Redesign the Solution

Respond to the questions in your Guide about how you would redesign your solution. The redesign should be based on the knowledge and information that you have gained during this activity.

⑧ Communicate Your Achievements

In your Guide, describe the plan you will use to present your solution to your class. Include any handouts and/or PowerPoint slides that you will use.

Technology: Design and Applications

Developer/Author:	R. Thomas Wright and Ryan A. Brown
Distributor/Publisher:	Goodheart-Willcox Company, Inc.
Publication date:	2004
Ordering information:	Goodheart-Willcox Publisher, 1-800-323-0440, www.goodheartwillcox.com/
Target audience:	Middle school (Grades 7–9)

BRIEF DESCRIPTION

The text for *Technology: Design and Applications* is very comprehensive, covers all twenty Standards for Technological Literacy (STL), is 81 percent standards-based, and addresses 98 percent of the middle school benchmarks. Its language and unusual organization reflect the influence of the STL—each instructional unit covers an STL theme, and a chapter is devoted to each of the designed world standards (14–20). The major laboratory activities occur at the end of each instructional unit. Of the products reviewed, *Technology: Design and Applications* has the most extensive and comprehensive coverage of STL Theme 3 (design). It has ten chapters and more than 200 pages dedicated to it.

The student experience, however, will be greatly curtailed if the teacher does not use either the *Teacher's Manual* or the *Teacher's Wraparound Edition*, especially when teaching the laboratory activities. The *Teacher's Wraparound Edition* is easier to use and provides many helpful teaching suggestions in the margins at the point they would be most beneficial.

Although the product supplies activities in many different resources, teachers need to consider several issues about using them. The student text provides activity procedures, but does not provide classroom context or connect the activity to the concepts they are intended to demonstrate or reinforce. The teacher materials provide some of that information for some of the activities, but not enough for an inexperienced teacher. This information can help experienced teachers decide which activities to implement, because the authors intended teachers to select activities that meet their students' interests and needs. The activities address Standard 11 (applying the design process) more than other standards, but only two of the laboratory activities take the students through three or more steps of the design process, as defined by the middle school benchmarks.

CURRICULUM COMPONENTS

- *Student Edition,* hardcover, 736 pp., $29.97
- *Teacher's Manual,* softcover, 187 pp., $30.00

- *Student Activity Manual*, softcover, 125 pp., $9.96
- *Teacher's Wraparound Edition*, hardcover, 736 pp., $49.98
- *Teacher's Resource Binder*, $94.50
- *Teacher's Resource CD*, $141.00

These prices are the school prices (as opposed to the list prices). Most of the teacher support content in the *Teacher's Manual* and the *Teacher's Wraparound Edition* is identical except for location of the information.

Materials/Equipment

The materials needed for each laboratory activity are usually listed as part of the activity. Most of the activities require materials from a typical classroom, art room, wood and electronics shop, and/or a computer and appropriate software. Except for some electronic equipment (digital camera, video camera, computer hardware and software), most of the materials appear inexpensive.

Some items may need to be purchased specifically for a project, such as a heat lamp, a thermometer going up to 200 degrees Fahrenheit, and some specific Radio Shack items (part numbers supplied). However, these items are reusable, which helps control costs. Many activities require computers and, depending on the focus of the activity, may require Internet connectivity and software such as CAD, video production, or photo editing software. Because the curriculum offers multiple activities from which to choose, teachers have the flexibility to choose activities requiring materials they already have or can easily access.

Special Preparations

As described earlier, some of the activities require electrical, woodworking, and other technical skills that nontechnology teachers may lack. Teachers need a working knowledge of any software, hardware, and Internet sites that will be used by the students.

CURRICULUM OVERVIEW

Topic Overview

The content of the twenty-seven chapters and their instructional organization follow the STL. The five instructional units parallel four of the STL themes, and the other STL theme is covered by the activities (Table 8.3.1). Within the intended designed world unit, there is a chapter for each of Standards 14–20.

All twenty of the STL are addressed and no other major technology topics are covered. The curriculum frequently offers even greater detail than the STL expects.

Instructional Model

As the title suggests, *Technology: Design and Applications* emphasizes the design and problem-solving processes and approaches technology from a systems perspective. It

Table 8.3.1   Unit and chapter alignment to STL themes for *Technology: Design and Applications*

Unit (Section)	# of chapters	Aligns to STL theme
Scope of Technology	3	The nature of technology
Resources and Technology	5	The nature of technology
Creating Technology	10	Design
Technological Contexts	7	The designed world
Technology and Society	2	Technology and society

was written specifically to support the STL and to "support the growing importance of technology in our democratic society."

The unique organization of the chapters into STL-themed units enables students to view technology as a "unified and purposeful human activity," not a group of "isolated concepts and series of facts." The authors expect the textbook to be read outside of class and to provide the basis for in-class discussions, laboratory activities, and presentations.

The placement of the large laboratory activities is unusual—they occur at the end of the thematic units rather than at the end of the chapters. The number of laboratory activities varies by unit. For example, the Technological Contexts unit ends with seven activities, yet the Technology and Society unit has only one. The authors intend for students to make connections from the textbook to the classroom through the "hands-on, minds-on" approach. In addition, the text offers ten Technology Student Association (TSA) activities in which students can experience "individual growth and leadership opportunities." As will be discussed in the Nature of Activities section, many of the major activities do not substantively support the unit themes without the help of the teacher support materials.

Each unit opens with a Technology Headline feature that describes an emerging or potential technology. Each chapter, averaging twenty-one pages, usually opens with 6–9 objectives, 15–30 key words, and a short list of Did You Know brief facts that are related to the topic and designed to engage students. Nearly every chapter has a two-page Technology Explained feature that provides an in-depth explanation of a technology. The text is written at a 7.7 grade level and has a Lexile score of 750L. Each chapter closes with

- A Summary—one to three paragraphs
- Curricular Connections—3–5 optional activities that tie the technology topic to related language arts, mathematics, science, or social studies skills
- Activities—3–4 short activities related to the chapter topic
- Test Your Knowledge chapter tests—10 or 15 questions

A TSA Modular Activity follows some chapters. The only career coverage is a few pages in Chapter 8, People, Time, Money, and Technology.

The book design has clearly demarcated section headers, chapter openings and closings, lab activities, and TSA activities. To explain concepts, the book appropriately and frequently uses drawings.

The content of the photographs and other graphics strongly reinforces, reflects, and expands students' understanding of the text by supplying concrete visuals to support the concepts being explained. The additional related information in the associated captions makes strong connections to the text. The photographs frequently have an industrial, rather than student-friendly, feel. Most do not include people, and when people are there, they are often adults.

Duration

The *Teacher's Manual* and the *Teacher's Wraparound Edition* provide course schedules to teach the curriculum as a 9, 12, 18, or 36 week course. They outline the number of weeks to spend on each of the five instructional units and propose a day-by-day schedule for each length of course. The amount of time recommended for the laboratory activities varies according to the length of the course.

The nine- and twelve-week course schedules appear very ambitious. This is especially true for the Creating Technology design unit, which recommends two weeks to cover more than 200 pages of material and three section activities.

Nature of Activities

We reviewed only the activities in the student textbook, which fell into three categories:

- 19 Laboratory Activities, located at the end of each of the five units
- 10 TSA Modular Activities, found after selected chapters
- 82 small end-of-chapter activities (two to four per chapter)

The curriculum provides additional laboratory activities in the *Student Manual* and in the teacher support materials. The *Teacher's Manual* and *Teacher's Wraparound Edition* suggest that teachers, as managers of their students' learning, use any of these activities or substitute their own, as long as the activities used are appropriate to the class, support the section concepts, and fit into the schedule.

The teacher support materials provide suggestions only for the laboratory activities. The TSA modular activities and the end-of-chapter activities are not addressed and do not appear to be calculated into the course schedules.

The organization of the laboratory activities is not consistent. They appear to follow one of two formats (sometimes adding, skipping, or varying the name of a section):

- Introduction, Equipment and Supplies, Safety, Procedure
- The Challenge, Background, Materials

Generally, the *Student Edition* does not explicitly connect what the student is doing in an activity with the concepts it is intended to support. The *Student Activity Manual* provides activity sheets for selected laboratory activities, and this can help students connect activities to concepts. However, these sheets are not provided for all the activities. The *Teacher's Manual* and *Teacher's Wraparound Edition* often provide concluding comments, evaluation suggestions, or links back to the concepts. Again these are useful, but providing more of them could help students make the connections. Because the *Teacher's Manual* and *Teacher's Wraparound Edition* contain the primary support for

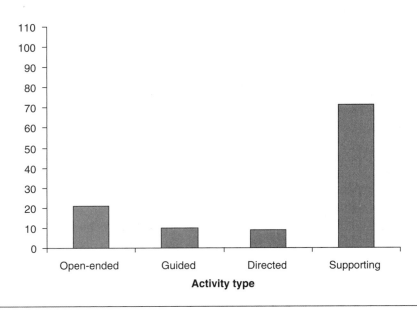

Figure 8.3.1   Number of activities by type in *Technology: Design and Applications*, N = 111

connecting the activities to the content in the text, the students' laboratory activities experience would be greatly enhanced by the teacher using those guides.

The short, end-of-chapter activities are almost all supporting or open-ended activities (Figure 8.3.1). Most of these short, end-of-chapter, open-ended activities occur in the Creating Technology design unit, in which a short project is continued from chapter to chapter, letting students focus on each step of the design process while completing a larger project. Conversely, almost all the guided and directed activities are either laboratory or TSA activities. The directed activities are often very detailed, do not allow much variation, and typically do not support the design process or the Abilities for a Technological World standards beyond following directions (Benchmark 12D).

The supporting activities are almost evenly divided between the investigate/ disassemble/evaluate and the short/focused/practical design approaches.

A third of the full-scale and all of the scaffolded design approach activities are laboratory activities. In fact, so much support was provided for many of the scaffolded design activities that they were almost "build-as-specified" activities, a category that does not exist in this analysis.

Some of the laboratory activities in the textbook have accompanying worksheets in the *Student Activity Manual*. However, the varying activity-naming protocol sometimes makes it difficult to locate the appropriate sheets.

Assessment

The *Teacher's Manual* and *Student Activity Manual* provide an evaluation procedure for each unit. This procedure states the unit's conceptual emphases and performance goals and lists the criteria on which students should be evaluated:

- Contributions to group activity
- Laboratory sheets, sketches, and designs created for activities
- Participation in activity discussions

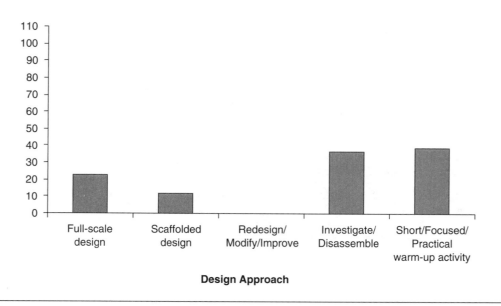

Figure 8.3.2 Number of Activities by Design Approach in *Technology: Design and Applications, N = 111*

- Scores on quizzes and chapter questions
- Creativity and divergent thinking shown during design activities (only for the Design and Designed World sections)

The teacher support materials do not provide substantive help on how to assess these items (e.g., how to score them or build an evaluation rubric). They do suggest teachers give primary emphases to instructional unit concepts and creativity, and secondary emphases should be placed on craftsmanship and the final product, memorization, and skills production workers use. The materials also suggest that contributions to group activities be assessed via daily student logs or diaries, teacher's observations, and student feedback, but they provide no further guidance.

Each chapter ends with a 10- or 15-question test, typically a mix of multiple-choice, fill-in-the-blank, and short-answer formats, and may include matching, true/false, and other questions. The answers to all questions, including the short-answer questions, are located in the *Teacher's Manual* and *Student Activity Manual*. The *Teacher's Resource CD*, available at an extra charge, contains test creation software.

STL STANDARDS AND BENCHMARK-LEVEL ANALYSES

As noted before, this product is strongly influenced by the STL, published a few years earlier. Besides the organization of the curriculum reflecting the thematic and chapter organization of the STL, the textbook even uses much language directly from the STL descriptions. All twenty standards are addressed in the curriculum.

Standards Coverage in the Overall Curriculum

This is a conceptually driven, text-based curriculum with supporting activities for each unit. The curriculum treats all of the standards in both the text and activities,

Table 8.3.2   Student assessment tools and their presence in *Technology: Design and Applications*

Assessment approach	Presence in the curriculum
Paper-and-pencil tests—multiple-choice, short answer, True/False, vocabulary, completion	◆ ◆ ◆ ◆
Projects/Products/Media—individual and group activities, projects, products, media	◆ ◆ ◆
Performance-based assessments—demonstrations, presentations, multimedia, performances	◆
Portfolios—student papers, notes, project reports, research, work samples	◆
Student work–workbook or lab journal pages, handouts, graphs, charts, etc.	◆ ◆ ◆
Open-ended questioning—essays, extended writing exercises, critical thinking questions, etc.	◆ ◆
Computerized assessment—electronic (online or CD-ROM) simulations, tests, etc.	◆ ◆ ◆
Evaluations—peer assessments, self-reflections, self-evaluations	◆
Rubrics/Checklists	◆
Informal observations/Discussions—teacher observations	◆ ◆ ◆ ◆

◆◆◆◆   Dominant—There are a large number of assessments of this type in the curriculum.

◆◆◆   Substantial—There are a substantial number of assessments of this type in the curriculum.

◆◆   Some/Moderate—There are a moderate number of assessments of this type in the curriculum.

◆   Marginal/Missing—There are very few or no assessments of this type in the curriculum.

except for Standard 11 (applying the design process), which is addressed only in the activities. Ninety-eight percent (all but two) of the middle school benchmarks are covered.

Table 8.3.3 shows the standards that appear most and least frequently in the overall curriculum. The five most frequently occurring standards account for 55 percent of the standards coverage in the curriculum, while the five least frequent account for about 7 percent. This is only one of two core technology products for which a Theme 3 (design) standard is one of the top three standards (Standard 9). On the other hand, Standard 11 has the lowest relative coverage for a core product.

Standards Coverage in the Text

The student text covers 19 of the 20 STL, and 81 percent of the coverage is standards-based; that is, more than four-fifths of the text coverage addresses STL

Table 8.3.3   Five most frequent and five least frequent standards in the overall curriculum (with percents) for *Technology: Design and Applications*

5 most frequent standards	5 least frequent standards
Standard 12 (14%)—using and maintaining technological products and systems	Standard 5 (1%)—the effects of technology on the environment
Standard 9 (13%)—engineering design	Standard 14 (1%)—medical technologies
Standard 17 (11%)—information and communication technologies	Standard 1 (1%)—the characteristics & scope of technology
Standard 2 (9%)—the core concepts of technology	Standard 15 (2%)—agriculture and related biotechnologies
Standard 11 (8%)—applying the design process	Standard 3 (2%)—the connections between technology & other fields

benchmarks in a way leading to technological literacy. The text misses only nine middle school benchmarks, most of which are for Standard 11 (applying the design process) and are treated in the activities.

Seventeen of the standards are more than 50 percent standards-based, and some have very high scores (Table 8.3.4). In fact, two standards are more than 91 percent standards-based, and seven have standards-based scores between 82 and 89 percent. Of the three lowest standards-based scores, two were for the Abilities for a Technological World standards, which are addressed in the activities, not the text. Refer to Appendix A for a standard-by-standard analysis of the benchmarks addressed in the text.

STL Theme 3 (design) and Theme 5 (the designed world) have the strongest coverage, in both the amount of text and overall level of standards-based coverage. With this strong presentation, the text definitely can lead students to technological literacy for all the standards in Theme 3, but not necessarily for all the standards in Theme 5.

The curriculum devotes ten chapters—more than 200 pages and nearly a third of the book—to the design process. Standards 9 (engineering design) and 8 (attributes of design) are 98 percent and 89 percent standards-based, respectively. Benchmark 9F (design involves a variety of steps) is the second most treated benchmark in the text.

Each of the Designed World standards has a chapter devoted to it in the Technological Concepts unit. Standards 16 (energy and power technologies), 17 (information and communication technologies), and 19 (manufacturing technologies) have concentrated treatment in other chapters as well. The standards-based scores for the Designed World standards range from 64 to 88 percent.

Benchmark 17K (use of symbols, measurements, and drawings provides clear communication by providing a common language to express ideas) accounts for more than half of the coverage for the standard and is the third most treated benchmark in the text. This benchmark is addressed frequently in the design chapters that discuss sketching, refining, and communicating solutions.

For Theme 4 (abilities for a technological world), students can gain technological literacy from the text only for Benchmark 12H (use information to see and understand how things work). Benchmark 12H is the most frequently occurring benchmark in the text. The text provides exceptionally clear explanations of how various technology

Table 8.3.4 Results of analyses of STL coverage in the text for *Technology: Design and Applications*

STL covered	Percent of text devoted to each STL	Percent of coverage that is standards-based for each STL	Primary benchmarks covered for each STL			
			K–2	3–5	6–8	9–12
Standard 1	2%	56%			G	
Standard 2	11%	73%		J		
Standard 3	2%	76%			E F	
Standard 4	4%	79%			D E G	
Standard 5	1%	83%			D E	
Standard 6	4%	47%			D	
Standard 7	3%	52%	—	—	—	—
Standard 8	7%	89%			F G	
Standard 9	17%	98%			F H	
Standard 10	3%	61%			G H	J
Standard 11	0%	—	—	—	—	—
Standard 12	11%	91%			H	
Standard 13	1%	0%			H	
Standard 14	1%	82%			G	
Standard 15	3%	87%			G J	
Standard 16	8%	83%			F	K
Standard 17	12%	85%			K	
Standard 18	3%	88%			F G	
Standard 19	5%	71%			F H J	
Standard 20	3%	64%			F G	

Primary benchmark coverage = 21% or more of total benchmarks for the standard

Benchmarks are not listed for standards that are covered in less than 0.5% of the text.

The highlighted standards are represented most often in the text.

processes, products, and concepts work, and thus students are gaining literacy in this benchmark as they read the text. Conversely, Benchmark 3F (the effect of knowledge gained from other fields on technology development) is not prevalent because the text provides technological explanations (Benchmark 12H) and not scientific and mathematical connections (3F) to describe how things work.

Of the Nature of Technology and Technology and Society standards, only Standard 2 receives comprehensive coverage, and more than two-thirds of that coverage is for the Grades 3–5 benchmarks. Standard 5 (effects of technology on the environment) has the weakest coverage of any standard.

Standards Coverage in the Activities

All standards are treated in at least two activities each, although sometimes those are the brief, end-of-chapter activities. All but one of the middle school benchmarks for Theme 4 (abilities for a technological world: Standards 11–13) are addressed by the activities.

As Table 8.3.5 reveals, the Abilities for a Technological World standards receive the most attention in the activities. However, treatments of Standard 11 (applying the design process) typically address an individual benchmark or two, rather than applying the entire design process using most of the middle school benchmarks. Only 11 of the 111 activities take students through three or more of the design steps as outlined in the middle school benchmarks. Of these, only two are laboratory activities, which are the only activities that the teacher materials support. Therefore, teachers need to make a special effort to assign other types of activities that address the entire design process in order for students to achieve Standard 11 technological literacy.

Students should develop technical abilities by completing activities that address Standard 12 (using and maintaining technological products and systems). Benchmark 12D (following directions) is the most frequently covered benchmark in the activities. Benchmark 12H (use information to see and understand how things work) and 12J (use computers and calculators) are also well addressed.

TEACHER MATERIALS REVIEW

The student text is very strong, but without the help of the *Teacher's Manual* and/or the *Teacher's Wraparound Edition*, the student experience could significantly suffer. Even a new or nontechnology teacher could use the text of this curriculum, but, even with the help of the teacher support materials, only an experienced technology teacher could effectively teach the laboratory activities.

Overview of Teacher Materials Components

The *Teacher's Manual* and the *Teacher's Wraparound Edition* share almost the same instructional information, but each has unique features. The *Teacher's Resource Binder* includes all of the information in the *Teacher's Manual* plus color transparencies in a three-ring binder, and the *Teacher's Resource CD* contains everything in the *Teacher's Resource Binder* plus test-making software.

The introductions to the *Teacher's Manual* and the *Teacher's Wraparound Edition* cover the following:

- Technology—A Societal Universe
- Technology Education: A Background
- Technology and Industry
- Systems (inputs, processes, outputs, feedback, impacts)
- Organizing the Content
- Scheduling the Program
- STL Correlation Chart
- Basic Skills Chart
- Scope and Sequence Chart

- Working with the Instructional System
  - Role of Teacher and Students
  - Accommodating Individual Differences
  - Role of the Textbook
  - Role of the Teachers Resource
  - Sections as Content Organizers

Table 8.3.5   Results of analyses of STL coverage in the activities for *Technology: Design and Applications*

STL covered	Percent of activities devoted to each STL	Primary benchmarks covered for each STL			
		K–2	3–5	6–8	9–12
Standard 1	1%		D	F	
Standard 2	5%		J		
Standard 3	3%			*F	
Standard 4	3%			*D E	
Standard 5	2%			*D	
Standard 6	1%			D	
Standard 7	3%			*	
Standard 8	2%			E F	
Standard 9	4%			F H	I
Standard 10	2%			G H	
Standard 11	26%			I	
Standard 12	23%		D	H	
Standard 13	6%			F H	
Standard 14	1%	C		G	
Standard 15	1%			*	
Standard 16	4%			*F	
Standard 17	8%			J K	
Standard 18	1%			*F G	
Standard 19	3%			F H K	
Standard 20	2%			C	F G

Primary benchmark coverage = 21% or more of total benchmarks for the standard.

An asterisk (*) in front of a benchmark indicates that, while the topic of the STL is addressed, no specific benchmarks are covered.

Benchmarks are not listed for standards that are covered in less than 0.5% of the activities.

The highlighted standards are represented most often in the text activities.

Table 8.3.6 shows five kinds, or categories, of teacher support and rates how strongly those categories are represented in the teacher support materials for this product.

Support for Teaching the Curriculum

The *Teacher's Manual* and the *Teacher's Wraparound Edition* do not supply traditional lesson plans for each chapter; rather, their support is organized by unit. For each unit, they provide the following:

- Teaching materials
- Introduction
- Objectives of the sections
- Suggested schedule and length of the section
- Preparing to teach the section
- Presenting the section

- Adjustments for special needs and gifted students
- Evaluation procedures
- Implementing the laboratory activities
- Procedures for directing each suggested activity

The *Teacher's Manual* uniquely offers the following:

- Answer key (by chapter)
- Answers to the study questions in the *Student Activity Manual*
- Alternative activities

- Activity sheets
- Transparency captions
- Reproducible masters and captions

The *Teacher's Wraparound Edition* features extensive margin notes covering

- Procedures for directing each suggested activity
- Answer keys to chapter tests
- Discussion starters, group activities, and writing assignments that open each unit

- Chapter outline
- Page-by-page STL correlations
- Teaching suggestions

Table 8.3.6   Categories of teacher support materials and adequacy ratings for *Technology: Design and Applications*

Categories of support found in teacher support materials	Adequacy of teacher support
Support for teaching the curriculum	◆ ◆ ◆
Support for pedagogy	◆ ◆ ◆
Support for assessment	◆
Support for teaching technology standards	◆ ◆
Support for teaching twenty-first-century knowledge and abilities	◆ ◆

◆◆◆◆   Dominant—Almost all of the criteria for support in this category are present.

◆◆◆   Substantial—Most of the criteria for support in this category are present.

◆◆   Some/Moderate—Some of the criteria for support in this category are present.

◆   Marginal/Missing—Very few or none of the criteria for support in this category are present.

Although the *Teacher's Manual* provides some valuable resources that the *Teacher's Wraparound Edition* does not, the latter is much easier to use and provides additional teaching ideas. The procedures for directing each suggested activity appear next to the activity they describe, helping to ensure its intended impact. The answer key also appears on the same page as the test itself. In addition to new opening activities and discussions for the units, nearly every page has two or more teaching suggestions. These teaching suggestions, labeled according to their purpose, fall into the following categories:

- Demonstrate
- Brainstorm
- Reinforce
- Research
- Extend

- Discussion
- Figure discussion
- Example
- Resource
- Tech terms

The teacher materials provide crucial support for teaching the laboratory activities in particular. While teachers will need to teach the entire unit as presented, they have flexibility in determining which of the varied laboratory activities to use (from the *Student Edition*, the *Teacher's Manual*, the *Student Activity Manual*, or their own). The procedures for directing each suggested activity appear in both the *Teacher's Manual* and the *Teacher's Wraparound Edition* and provide critical support for choosing laboratory activities. This support is not provided anywhere else.

Support for Pedagogy

The curriculum assigns the teacher three distinct roles—curriculum planner, technical expert, and manager of education. The *Teacher's Manual* provides such information for each instructional unit, albeit not explicitly. In addition, the introduction and the smaller sections in each instructional unit provide general support and suggestions for accommodating individual differences for the entire unit, rather than specific lesson and activity suggestions along the way. The teaching suggestions in the margin notes of the *Teacher's Wraparound Edition* strongly facilitate a teaching environment that promotes inquiry, student-generated knowledge, problem solving, and grappling with technology concepts.

Support for Assessment

The student assessment component of the teacher support materials provides general guidance that would be most appreciated by a new teacher. It does not provide advanced suggestions for veteran teachers nor does it discuss portfolio assessment or performance-based assessments. As discussed earlier, it offers no guidance on how to use student projects and student work or informal observations and discussions as means of assessment.

Support for Teaching Technology Standards

This textbook was published after the national STL were released. The *Teacher's Manual* and the *Teacher's Wraparound Edition* provide a chapter and page-level correlation to the STL, and the *Teacher's Wraparound Edition* margin notes report the STL standards addressed on every page. The introduction to the teacher materials begins with an overview of technology, technology education, technology industry, and systems, all of which address principles of the STL.

Support for Teaching Twenty-First-Century Knowledge and Abilities

This curriculum does not address specific workplace skills beyond the overarching principle that students need to be literate in technology in order to be successful in our society. The curriculum and teaching support materials strongly promote design and problem solving as well as technological and digital-age literacy.

Table of Contents—*Technology: Design and Applications*
(Number of pages indicated in parentheses)

Section 1 Scope of Technology (2)

1. What Is Technology (12)
2. Technology as a System (20)
3. Contexts of Technology (20)
   Section 1 Activities A—B (4)

Section 2 Resources and Technology (2)

4. Tools and Technology (26)
5. Materials and Technology (22)
6. Energy and Technology (22)
7. Information and Technology (13)
   TSA Modular Activity (3)
8. People, Time, Money, and Technology (20)
   Section 2 Activities A—F (24)

Section 3 Creating Technology (2)

9. Invention and Innovation (18)
   TSA Modular Activity (2)
10. The Design Process (19)
    TSA Modular Activity (3)
11. Identifying Problems (14)
12. Researching Problems (16)
13. Creating Solutions (26)
14. Selecting and Refining Solutions (20)
15. Modeling Solutions (30)

16. Testing Solutions (19)
    TSA Modular Activity (3)
17. Communicating Solutions (25)
    TSA Modular Activity (3)
18. Improving Solutions (16)
    Section 3 Activities A–C (6)

Section 4 Technological Contexts (2)

19. Agricultural and Related Technology (32)
20. Construction Technology (23)
    TSA Modular Activity (3)
21. Energy Conversion Technology (22)
22. Information and Communication Technology (37)
    TSA Modular Activity (2)
    TSA Modular Activity (3)
23. Manufacturing Technology (24)
    TSA Modular Activity (2)
24. Medical Technology (22)
25. Transportation Technology (24)
    Section 4 Activities A–G (24)

Section 5 Technology and Society (2)

26. Technological Impacts (22)
    TSA Modular Activity (3)
27. Technology and the Future (13)
    Section 5 Activity (A) (2)

SAMPLE PAGES

The first two sample pages, selected from the Creating Technology design unit, demonstrate the book's clean layout, use of graphics and photographs, and the amount of detail in the writing. Activity 3C is a typical laboratory activity in terms of the organization, graphics, and directions.

286 Section 3 Creating Technology

The design process can be divided into two sections: problem seeking and problem solving. The first two steps of the process are problem seeking. In step one, the problem is identified, and a design brief is created. The problem is then researched in step two. Both of these steps deal with seeking information about the problem. Step three is the first step to involve solving the problem. In this step, the designers begin to think of ways the problem can be solved. They will develop many ideas and draw sketches for each of the ideas. See **Figure 13-1.** The sketches will help to explain their ideas to others. The ideas and sketches developed will then be refined, modeled, and tested in the next steps of the design process.

Exploring Ideas

Some people may come to this step and think they already know what their final solution will be. They might

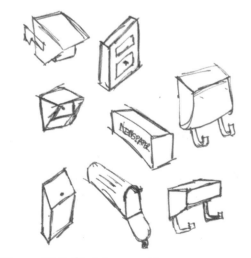

Figure 13-1. Sketches are ideas on paper.

Figure 13-2. Broad thinking leads to new solutions to problems. (Motorola, Inc.)

feel that developing a number of solutions is a waste of time. This is the wrong attitude to have. Designers must explore a number of ideas. The more ideas explored, the better the design will be. Designers should generate original and creative ideas. They have to think broadly and develop a wide variety of ideas. If designers use narrow thinking, their designs will not be unique. For example, imagine you are designing a telephone. You should explore many different ideas (broad thinking). One idea may be a phone fitting in your ear like a hearing aid. Another idea could be a digital phone with a computer video display. See **Figure 13-2.** These are two unique solutions to the problem of a new telephone. You would not want to create ideas like a red desk phone and a black desk phone. That would be narrow thinking. These ideas are essentially

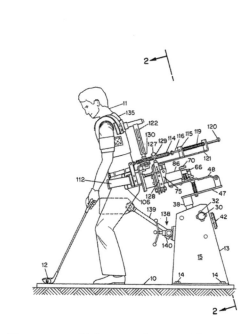

Figure 13-3. Unique products are the results of creativity and imagination. (Patent No. 5,050,855, U.S. Patent and Trademark Office)

the same thing, with only the color differing. The small changes, like color, can be made later. It is important that designers explore many ideas. Exploring ideas is called *ideation.*

Ideation

Creating a number of new ideas to solve a problem is ideation. The process of ideation is creative and imaginative. See **Figure 13-3.** Creativity leads to new ideas and solutions. The solutions created at this step should be simple and rough. Later in the process, the solutions will be revised and refined. Ideation begins by reviewing the problem and design brief. Remember, the solutions developed must solve the problem. The solution must also fit the criteria and

limitations. After reviewing the design brief, the research conclusions must be reviewed. This review will help the designer understand what others have done and what people want from the solution.

Ideation is a free flowing activity. Ideas must be able to flow without others shooting them down. In ideation, all ideas are good ideas. There are no right or wrong answers. It is important to record (sketch or write down) all ideas. Ideas seeming silly or wild at first may make more sense later. If you do not record them, you may forget some good ideas.

The environment you use to create solutions is very important. You must be able to concentrate on the problem. In front of the television at home may not be the best place to focus on creating ideas. Many designers find quiet places to work. They may leave their offices and work outside or in a library. See **Figure 13-4.** The only

Figure 13-4. Designers often work best in quiet areas away from their offices and desks. (Tony Gothard)

Activity 3C

Design for Space

Introduction

Technology has given us the life we have today. This life is very different from what our grandparents had. Likewise, life for future generations will be very different from life today. People may be living in deep space or undersea settlements. This activity will allow you to consider a life in space. You will design a self-contained space station.

Equipment and Supplies

➤ No. 10 tin cans (large cans found in most school cafeterias)
➤ Paper towel tube
➤ Five 6″ cardboard or poster board squares
➤ 1½″ wide strips of poster board
➤ Compass
➤ Ruler and pencil
➤ Scissors or small tin snips
➤ Glue
➤ Masking or transparent tape
➤ Wallpaper samples or scraps of cloth

Procedure

Your teacher will divide the class into groups of three to four students. Each group should perform the following steps:

1. Obtain the materials listed above.
2. See **Figure 3C-1** to determine the basic structure of the space station.

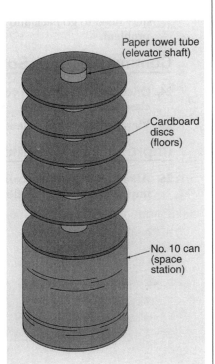

Figure 3C-1. Here is the basic structure of the model space station.

Design for Space **431**

3. List the basic areas needed for complete, comfortable living. These may include the following areas:

 a. Living quarters.

 b. Recreation areas.

 c. Agriculture, production, or factory areas (the reason for the space station).

 d. Mechanical support areas (such as areas for heating, air conditioning, and waste disposal).

 e. Office or managerial areas.

 f. Flight control areas.

NOTE: Be sure to consider other types of facilities. This is not a complete list!

4. Assign each basic area to one of the four floors of the space station.

Each member of the group should select one or two floors to develop. All group members should complete the following steps:

5. Cut a 5⅞″ disc from a square of cardboard or poster board.

6. Cut a 1½″ hole in the center of the disc.

7. Draw a floor plan on the disc. Be sure to consider the wise use of space, ease of movement from different areas, and grouping like activities together. Remember, 1″ = 8′.

8. Cut walls from the 1½″ strips of poster board.

9. Cut doorways in the wall sections.

10. Attach the walls to the floor.

11. Decorate the walls and floors with wallpaper samples and cloth to represent actual surface treatments.

The group should complete their space station by completing these steps:

12. Cut openings in the elevator shaft (paper tube).

13. Attach the floors to the elevator shaft. See **Figure 3C-2.**

14. Insert the space station into the launch shell (tin can).

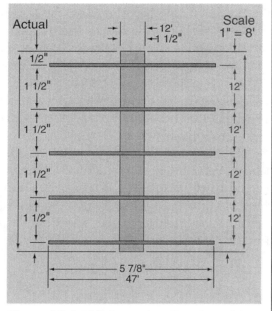

Figure 3C-2. This is an elevation view of the space station.

Technology Interactions, Second Edition

Developer/Author:	Henry R. Harms and Neal R. Swernofsky
Distributor/Publisher:	Glencoe/McGraw-Hill
Publication date:	2003
Ordering information:	Glencoe/McGraw-Hill, 1-800-334-7344, www.glencoe.com
Target audience:	Middle school

BRIEF DESCRIPTION

This introductory textbook covers twenty-two technology topics, or modules, each in a stand-alone chapter that can be covered in any order. Although designed to be used in classrooms with modular learning stations through which student pairs rotate, this textbook also can be used easily in a traditional classroom arrangement.

The curriculum balances theory and activities relatively evenly as it solidly covers the twenty-two topics. Overall, 61 percent of the content is standards-based. Primarily through the activities, this book provides the strongest coverage for Standards 11 and 12 from the Standards for Technological Literacy (STL) theme Abilities for a Designed World. Students completing this curriculum should be technologically literate in Standard 11. The major activities, organized by a design process, also strongly support Standard 9 (engineering design).

The teacher materials provide helpful support for day-to-day technology teaching through the lesson plans. However, newer teachers may need to use outside resources for additional support. The curriculum especially promotes teaching twenty-first-century knowledge and abilities—from the reality-based help wanted ads and activities in the student text to the additional Career Investigations worksheets and Career Readiness Skills chapter in the *Teacher Resource Guide (TRG).*

CURRICULUM COMPONENTS

- *Student Edition*, hardcover, 496 pp., $38.97
- *Teacher Resource Guide*, softcover, 335 pp., $55.98
- *Teacher Productivity CD-ROM*, $129.99

Materials/Equipment

Each activity lists the materials and equipment to collect prior to starting. There is much variation in the type of materials and equipment needed. Depending on the activity, the materials required may be found in a regular classroom, a wood or electronics shop, a computer lab, a basic technology education classroom, or a fully loaded modular technology education laboratory. Most of the equipment can be obtained from a science or technology education supply catalog. A few of the activities require advanced equipment, such as a plastics oven, which might be expensive or difficult to find. Some activities specify "materials processing" equipment, tools, or machines without elaborating. Note that many of the activities have computer requirements such as CAD, desktop publishing software, and Internet connectivity.

Special Preparations

No special preparations are required. However, teachers need a working knowledge of any software, hardware, and Internet sites that will be used by the students.

CURRICULUM OVERVIEW

Topic Overview

The twenty-two chapters are divided into the following seven sections, each covering a major area of technology. Each section opens with a page addressing technology and society issues.

- Introduction to Technology
- Communication Technologies
- Production Technologies
- Power Technologies

- Bio-Related Technologies
- Control Technologies
- Integrated Technologies

All twenty of the STL are addressed to some degree. The curriculum also covers technology topics not found in the STL, such as computer software and hardware, desktop publishing, animation, the Internet, fluid power, circuits (electronics and electricity), lasers, engineering, and weather.

Instructional Model

This curriculum was developed specifically to support a modular technology education (MTE) program, although it can easily be used in any type of technology education program. The authors define MTE as "a teaching system in which the classroom is divided into modular learning stations, each populated by a team of two students. Student teams rotate through a series of self-directed instructional units . . . students take an active role in the learning process and gain practical knowledge through hands-on activities." Other characteristics of MTE include teachers as facilitators of the learning process rather than deliverers of information; "an investigative, design-and-construct, problem-solving approach"; and "real-world, action-based activities that challenge students to achieve their highest potential." Students can choose the technology topics of interest to them to study in whatever order they want. The MTE laboratory can be created by the teacher or school or can be purchased as a turnkey system. Despite the flexibility of the curriculum and its MTE design, this product still can be used in the most traditional of technology classroom setups, and the text can be successfully followed in a linear fashion. The only requirement is that a well-equipped, modern technology laboratory needs to be available.

Each chapter averages twenty pages and includes two to three major activities, several Fascinating Facts boxes, a section on impacts, a section on the future, a page on careers, and a chapter review. In addition, each chapter has several Linking to Science, Math, and Communications activities that engage students in brief exercises. The page on careers displays sample help wanted ads for a variety of jobs and supplies a Linking to the Workplace activity. The chapter review includes a chapter summary and both fact-based and critical thinking questions. The text is written at a 6.0 grade level and has a Lexile score of 940L. The major activities provide students with hands-on experience for each chapter topic. The smaller activities provide opportunities for students to make further connections across the curriculum.

The product also connects the technology content to the student's world whenever possible. This happens mostly through the text features just mentioned, the career pages, and the chapter introductions. The real-world nature of the help wanted advertisements emphasizes that technology education has direct application outside of school. In addition, many chapters begin by encouraging students to make connections with their lives or to draw upon preexisting knowledge. For example, chapters open with thought-provoking scenarios such as imagining that you lived 200 years ago without electricity, considering how you got to school today, or vividly describing a skateboard run to introduce the concept of flight.

The instructional flow for this book is established through its clearly demarcated chapter openers, closings, heads, subheads, text box features, and very structured format for Explore and Apply What You've Learned activities. The page layout, graphics and photographs, and nonlinear design elements provide a sense of excitement and encouragement to look to the future, but do not add to the content. Nearly every page has a photograph, graphic, and/or text box feature. Photographs typically provide visual context, are multicultural, and show a balance of male and female subjects. The drawn graphics often add new information, especially when explaining or demonstrating a concept.

Duration

The authors recommend ten days per chapter, although each can be shortened or lengthened easily. Lesson plans estimate the number of days required by each individual major activity. Typically this is from one to three days, although a few activities need a week or more. The numerous brief activities require a class period or less.

Nature of Activities

Technology Interactions has major activities as well as substantially shorter ones. Each chapter has one or two major Explore activities and closes with an Apply What

You've Learned activity. The titles for all of these major activities start with "Design and Build a. . . ." Very brief activities, called Linking to Science, Math, and Communications, are scattered throughout each chapter.

All 61 major Explore and Apply What You've Learned activities use the following format, which generally maps to the middle school benchmarks for Standard 11 (students will develop abilities to apply the design process).

- State the problem
- Develop alternative solutions
- Select the best solution

- Implement the solution
- Evaluate the solution

Of the 130 activities in this book, most of the 61 major activities are either guided explorations or directed activities, and a few are open-ended explorations. Almost all of the brief Linking activities are supporting exercises (Figure 8.4.1).

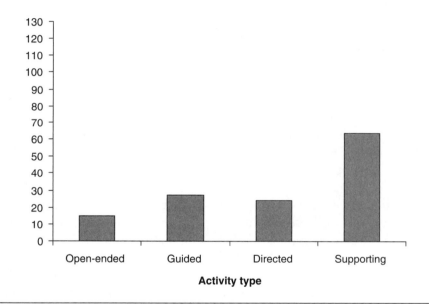

Figure 8.4.1 Number of activities by type in *Technology Interactions, 2nd Edition, N = 130*

Most major activities use a full-scale design approach, scaffolded design approach, or investigate/disassemble/evaluate approach (Figure 8.4.2). Nearly all of the open-ended activities engage students in the full-scale design process, as do about 40 percent of the guided activities. Another 40 percent of the guided activities use the scaffolded design approach, in which students create a product but are given a substantial part of the design.

The frequently occurring brief Linking activities use the two most common design approaches—short/focused/practical and investigate/disassemble/evaluate. In fact, all the short/focused/practical activities and nearly three-quarters of the investigate/disassemble/evaluate activities are the brief Linking activities.

The directed activities usually use the investigate/disassemble/evaluate approach, in which students choose the best method, material, or design, or the scaffolded design approach, in which most of the design is provided or given.

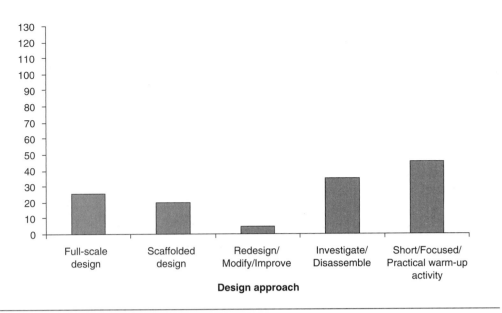

Figure 8.4.2 Number of activities by design approach in *Technology Interactions, 2nd Edition*, N = 130

Assessment

Assessment is supported primarily through end-of-chapter tests. The chapter summary features five to ten short answer questions (Check Your Facts) and two to six open-ended questions (Critical Thinking). The *TRG* provides answers for the Check Your Facts questions, but not the Critical Thinking questions. It also provides chapter study guides consisting of questions and paper activities to review chapter vocabulary and concepts. Furthermore, the *TRG* provides chapter tests, each consisting of twelve matching and eight multiple-choice questions. Expanded tests and a test generator on CD-ROM can be purchased separately. See Table 8.4.1.

The Assessment Materials section of the *TRG* has three short paragraphs suggesting hands-on activities that can be used for assessment. It further provides a one-page review of the advantages and disadvantages of various assessment strategies (objective measures, written measures, oral measures, simulated activities, portfolio and product analysis, performance measures, performance records, and self-evaluation). No specific support for implementing any assessment strategies is included, even in the Assess section of the lesson plans. The *TRG* provides support for informal observation and discussion, but not in an assessment capacity. The *TRG* also features a safety test that students should pass before they are allowed to work in the lab.

STL STANDARDS AND BENCHMARK-LEVEL ANALYSES

This edition was released after the STL were published. All twenty of the STL are covered to various degrees. The *TRG* provides a correlation of the curriculum to the STL.

Standards Coverage in the Overall Curriculum

This curriculum is 61 percent standards-based and addresses 80 percent of the middle school benchmarks. Middle school students will gain a solid understanding of the

Table 8.4.1 Student assessment tools and their presence in *Technology Interactions, 2nd Edition*

Assessment approach	Presence in the curriculum
Paper-and-pencil tests—multiple-choice, short answer, true/false, vocabulary, completion	◆◆◆◆
Projects/Products/Media—individual and group activities, projects, products, media	◆◆◆◆
Performance-based assessments—demonstrations, presentations, multimedia, performances	◆◆
Portfolios—student papers, notes, project reports, research, work samples	◆
Student work—workbook or lab journal pages, handouts, graphs, charts, etc.	◆◆
Open-ended questioning—essays, extended writing exercises, critical thinking questions, etc.	◆◆◆
Computerized assessment—electronic (online or CD-ROM) simulations, tests, etc.	◆◆◆
Evaluations—peer assessments, self-reflections, self-evaluations	◆
Rubrics/Checklists	◆
Informal observations/Discussions—teacher observations	◆

◆◆◆◆ Dominant—There are a large number of assessments of this type in the curriculum.

◆◆◆ Substantial—There are a substantial number of assessments of this type in the curriculum.

◆◆ Some/Moderate—There are a moderate number of assessments of this type in the curriculum.

◆ Marginal/Missing—There are very few or no assessments of this type in the curriculum.

twenty-two topics covered and will encounter material addressing all of the standards; however, it is unclear whether students will achieve technological literacy for the twenty standards. The five most frequent standards comprise 64 percent of the standards coverage, and the five least frequent standards account for less than 5.5 percent (Table 8.4.2.).

Standards Coverage in the Text

Almost two-thirds (61 percent) of the coverage addresses STL benchmarks in a way that strongly encourages technological literacy. The text coverage for STL Themes 1 (nature of technology) and 2 (technology and society) is more standards-based than standards-referenced, and coverage for the other STL themes is standards-based about half the time.

Table 8.4.2 Five most frequent and five least frequent standards in the overall curriculum (with percents) for *Technology Interactions, 2nd Edition*

5 most frequent standards	5 least frequent standards
Standard 11 (28%)—applying the design process	Standard 1 (< .5%)—the characteristics & scope of technology
Standard 12 (13%)—using and maintaining technological products and systems	Standard 6 (1%)—the role of society in the development and use of technology
Standard 3 (8%)—the connections between technology & other fields	Standard 18 (1%)—transportation technologies
Standard 9 (8%)—engineering design	Standard 7 (1%)—the influence of technology on history
Standard 17 (7%)—information and communication technologies	Standard 14 (2%)—medical technologies

All of the standards are touched upon; some are diffused throughout the book, and others are concentrated in specific chapters. For example, within Theme 2 (technology and society), Standard 4 (role of technology on society) is distributed across the entire book and is featured in each of the seven section openers, while Standards 5 (effects of technology on the environment) and 7 (influence of technology on history) are concentrated in specific chapters. Table 8.4.3 reports the breakout of coverage for all of the standards in the text.

This book emphasizes how technology works, providing copious scientific and technological explanations. The most frequently occurring benchmark in the text, Benchmark 3F (knowledge gained from other fields of study has a direct effect on the development of technological products and systems) is invoked when scientific concepts are covered in order to explain Designed World topics. Benchmark 3F accounts for nearly all coverage of Standard 3 (connections between technology and other fields) and is standards-based more than two-thirds of the time. Further connections are made with other fields in the Linking to Science, Math, and Communications activity boxes.

The second most frequently occurring benchmark in the text, Benchmark 12H (use information provided in manuals, protocols, or by experienced people to see and understand how things work) is invoked for the many explanations of how technological products work. Benchmark 12H accounts for almost all of the coverage for Standard 12 and is standards-based about half the time. Benchmark 12H is also the only benchmark in Theme 4 (abilities for a technological world) that is substantially covered in the text.

While the Abilities for a Technological World standards (11–13) are well covered by the activities, the text provides little coverage for the formalized concepts in the Design standards (8–10), in terms of both the number of occurrences in the text and their treatment being standards-based (less than half of the time). For example, the text does not significantly discuss concepts such as working as a team, creativity, troubleshooting, making design revisions, or brainstorming.

All the Designed World standards (14–20) are addressed in the text, usually in individual chapters dedicated to each specific topic; yet the amount of standards-based coverage varies widely (Table 8.4.3). Standard 17 (information and communication technologies), the third most covered standard in the text, is concentrated in the five

Table 8.4.3   Results of analyses of STL coverage in the text for *Technology Interactions, 2nd Edition*

STL covered	Percent of text devoted to each STL	Percent of coverage that is standards-based for each STL	Primary benchmarks covered for each STL			
			K–2	3–5	6–8	9–12
Standard 1	< .5%	0%	—	—	—	—
Standard 2	7%	58%		K	M	
Standard 3	15%	63%			F	
Standard 4	6%	66%			D E G	
Standard 5	8%	68%			D	I
Standard 6	1%	63%			D E F	
Standard 7	3%	38%			D	
Standard 8	2%	36%			E G	
Standard 9	5%	57%			F G H	
Standard 10	1%	20%			H	
Standard 11	1%	0%			H J L	
Standard 12	12%	54%			H	
Standard 13	1%	67%			F G H	
Standard 14	3%	63%			G	
Standard 15	4%	95%			G H	
Standard 16	8%	38%			F	
Standard 17	11%	44%			H K	
Standard 18	1%	40%			F	
Standard 19	6%	62%			H	
Standard 20	7%	62%			F G	

Primary benchmark coverage = 21% or more of total benchmarks for the standard

Benchmarks are not listed for standards that are covered in less than 0.5% of the text.

The highlighted standards are represented most often in the text.

communications technology chapters that focus on computer applications. However, because they address Standard 17 via computer technology, they directly address the standard itself only slightly more than half the time. On the other hand, Standard 15 (agriculture and related biotechnologies) has the most standards-based coverage in the book (95 percent). The medical, manufacturing, and construction standards (14, 19, and 20) are standards-based approximately two-thirds of the time. Many other chapters are related to Designed World standards and provide interesting technology information on topics and concepts such as how something works or why something happens, but do not address the technological literacy concepts called for by the STL.

Refer to Appendix A for a list of all benchmarks addressed in the text. The vast majority of the benchmarks present are at the middle school level, but the book slants slightly toward Grades 9–12 coverage. High school benchmarks for Standards 5 (effects of technology on the environment), 7 (influence of technology on history), 17 (information and communication technologies), and 19 (manufacturing technologies) are invoked at least a quarter of the time for each of these standards. The coverage for Standard 2 (core concepts) and Standard 12 (using and maintaining technological products and systems) addresses elementary grade benchmarks a significant amount of the time (about a third).

Standards Coverage in the Activities

Activities generally support the topic of the chapter in which they appear. However, the topic of the activity frequently does *not* address any STL benchmark other than those for Theme 4 (abilities for a technological world). Yet 18 of the standards are addressed at least once in the activities, but only eight of the standards are addressed 2 percent or more of the time. Table 8.4.4 reports the breakout of coverage for all of the standards in the text.

The structure and format of the Explore and Apply What You've Learned activities transparently teach Standard 9 (engineering design) and Benchmark F (design involves a set of steps) while taking students through all of the middle school benchmarks for Standard 11 (applying the design process). Many of the brief Linking activities also require Standard 11 skills. Students will be technologically literate in Standard 11 upon finishing this curriculum. In addition to Standard 11, Standard 12 is a frequently addressed standard in Theme 4 (abilities for a technological world).

Most of the Explore and Apply What You've Learned activities in this textbook include the five middle school benchmarks for Standard 11. The research benchmark is especially strong in activities where students are doing research in the form of tests or experiments. Students are required to make multiple sketches (J). Benchmark K (test, evaluate, and refine) is the most frequently occurring benchmark in the entire curriculum. Because the text usually supplies the requirements for a design, students do not develop requirements and thus do not gain technological literacy for that benchmark (I) to the same extent as for the others.

Standard 12 (using and maintaining technological products and systems) is the second most frequently occurring standard in the activities. It is particularly strong for following directions (D). Using computer technology (J and P) also is strongly addressed.

Benchmark 9F (design involves a set of steps) accounts for almost all of the coverage for Standard 9. Each Explore and Apply What You've Learned activity in effect teaches the benchmark by using the design steps noted earlier:

Refer to Appendix A for a list of all benchmarks addressed in the activities.

TEACHER MATERIALS REVIEW

The lesson plans in the *TRG* provide support for day-to-day teaching of the curriculum, although an experienced technology education teacher could implement much of this curriculum without relying on them. A teacher new to science or technology education would find the lesson plans helpful, but would need extra self-education for unfamiliar topics.

Table 8.4.4   Results of analyses of STL coverage in the activities for *Technology Interactions, 2nd Edition*

STL covered	Percent of activities devoted to each STL	Primary benchmarks covered for each STL			
		K–2	3–5	6–8	9–12
Standard 1	0%	—	—	—	—
Standard 2	1%		J K	V	
Standard 3	2%			F	
Standard 4	0%	—	—	—	—
Standard 5	1%			D	I
Standard 6	< .5%	—	—	—	—
Standard 7	< .5%	—	—	—	—
Standard 8	1%			E G	
Standard 9	11%			F	
Standard 10	3%			H	
Standard 11	55%			K	
Standard 12	15%		D	J	
Standard 13	3%			G H	
Standard 14	< .5%	—	—	—	—
Standard 15	1%			H I	
Standard 16	2%			E F G	
Standard 17	3%			J K P	
Standard 18	1%			*G	
Standard 19	1%			H K	
Standard 20	1%			F	

Primary benchmark coverage = 21% or more of total benchmarks for the standard

An asterisk (*) in front of a benchmark indicates that, while the topic of the STL is addressed, no specific benchmarks are covered.

Benchmarks are not listed for standards that are covered in less than 5% of the activities.

The highlighted standards are represented most often in the activities.

Overview of Teacher Materials Components

The *TRG* features the following:

- Correlations to the standards
- Teaching modular education
- Teaching safety first
- Computer and Internet use
- Career readiness skills

- Lesson plans
- Career investigations
- Study guide worksheets
- Chapter tests

Table 8.4.5   Categories of teacher support materials and level ratings in *Technology Interactions, 2nd Edition*

Categories of support found in teacher support materials	Level of teacher support
Support for teaching the curriculum	◆◆
Support for pedagogy	◆◆
Support for assessment	◆◆
Support for teaching technology standards	◆◆
Support for teaching twenty-first-century knowledge and abilities	◆◆◆◆

◆◆◆◆   Dominant—Almost all of the criteria for support in this category are present.

◆◆◆   Substantial—Most of the criteria for support in this category are present.

◆◆   Some/Moderate—Some of the criteria for support in this category are present.

◆   Marginal/Missing—Very few or none of the criteria for support in this category are present.

The *TRG* also provides a list of technology education resources, including associations, material and equipment suppliers, publications, and contests and projects. A *Teacher Productivity CD-ROM* contains the lesson plans and correlations to the STL in Microsoft Word, PowerPoint slides, and a test-generation program.

Table 8.4.5 shows how strongly *Technology Interactions* treats each major category of teacher support.

Support for Teaching the Curriculum

The lesson plans in the *TRG* provide the bulk of support for teaching the curriculum. Each chapter's two-page lesson plan is divided into four sections, plus handouts: Focus, Teach, Assess, Close (Table 8.4.6).

The support in the lesson plans is uneven. The Tying to Previous Knowledge sections provide great discussion or activity starters for tying the current topic to previous knowledge and will enrich the student experience. Each suggestion in the Teach section, including the support for the major design and build activities, is typically only two to four sentences. The suggestions supply background information for selected items and good ideas for introducing the concepts and helping students make connections. The brief suggestions for the major activities only give the amount of time to complete, additional information about using the materials, and possible problems the student may encounter. The Enrich subsection in Assess provides broad-brush ideas for further ideas that students can pursue further if done early or if a more challenging activity is needed. None of the Teach or Enrich suggestions provide the detail necessary to help the teacher implement the suggestions. They appear to assume that the teacher will have the necessary content and pedagogical knowledge.

The *TRG* comprehensively addresses two areas in which the student edition is weak: safety and computer and Internet usage. The Safety First chapter in the *TRG*

Table 8.4.6 Outline of lesson plans in *Technology Interactions, 2nd Edition*

Lesson plan section	*Provides*
Focus	• chapter overview • objectives • opportunities for tying to previous knowledge

Teach	teaching suggestions such as:
	  • demonstration
	  • reinforcement
	  • design and build activity
	  • careers
	  • problem solving
	  • background
	  • discussion

Assess	• meeting chapter objectives • evaluate • reteach • enrich
Close	implementation information for the Apply What You've Learned Activity

includes extensive student handouts, safety signs for the classroom, and general information that can ensure a safe technology environment. The Computer and Internet Use chapter provides multiple student handouts and information about Internet safety, netiquette, and research organizers.

Support for Pedagogy

The first 94 pages of the *TRG* provide a great deal of pedagogical support but do not embed it in, or connect it to, the lesson plans teachers use on a daily basis. The *TRG* particularly stresses the idea that teachers be facilitators of student learning rather than the purveyors of it. However, it does not connect this comprehensive chapter with the lesson plans that follow it or with the student edition. The pedagogical discussion includes

- Suggestions for increasing attention, relevance, confidence, and satisfaction;
- A brief discussion of intrinsic and extrinsic motivation;
- Overviews of thinking skills, brain-based learning, the Gregorc learning style model, and Howard Gardner's multiple intelligences theory;
- Brief suggestions for working with students with special needs;
- A chart reviewing advantages and disadvantages of various assessment strategies;
- The importance of team and collaboration skills for career readiness.

The teacher support materials also include an entire chapter on teaching in a modular classroom, including sections such as

- Starting a modular technology education program,
- Developing curriculum for it,

- Building your own program,
- Designing and furnishing it,
- Funding it, and
- Managing the laboratory classroom.

Support for Assessment

For assessing student understanding, this product relies primarily on end-of-chapter tests, projects, and products and secondarily on end-of-chapter critical thinking questions. However, the *TRG* supports assessment only by offering a student study guide worksheet for every chapter and by giving the answers to those worksheets and to the chapter tests. The *TRG* does not assist teachers in assessing student projects and products and does not provide the answers to the critical thinking questions.

The Focus section of the lesson plans supplies very good ideas for engaging students in the Tying to Previous Knowledge section. Although it does not make connections to assessment, a good teacher can easily use the information students provide to guide instruction for the chapter.

The Meeting Chapter Objectives, Evaluate, Reteach, and Enrich suggestions in the Assess section of the lesson plans do not make connections to assessment practices. They tell teachers to complete the chapter study guide worksheets to meet chapter objectives, take the chapter test for evaluation, reteach a specific concept or exercise, and do an enrichment activity.

Support for Teaching Technology Standards

This textbook was published after the STL. The curriculum was correlated to several sets of standards, which appear at the beginning of the *TRG:*

- National Standards for Technological Literacy
- National Science Education Standards
- National Council of Teachers of Mathematics

The lesson plans do not relate the chapter content to the STL, and the *TRG* does not discuss the STL or the importance or role of technology education.

Support for Teaching Twenty-First-Century Knowledge and Skills

Of the five core products reviewed in this book, this curriculum most strongly emphasizes technology careers and related workplace skills. In addition to the help wanted advertisements and investigations on the career pages at the end of each chapter in the student text, the *TRG* provides Career Investigations worksheets to augment the career pages in each chapter. Students select a career in the technology topic area and then research the nature of the work, employment information, training necessary, job outlook, earnings potential, and pros and cons. Students then relate what they learned in the chapter to this career.

The *TRG* also includes a thirteen-page Career Readiness Skills chapter that includes the following topics:

- Interests, Aptitudes, and Abilities
- Entrepreneurship
- Taking an Interest Inventory
- Keys to a Positive Attitude

- Teamwork
- Work Habits
- Personal Employability Traits
- Work Habits Checklist

Table of Contents—*Technology Interactions, 2E*
(Number of pages indicated in parentheses)

Introduction to Technology (2)
1. How Technology Works (14)
2. Design and Problem Solving (16)

Communication Technologies (2)
3. Computer-Aided Drafting (CAD) (18)
4. Desktop Publishing (18)
5. Computer Animation (14)
6. Internet (16)
7. Audio, Video, and Multimedia (22)

Production Technologies (2)
8. Manufacturing (20)
9. Structures (22)

Power Technologies (4)
10. Flight (20)
11. Land and Water Transportation (24)
12. Fluid Power (18)

Bio-Related Technologies (2)
13. Health Technologies (16)
14. Environmental Technologies (22)

Control Technologies (2)
15. Electricity and Electronics (20)
16. Computer Control Systems (18)
17. Robotics (22)

Integrated Technologies (2)
18. Lasers and Fiber Optics (20)
19. Engineering (20)
20. Applied Physics (22)
21. Weather (30)
22. Recycling (24)

SAMPLE PAGES

Many of the textbook's regular features appear on the following sample pages: state-of-the art pictures, Fascinating Facts, and the Impacts and The Future sections that close each chapter. The Explore and Apply What You've Learned activities follow the same format as the Explore activity included here. Note that its heads follow a design loop.

cameras and angle sensors to tell the computer its position. The arm can be used to release satellites into space as well as retrieve items already in orbit. The RMS can also serve as a remote work platform for doing repair work on space vehicles.

Robots may also use microphones to sense sounds. They may use sonar to measure distances. They use sensors to detect poisonous materials in the work envelope. These sensors are called non-contact sensors.

Robot Generations

The first generation of robots was designed by industry to perform a variety of tasks. Known as steel collar workers, these robots did simple tasks that were dangerous or unpleasant for human workers. Early robots were used to handle hot metal, weld metal parts, spray-paint, move parts, and load pallets. These early robots were large and not very flexible.

The second-generation robots used today can perform tasks more complex than the tasks performed by early robots. Today's robots are flexible. Fig. 17-11. They can

▶ **Fig. 17-11** IT (Interactive Technology) is demonstrated here as an interactive robot. It mimics the human emotions of happiness, sadness, surprise, boredom, sleepiness, and anger.

quickly be taught to do several different operations. With movements accurate to a fraction of a millimeter, robotic arms can assemble intricate electronic circuits. They can solder wires as thin as a human hair.

IMPACTS

Are there negative impacts to the use of robot technology?

What if your friend worked in a factory that assembled automobiles? She performs her job with the greatest accuracy and never misses work. Her supervisor often tells her that she is the most productive and reliable employee in the company. One day when your friend goes to work, she walks onto the assembly line floor to find a shiny robotic arm in her spot. The arm works twice as fast as your friend. It takes no breaks and works twenty-four hours a day. Fig. 17-12.

Your friend has just been displaced. "Displaced" is a term used to describe a person whose job has been taken over by automation or new technology. Many experts tell us that robotic technology may cause increased unemployment as companies switch to automation.

Others say that being displaced is not the same as being dismissed. Displaced employees may find new work within the same company or with other companies that are not yet automated.

THE FUTURE

The use of robots in business and industry is part of the automation revolution. Automation is the process by which computers control a series of tasks in manufacturing. Automated factories can operate with very few people. Automated machines can usually work faster, at lower cost, and more accurately than human workers. Remember that robots are not paid a salary, are never late, never call in sick, never need health insurance, and never take vacations.

Robotic automation now allows manufacturers to produce products more cheaply. This allows products to be sold for less. This allows the manufacturer to become more competitive in the world market. In the future, the use of robots will increase.

Fig. 17-12 Welding is commonly done by robots. Weld placement can be precisely controlled.

Explore

Design and Build a Cam Operating System

Engines used in transportation change motion from one direction to another. For example, an automobile engine changes the up-and-down motion of its pistons (linear motion) into rotary motion (circular motion). The direction of motion is changed by using a mechanical device called a *cam*. Cams are arranged along the *camshaft* in the car's engine.

A cam is an offset wheel. Cams are connected to rods. Fig. A. A second rod, or follower, rests on the top of the cam. As the cam turns, the top rod moves up-and-down.

State the Problem
Design and build a cam system that operates a device by changing rotary motion into linear motion. At least one part of the device must move as a result of the cam's action.

Develop Alternative Solutions
Develop three sketches of devices that can be operated by a cam system.

Collect Materials and Equipment
1/4" dowel rod
container for cam operating system (orange juice can or milk carton)
plastic tubing (must fit snugly over the dowel rod)
cardboard
foamcore board
construction paper
brass paper fasteners
pipe cleaner
glue
scissors
pliers

Safety Note
Follow all safety rules given by your teacher when using hand or power tools.

Fig. A

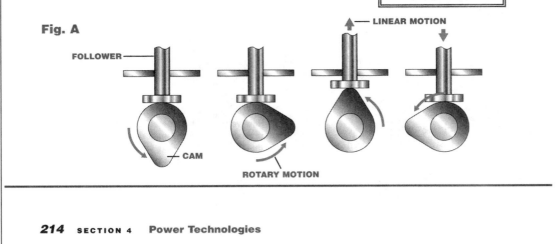

FOLLOWER

LINEAR MOTION

CAM

ROTARY MOTION

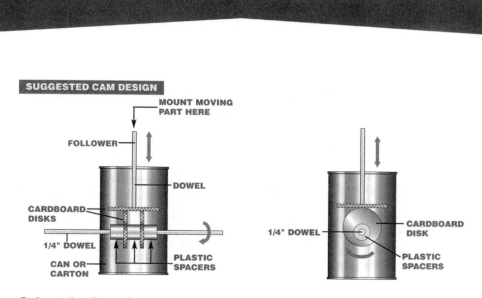

SUGGESTED CAM DESIGN

Select the Best Solution

Consider the complexity of the design and the amount of time you have to build. Review your sketches. Select the design you feel best meets the specifications and solves the problem.

Implement the Solution

1. Prepare any patterns you might need for the construction of the device.
2. Construct the cam system.
3. Place the cam system within the device.
4. Attach the device to the shaft of the follower.

Evaluate the Solution

1. Test your system. Does the device move in the expected way?
2. Make any needed changes.
3. Test the system again.

Technology in Action, Second Edition

Developer/Author:	Brad and Terry Thode
Distributor/Publisher:	Glencoe/McGraw-Hill
Publication date:	2002
Ordering information:	Glencoe/McGraw-Hill, 1-800-334-7344, www.glencoe.com
Target audience:	Middle school

BRIEF DESCRIPTION

This introductory textbook for middle school students focuses heavily on activities. It has sixty-six fully elaborated action activities, which are the book's major activities, and 120 other minor activities. According to the scope and sequence, 93 percent of the class periods are devoted to doing activities. The curriculum, through the activities alone, most strongly supports Standard 11 (applying the design process) and Standard 12 (using and maintaining technological products and systems) from the *Standards for Technological Literacy* (STL) theme Abilities for a Design World.

This curriculum emphasizes building and making things, but often does not explicitly connect the activities to the concepts they are trying to teach. The text, which serves to introduce and support the activities, is 53 percent standards-based, but it is not the focus of the curriculum—the scope and sequence devotes only 7 percent of the class periods to addressing the text. Though all of the standards are present in the text, most are not covered in great depth. Standards 5 and 16 are exceptions; their environmental and conservation issues infuse the curriculum.

The teacher support information, particularly for the Action Activities, is too broadbrush for an inexperienced technology teacher or one who is not familiar with the technology content and pedagogical assumptions. An experienced technology teacher could teach this curriculum without the teacher support materials, but the student experience would be curtailed, especially if the teacher does not implement the Focus and Close sections in the lesson plans, the TechNotes, or the portfolio assessment.

CURRICULUM COMPONENTS

- *Student Edition*, hardcover, 512 pp., $29.97
- *Teacher Resource Guide*, softcover, 320 pp., $67.98
- *Interactive CD-ROM*, $49.98

Materials/Equipment

Because there are so many activities, teachers could elect to implement only those activities for which they have the materials. Materials needed for the Action Activities are listed in each activity and at the beginning of the lesson plans for the chapter. Many activities require shoplike technology labs with expensive equipment that requires much floor space. Examples of advanced or expensive equipment include a direct-TV satellite dish, a GPS receiver, a satellite receiver, an audio mixer, a digital camera, a remote-controlled four-wheel-drive model truck with radio controller, a 12 volt DV rechargeable power-tool battery and plastic cap, lights for video recording, and a vacuum jar, pump, and tubing. The *Teacher Resource Guide (TRG)* provides a list of possible suppliers.

On the other hand, many activities require materials that may be found in a regular classroom, a wood or electronics shop, a computer lab, or a basic technology education classroom. Many of the activities have computer requirements such as CAD, desktop publishing software, and Internet connectivity.

Special Preparations

Some activities require teachers to know how to operate unusual or advanced technical equipment. Many Action Activities require electrical, woodworking, and other technical skills that a nontechnology teacher may not have. Teachers need a working knowledge of any software, hardware, and Internet sites that will be used by the students.

CURRICULUM OVERVIEW

Topic Overview

This book has twenty chapters covering different technology topics (see the table of contents). All twenty of the STL are addressed. The curriculum also covers technology content that is not included in the standards, including the business process, production of TV/radio programs, and traveling, living, and working in space.

Instructional Model

In *Technology in Action,* the text supplies the context for the numerous small and large activities. Through the activities, students build things and get practice in design and problem solving while gaining hands-on experience with technology and how it applies to the real world. The topics can be covered in order, according to student interests. The text is written at a 7.0 grade level and has a Lexile score of 1040L.

Chapters typically have four sections, average twenty-two pages, and open with TechnoTerms (vocabulary) and a list of objectives. Each section has

- At least one Action Activity (except for the first section in the chapter)
- TechnoFacts—fact boxes written to motivate students to learn more
- InfoLinks—connections to related information in other chapters

- Cross-Curricular Connections—explanations of how science, mathematics, or communications relate to technology, plus an activity
- TechCheck box—three questions and an Apply Your Knowledge question or activity, closing each section

The chapter review includes a section-by-section summary, fact-based review questions, and short-answer and activity-based critical thinking questions. The last page of each chapter provides Cross-Curricular Extensions and a section on Exploring Careers. The latter includes an exploration of two careers in that area of technology and an activity intended to draw on skills or knowledge required in those careers.

The curriculum makes real-world connections primarily in three ways: in every chapter, through the Exploring Careers section and other text features such as TechnoFacts, InfoLinks, and Cross-Curricular Connections; through the numerous activities designed for real-world application; and through the use of photographs and graphics. One of the stated purposes of the activities is to learn how technology applies to real-world situations. To that end, each Action Activity opens with a Real World Connection section that supplies background information or has students make connections to their lives through questions such as the following: Have you ever searched for a book in the library; have you ever watched an educational program on TV; you have seen animated cartoons, but have you ever thought about the technology behind making them? The environment—a popular middle school topic—is an ongoing theme of the curriculum.

The photographs and graphics provide contextual support but rarely add information or make explicit connections to the text around them. The captions often serve as discussion or activity starters through which teachers can make those connections explicit, but they don't provide enough detail for students to understand the points on their own. The photographs are crisp, up-to-date, and feature a lot of adult men, although there is a relatively good mix of cultures. Hand-drawn graphics, though not as many as in other texts, are somewhat playful and generally explain the scientific or technical topic.

The textbook has a clear structure but a busy feel. The openings and closings of chapters, text features, and Action Activities are clearly demarcated and follow a consistent format. The sections tend to be short, only two to four pages. Each two-page spread usually has at least one picture, and each page usually has at least one text box feature.

Duration

The scope and sequence estimates the number of forty-five-minute class periods needed to complete each chapter. It states that the concepts presented in the text of each chapter can be covered in one to two periods. It then estimates the number of forty-five-minute class periods needed to complete each of the 66 Action Activities. For example, Table 8.5.1 indicates that there are eight activities, each requiring one to two periods.

In total, 25 periods are devoted to the chapter background information, and 349 periods are used to complete the Action Activities. Recognizing that most teachers cannot cover all the Action Activities, the scope and sequence recommends some activities over others. No estimates are provided for the numerous other activities in the book, which have a very wide range of completion times.

Table 8.5.1 Action activities by number of class periods in *Technology in Action, 2nd Edition*

# of class periods required	# of action activities
1–2	8
3–5	33
6–10	17
11+	7

Nature of Activities

This book has 193 activities, of which 66 are Action Activities, covering one or more pages and using the following format:

- Real World Connection
- Design Brief
- Materials/Equipment
- Procedure
- Evaluation

Each Action Activity tells students to fill out a TechNotes form, which can be reproduced by the teacher from the *TRG*, and to place it in their portfolio. Each activity also has a brief Safety First box that refers students to the safety rules on pages 42–43 and sometimes provides additional information. Note that the Evaluation section does not typically ask students to evaluate their designs (Benchmark 11K), but to think about and answer questions about what they did or something related to the activity.

The 120 remaining activities are described in a paragraph or less. They are found in picture captions, Connections Activities, Apply Your Knowledge questions in the TechChecks section, or in the Critical Thinking questions at the end of the chapter. Although shorter in text space, these unelaborated activities are not necessarily shorter, smaller, or simpler activities than the Action Activities. For example, several Apply Your Knowledge TechCheck activities have seemingly simple instructions, such as "Design and build a scale model of a car" that spark very complex and lengthy activities.

The most common type of Action Activity is the guided activity (Figure 8.5.1). Because guided design activities require directions and design and process suggestions, the one-plus page Action Activities provide a perfect venue for them. The next most frequently occurring Action Activity is the directed type, whose directions are often detailed and lengthy. Although these activities appear fun to do, they are time-consuming and often little conceptual knowledge is drawn from the experience. Other activities (not Action Activities) build a lot of conceptual knowledge, but the text structure does not devote enough space to these other activities to support the connections and ensure learning.

One might anticipate that Action Activities could be open-ended explorations because they tend to require the most from students conceptually and are frequently the most time-consuming, yet few of the Action Activities are open-ended.

The most common design approach for Action Activities is the scaffolded design (Figure 8.5.2). This makes sense, considering the amount of page space required to provide the design guidance and suggestions required of this approach. Consistent with the results discussed earlier, this approach is most often coupled with the guided exploration type of activity.

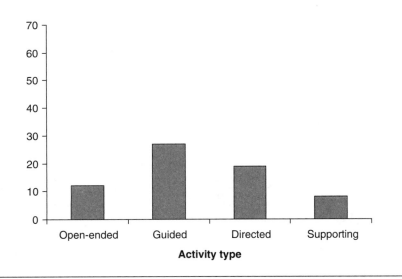

Figure 8.5.1 Number of action activities by type in *Technology in Action, 2nd Edition*, $N = 66$

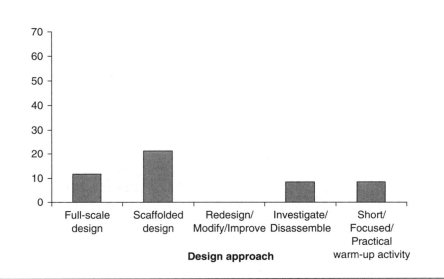

Figure 8.5.2 Number of action activities by design approach in *Technology in Action, 2nd Edition N = 66*

The second most common Action Activity design approach is full-scale design. A full-scale design approach requires students to be involved in all the design steps and results in a product and is typically coupled with the open-ended exploration activity type.

Assessment

The *TRG* recommends several types of assessments: review questions and activities, chapter tests, portfolio assessment, and team evaluations (Table 8.5.2). The *Student Edition* prominently features end-of-section and end-of-chapter review questions. The end-of-section TechCheck box consists of three fact-based questions followed by an Apply Your Knowledge question or activity. The end-of-chapter assessments consist of approximately five short-answer factual Review Questions and five short-answer or activity-based Critical Thinking questions.

Table 8.5.2 Student assessment tools and their presence in the curriculum in *Technology in Action, 2nd Edition*

Assessment approach	Presence in the curriculum
Paper-and-pencil tests—multiple-choice, short answer, true/false, vocabulary, completion	◆◆◆◆
Projects/Products/Media—individual and group activities, projects, products, media	◆◆◆◆
Performance-based assessments—demonstrations, presentations, multimedia, performances	◆◆
Portfolios—student papers, notes, project reports, research, work samples	◆◆◆
Student work—workbook or lab journal pages, handouts, graphs, charts, etc.	◆◆◆◆
Open-ended questioning—essays, extended writing exercises, critical thinking questions, etc.	◆◆◆
Computerized assessment—electronic (online or CD-ROM) simulations, tests, etc.	◆◆◆
Evaluations—peer assessments, self-reflections, self-evaluations	◆◆◆
Rubrics/Checklists	◆◆
Informal observations/Discussions—teacher observations	◆◆

◆◆◆◆ Dominant—There are a large number of assessments of this type in the curriculum.

◆◆◆ Substantial—There are a substantial number of assessments of this type in the curriculum.

◆◆ Some/Moderate—There are a moderate number of assessments of this type in the curriculum.

◆ Marginal/Missing—There are very few or no assessments of this type in the curriculum.

In addition, the *TRG* provides ten-question, multiple-choice tests for each chapter. More test questions, vocabulary quizzes, and a test generator are available on the *Interactive CD-ROM*, which can be purchased separately. Although supported in the *TRG*, some of the activities and exercises in the text (e.g., performance-based activities and informal observations and discussions) were not presented as assessment opportunities.

The *TRG* provides suggestions for using portfolios and an example of how performance-based portfolio assessment can be used in a typical day. For every Action Activity, students are directed to fill out a TechNotes form in which they record the topic, a design brief, safety rules, procedure, and sketches and then answer four questions designed to help teachers assess their understanding. Students place their TechNotes in their own binders, which serve as portfolios. Typically, however, TechNotes are only mentioned in the tag line of every Action Activity header: "Be sure to fill out your TechNotes and place them in your portfolio." No further instructions or reminders to use them as assessments are given.

The *TRG* also provides rubrics for individual and team evaluations, but these are not mentioned in the lesson plans or student edition. In the rubrics, students and teachers rate participation in the problem-solving strategy, contribution of ideas, resolving differences, successful and timely completion, safety, and testing and experimenting with the design. The *TRG* also provides a safety test.

STL STANDARDS AND BENCHMARK-LEVEL ANALYSES

Released after the STL were written, *Technology in Action* addresses all twenty of the standards, is 53 percent standards-based, and covers 76 percent of the middle school benchmarks. It is an activity-based curriculum, and upon completion, students could be technologically literate in Standard 11 (applying the design process) and selected benchmarks for Standard 12 (using and maintaining technological products and systems). This is most likely to be the case for students who use the text *and* complete a large proportion of the activities. From the text alone, it is unlikely that students would attain technological literacy for any of the twenty standards. The curriculum involves students in building and making, but often doesn't provide strong enough connections back to the standards and concepts being taught.

Standards Coverage in the Overall Curriculum

Table 8.5.3 shows the standards that appear most and least frequently in the curriculum overall. For more details about the specific benchmarks covered in the text and activities, see Appendix A.

The five most frequently occurring standards account for 66 percent of the standards coverage in the curriculum, while the five least frequent account for less than 5 percent. With the heavy emphasis on activities in this curriculum, it is not surprising that the two most addressed standards, 11 and 12, are part of Theme 4 (abilities for a technological world).

Table 8.5.3   Five most frequent and five least frequent standards in the overall curriculum (with percents) for *Technology in Action, 2nd Edition*

5 most frequent standards	5 least frequent standards
Standard 11 (25%)—applying the design process	Standard 6 (<.5%)—the role of society in the development and use of technology
Standard 12 (18%)—using and maintaining technological products and systems	Standard 15 (1%)—agriculture and related biotechnologies
Standard 2 (8%)—the core concepts of technology	Standard 14 (1%)—medical technologies
Standard 17 (8%)—information and communication technologies	Standard 7 (1%)—the influence of technology on history
Standard 3 (7%)—the connections between technology & other fields	Standard 1 (1%)—the characteristics & scope of technology

Standards Coverage in the Text

Slightly more than half (53 percent) of the text coverage is standards-based; that is, it addresses STL benchmarks in a way that should lead to technological literacy. The best-covered theme in the text—Theme 5 (the designed world)—is also the only theme that is standards-based less than half the time. Conversely, the themes that are most standards-based—Theme 2 (technology and society) and Theme 4 (abilities for a technological world)—do not have as much coverage. See Table 8.5.4 for a breakout of the coverage of each standard in the text.

Technology in Action strongly emphasizes environmental and conservation issues, Standards 5 and 16. The strong standards-based ratings for Standard 5 (effects of technology on the environment) in large part accounts for the generally high overall standards-based rating for the curriculum.

Standard 5 is the only standard that is 100 percent standards-based.

The most often cited Standard 16 (energy and power technologies) benchmarks are I (energy is not used efficiently) and M (renewable and nonrenewable resources), which are more than two-thirds standards-based.

The authors emphasize environmental and conservation issues as they discuss how technology affects students; using energy, chemical, and bio-related technology; and making, building, and moving things. Furthermore, they ask students to apply Standard 5 environmental concepts in activities throughout the book.

The 80 percent standards-based treatment of Standard 4 (cultural, social, economic, and political effects of technology) further reinforces student awareness of issues relating to technology use.

The technology and society STL theme, which includes Standards 4 and 5, receives one of the higher standards-based scores, but it is the third most frequently occurring theme.

While Benchmark 12H is invoked for explanations of *how* things work, 3F (connections between technology and other fields) is invoked for the frequent explanations from other subjects, especially science, about *why* things work. In both cases, the student can most likely achieve the benchmark through reading the text alone.

Benchmark 12H accounts for almost all of the Standard 12 occurrences and is 87 percent standards-based. This benchmark is concentrated in five chapters. While it is the second most covered benchmark in the text, the other Theme 4 standards (11 and 13) are not addressed in the text at all.

Benchmark 3F is the best-covered benchmark in the text, is about 50 percent standards-based, and is concentrated in the chapters about space, chemical and bio-related technology, and moving things. Unlike 12H, Benchmark 3F is standards-based only half the time, usually because connections between technology and the other subject are not explicitly made.

The treatment of the Designed World standards varies both in terms of the amount of coverage and in terms of how standards-based it is. For example,

Standard 17 (information and communication technologies) is the most covered Designed World standard, but it is only 39 percent standards-based.

Table 8.5.4 Results of analyses of STL coverage in the text for *Technology in Action, 2nd Edition*

STL covered	Percent of text devoted to each STL	Percent of coverage that is standards-based for each STL	Primary benchmarks covered for each STL			
			K–2	3–5	6–8	9–12
Standard 1	4%	23%			F G	
Standard 2	14%	64%		K		
Standard 3	11%	53%			F	
Standard 4	4%	80%			D E	
Standard 5	4%	100%			D	
Standard 6	1%	33%			D F	
Standard 7	3%	11%		B		
Standard 8	3%	18%			E G	
Standard 9	4%	71%			F H	
Standard 10	2%	57%			G	
Standard 11	0%	—	—	—	—	—
Standard 12	9%	70%			H	
Standard 13	0%	—	—	—	—	—
Standard 14	2%	67%			G J	
Standard 15	1%	40%			H	
Standard 16	11%	54%			I	M
Standard 17	12%	39%			K	
Standard 18	6%	25%		D		
Standard 19	6%	58%			H	O
Standard 20	4%	50%			F	L

Primary benchmark coverage = 21% or more of total benchmarks for the standard.

Benchmarks are not listed for standards that are covered in less than 0.5% of the text.

The highlighted standards are represented most often in the text.

Standards 14 (medical technologies) and 15 (agricultural and related bio-technologies) have minimal coverage.

The conservation benchmarks account for most of the Standard 16 (energy and power technologies) occurrences and its standards-based record.

The text primarily addresses middle school benchmarks, but for a few standards it concentrates on benchmarks for either younger or older grades. For example, nearly three-fourths of the coverage for Standard 2 (understanding core concepts of technology) and half of the coverage for Standard 18 (transportation) addresses

Grades 3–5 benchmarks. About a quarter of the coverage for Standard 16 (power and energy technologies) and for Standard 17 (information and communication technologies) addresses Grades 9–12 benchmarks. Again, refer to Appendix A for more detailed information on the benchmarks.

Standards Coverage in the Activities

This is an activity-centered curriculum in which the text introduces and supports the activities. However, the activities often do not make strong connections to the standards and thus cannot be considered as really addressing them outside of a thematic connection. See Table 8.5.5 for a breakout of the coverage for each standard in the activities.

Students should be able to achieve technological literacy in Standard 11 (applying the design process). It is addressed in 19 of 20 chapters. Benchmark K (test and evaluate design) is the most frequently treated benchmark in the book and in the activities. Benchmark 11I (specify criteria and constraints) is not as strongly addressed because nearly all Action Activities provide the design requirements. Although not a focus of the Evaluation section of the Action Activities (despite its name), design evaluation (11K) is still heavily treated. Sometimes the questions in the Evaluation section address Standard 13 (assessing the impacts of products and systems).

The next most frequently addressed standard in the activities is Standard 12 (using and maintaining technological products and systems), which appears in every chapter. Many Action Activities emphasize the Grades 3–5 Benchmark 12D (following directions), which is the second most frequently occurring benchmark in the activities.

Design Standards 8–10 are among the least covered in the text and the activities. While the activities tell students to work in teams, to brainstorm, and to use requirements, experiment, and so on, the activities do not provide instruction and support on how to do these things at the point students would most benefit from it—in the activities themselves. Although some of this is covered in the text, the coverage is only peripheral. Implementing teamwork and cooperative learning in the classroom, however, are addressed for the teacher in the *TRG*.

Some standards are well covered by the activities while others are not. In keeping with the book's awareness of environmental issues, Standard 5 appears in many activities throughout the book. Standards 2, 3 (particularly 3F), 16, and 17 also appear more frequently than others in the activities. Standards 1, 6, 7, 14, and 15 occur infrequently in the activities. Refer to Appendix A for a list of all benchmarks addressed in the activities.

TEACHER MATERIALS REVIEW

Students whose teachers follow the lesson plans in the *TRG* will have a richer experience than students whose teachers do not use the lesson plans. Conversely, experienced technology teachers could teach the curriculum straight out of the *Student Edition* but would miss the pedagogical richness it supplies, especially in the Focus and Close sections. The lesson plans have many teaching suggestions, but not in much detail. They seem to assume that teachers have the requisite content background and implementation knowledge to teach the text and activities and that they have the pedagogical knowledge to take full advantage of all the *TRG* has to offer.

Table 8.5.5   Results of analyses of STL coverage in the activities for *Technology in Action, 2nd Edition*

STL covered	Percent of activities devoted to each STL	Primary benchmarks covered for each STL			
		K–2	3–5	6–8	9–12
Standard 1	1%			F	
Standard 2	4%		I J		
Standard 3	4%			F	
Standard 4	1%			*E	
Standard 5	3%			D	
Standard 6	< .5%	—	—	—	—
Standard 7	< .5%	—	—	—	—
Standard 8	2%			E	
Standard 9	1%		C	G	
Standard 10	2%			G H	
Standard 11	40%			K	
Standard 12	24%		D		
Standard 13	4%			F G H	
Standard 14	< .5%	—	—	—	—
Standard 15	0%	—	—	—	—
Standard 16	3%			F I	
Standard 17	5%			J K	
Standard 18	2%			*G I	
Standard 19	2%			H K	
Standard 20	2%		C	*F	

Primary benchmark coverage = 21% or more of total benchmarks for the standard

An asterisk (*) in front of a benchmark indicates that, while the topic of the STL is addressed, no specific benchmarks are covered.

Benchmarks are not listed for standards that are covered in less than 0.5% of the activities.

The highlighted standards are represented most often in the activities.

Overview of Teacher Materials Components

Table 8.5.6 shows the level of support the teaching materials provide in five categories. The *TRG* supplies this support through the following features:

- Teaching technology education
- Scope and sequence
- Lesson plans
- Action activities (additional)
- 40 transparency masters and 20 handouts
- 20 chapter tests and answer keys

Table 8.5.6   Categories of teacher support materials and level ratings for *Technology in Action, 2nd Edition*

Categories of support found in teacher support materials	Level of teacher support
Support for teaching the curriculum	◆◆◆
Support for pedagogy	◆◆
Support for assessment	◆◆
Support for teaching technology standards	◆◆
Support for teaching twenty-first-century knowledge and abilities	◆◆◆

◆◆◆◆ Dominant—Almost all of the criteria for support in this category are present.

◆◆◆ Substantial—Most of the criteria for support in this category are present.

◆◆ Some/Moderate—Some of the criteria for support in this category are present.

◆ Marginal/Missing—Very few or none of the criteria for support in this category are present.

The teacher portion of the *Interactive CD-ROM* includes presentation materials for every chapter, tips and solutions for the activities and the TechNotes activities, rubrics for assessing team and individual performance, vocabulary quizzes, and a test-generator program.

Support for Teaching the Curriculum

The lesson plans and the scope and sequence (which estimates the length of lessons) are perhaps the most helpful day-to-day logistical resources. Each chapter has a chapter lesson plan, a list of materials and equipment needed, and individual lesson plans for each section.

The one-page lesson plans for each section bookend the student edition nicely, introducing and closing each section and making connections to students' lives. Each lesson plan is divided into six sections: Objectives, Focus, Teach, Assess, Close, and TechCheck Answers (Table 8.5.7).

In the Focus section, the gaining attention and orientation activities and discussions engage students in the topic, have them recall how they may have encountered the upcoming concepts in their lives, and draw out any previous knowledge they may have. The Close activities and discussion give students a chance to apply what they just learned to their lives, sometimes following up on a Focus activity.

The support in the Teach and Assess sections, while labeled in accord with what students do, are very brief (typically one to three sentences). They often suggest creative approaches to conveying the concepts, prompting students to reflect on their work and think about what they have learned. For teachers who need support teaching the content in the section, the Teach section probably does not give the kind of in-depth content or implementation support that a new technology teacher would need, especially for the Action Activities. In either case, the *TRG* assumes that teachers

Table 8.5.7 Outline of lesson plans, *Technology in Action, 2nd Edition*

Lesson plan section	*Provides*
Focus	• gaining attention • orientations
Teach	teaching suggestions such as: • captions • action activity • key terms • specific topics for section • summarizing • sequencing • comparing • brainstorming • demonstrating
Assess	• TechCheck • reteach • enrichment
Close	• additional activity given

have the background in technology and in pedagogy to know how to implement the quickly sketched ideas.

In addition to the 193 activities in the *Student Edition*, the *TRG* provides twelve additional Action Activities. The scope and sequence in the *TRG* somewhat prioritizes the Action Activities in the *Student Edition*, but no support is provided to help teachers decide which of all the other activities (*Student Edition* other activities, *TRG* additional Action Activities, lesson plan activities) would be most advantageous to do and under what circumstances.

Support for Pedagogy

The beginning of the *TRG* (Table 8.5.8) provides support for cooperative learning, encouraging student autonomy and multiple solution pathways through a nonlinear approach to teaching and setting up and teaching a technology education curriculum. While all potentially helpful in the classroom, most of the topics covered in this part of the *TRG* are not picked up again elsewhere in the *TRG*, the lesson plans, or the *Student Edition*.

Support for Assessment

The beginning of the *TRG* also describes a number of assessment options and supplies rubrics, a portfolio assessment vignette, and evaluation forms. However, most of the assessment information is not mentioned elsewhere in the product. The TechNotes are the only assessment item that is woven throughout the curriculum. They are referenced at the start of every Action Activity in the *Student Edition* and in some of the *TRG* lesson plans, but are not further incorporated into the activity.

Table 8.5.8 Teaching technology in education chapter in *TRG*, *Technology in Action*, *2nd Edition*

Topics	Description of coverage
Rationale for technology education	Introduces the role of technology in society and in the curriculum, SCANS, and the *Technology for All Americans* project.
Suggestions for nonlinear delivery of technology education	Suggests teachers assign multiple activities and allow students to complete them in any order they choose. Provides teaching and classroom management ideas, benefits of the approach, and a classroom example. Stresses the connection to the portfolio assessment system (see Assessment section).
Designing technology education facilities	Presents curricular, architectural, and logistical challenges for setting up a technology education facility.
Cooperative learning	Discusses the essential components (positive interdependence, face-to-face interaction, accountability, and social skills) of cooperative groups and provides guidelines for incorporating it into the curriculum.
Student diversity	Provides general suggestions for teaching students with different needs. Discusses how children with different sensory mode preferences and types of intelligences typically learn.
Assessment and assessment forms	Discussed earlier in the Assessment section.
Resources	Lists associations, material and equipment suppliers, and publications that support technology education.
Using *Technology in Action* in a modular setting	Lists topics typically addressed in modular labs and the chapters/sections that address them.
Technology, mathematics, and science standards	Identifies the chapters/sections that address the ITEA, NSES, and NCTM standards.

The TechCheck, Reteach, and Enrich suggestions in the Assess section of the lesson plans do not make explicit connections to assessment practices. For example, the *TRG* tells teachers to reteach specific concepts but does not make alternative suggestions. The chapter lesson plan provides answers to the fact-based chapter Review Questions, but does not mention the Critical Thinking questions and activities. The product also provides a pre and posttest that has 50 multiple-choice questions.

Support for Teaching Technology Standards

This textbook was released after the STL were published. The *TRG* provides a chapter/section level correlation to the following sets of standards:

- National Standards for Technological Literacy
- National Science Education Standards
- National Council of Teachers of Mathematics

Although the *TRG* explicitly explains what the STL are, the lesson plans do not relate the chapter content to the STL.

Support for Teaching Twenty-First-Century Knowledge and Abilities

This curriculum emphasizes technology careers and the importance of workplace skills. Each chapter closes with an exploration of two careers in that area of technology and an activity that is supposed to draw upon skills or knowledge required in those careers. The chapter lesson plans provide discussion starters or additional activities related to the careers. In addition, many of the handouts address Secretary's Commission on Achieving Necessary Skills (SCANS) and workplace skills (e.g., succeeding at work, values, an interest inventory, entrepreneurship, job applications and interviews, and working in teams).

The opening chapter of the *TRG* discusses the skills needed in a technological world in terms of understanding the impacts of technology on individuals, society, the world of work (SCANS), and education (*Technology for All Americans*). The *TRG* does not provide additional support for teaching inventive thinking, design, and problem solving.

Table of Contents—Technology in Action, 2E
(Number of pages indicated in parentheses)

1. Getting Started in Technology (24)
2. Using Technology (20)
3. How Technology Affects You (18)
4. Introducing Computers (22)
5. Using Computers (20)
6. Inventing Things (20)
7. Making Things (16)
8. How Things Work (28)
9. Designing Things (24)
10. Exploring Automation (24)
11. How Business Works (26)
12. Building Things (22)
13. Using Energy (24)
14. Moving Things (26)
15. Finding and Using Information (24)
16. Producing TV/Radio Programs (22)
17. Traveling in Space (22)
18. Living and Working in Space (26)
19. Exploring Chemical and Bio-Related Technology (22)
20. Technology and Your Future (21)

Sample pages 78–79 display a typical section in its entirety. Note the Things to Explore objectives, the vocabulary, multiple pictures, TechnoFacts boxes, and four-question TechCheck, which includes a student activity. The Action Activity has five main sections plus a safety first box, an InfoLink, explanatory graphics, and a reminder to place TechNotes in the portfolio.

SECTION 4

The Ecology of a Product

THINGS TO EXPLORE

- Explain what ecology is.
- Tell why recycling is important.
- Compare the time it takes different materials to decompose.

TechnoTerms

ecology
landfill
recycling

We live in a "throwaway" world. When we're finished with a product, we often just throw it away instead of fixing it or **recycling** (reusing) it. Did you know that every man, woman, and child in the United States creates an average of 5 pounds of garbage a day? That's 230 million tons of garbage every year!

Ecology is the study of how things interact with the environment. Part of designing a product is planning ahead for what will happen to it after it is no longer useful. That includes every product from newspapers to jet airplanes. Fig. 3-5.

Fig. 3-5. Old cars and trucks are a big waste problem because they take up so much space. How does your community dispose of old vehicles?

TechnoFact

FROM OLD JUNKER TO SHINY NEW MODEL Nationwide, 20,000 cars are junked each day. Researchers are taking apart cars to experiment with reusing the materials. They are making glove compartments from waste products and using fabric scraps to make sound insulation. In the future, more plastics will probably be used in cars, because plastics can easily be reused.

78 · Chapter 3, Section 4

Fig. 3-6. Materials like aluminum, which can be recycled, must be separated from other waste. Research how recycling plants sort waste. Report your findings to the class.

Why Recycle?

Do you ever stop to think what happens to the things you throw away? Many of them end up in **landfills** (garbage dumps) where they are buried or burned. Others are sometimes dumped into the oceans. Disposing of materials in these ways can eventually cause air or water pollution.

Whenever possible, the best alternative is to use materials that are biodegradable. Biodegradable materials break down naturally and return to the earth. Those materials that take a long time to decompose (break down), such as aluminum, plastic, and glass, should be recycled. Fig. 3-6. Some products, such as the batteries in flashlights, transistor radios, and other electronic devices, should always be recycled.

SECTION 4
TechCHECK

1. What is ecology?
2. Why is recycling necessary?
3. Name some items at school you can recycle.
4. **Apply Your Knowledge.** Contact the agency that operates your local landfill. Ask about their five-year and ten-year plans for managing the landfill.

TechnoFact

MONEY THROWN AWAY The cost of throwing away our trash is going up fast because of new rules to protect the environment and because of lack of landfill space. It can cost $50 per ton to throw away trash. If you multiply the 230,000,000 tons of garbage we throw away each year by $50, we spend $11,500,000,000 just on garbage!

Chapter 3, Section 4 · 79

ACTION ACTIVITY

Designing a Robot's End Effector

Be sure to fill out your TechNotes and place them in your portfolio.

Real World Connection

Did you ever have trouble grabbing a bar of soap in the bathtub? Imagine that the thing you are trying to grab is worth hundreds or millions of dollars and the slightest wrong move would destroy it. This is part of the difficulty in using robots. Their end effectors must be sensitive and able to grab without causing damage. Satellites, for example, that need repair in orbit require careful handling by astronauts in the Space Shuttle. The grapple device on the shuttle's robot arm was designed for this purpose.

The robot arm is called the Remote manipulator system (RMS). Eventually, it will find uses in manufacturing or in underwater robotic exploration. It will be used to grip large, delicate objects and materials.

In addition to a gripper with fingers, special cup-shaped devices can make it much easier to grab objects.

> **INFOLINK**
>
> See Chapter 18, "Living and Working in Space."

Design Brief

Design, build, and test a gripping device that might be used on a robot arm.

Materials/Equipment

* plastic cups
* sharp knife
* tape
* string

> **SAFETY FIRST**
>
> Follow the safety rules listed on pages 42-43 and the specific rules provided by your teacher for tools and machines. Use hand tools such as sharp knives with caution.

Procedure

1. Put two plastic cups together and cut them as shown in Fig. A.
2. Cut three pieces of string 5 inches long.
3. Tape the strings to the outside of one cup and the inside of the other cup as shown.
4. Put the cups together and adjust the lengths of the strings to cross the diameter of the cup.
5. Test your end effector by turning one cup in the opposite direction of the other. The strings should cross in the center.
6. Try to grab a pencil or other object using your grapple device. (The pencil simulates the grapple point on an object such as a satellite.)

Evaluation

1. What makes this device better than a gripper?
2. What does it mean to grapple something?
3. Why is it important for astronauts to be able to grab satellites in orbit?
4. **Going Beyond.** Design, build, and test a grapple device like the one in this activity that would fit on a robot arm in your school.
5. **Going Beyond.** Research other types of end effectors. Make a chart or a poster of various types and describe their uses.

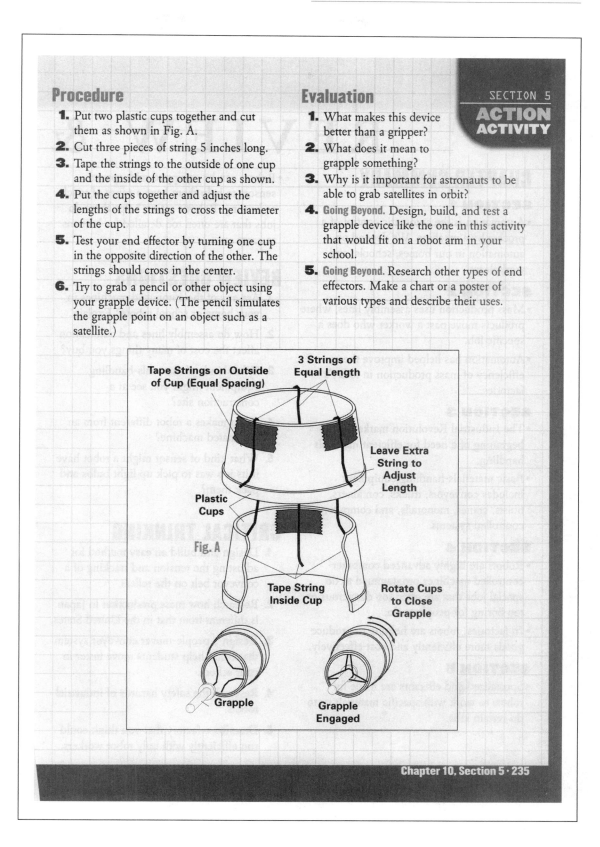

Tape Strings on Outside of Cup (Equal Spacing)

3 Strings of Equal Length

Leave Extra String to Adjust Length

Plastic Cups

Fig. A

Tape String Inside Cup

Rotate Cups to Close Grapple

Grapple

Grapple Engaged

9

Cross-Curricular Products

This chapter provides extensive reviews of seven products that integrate technology with other subjects: four are for the elementary grades, and three others are for the middle grades. Between two and four sample pages are reproduced from each product, as well as the products' tables of contents. Newer products are provided before older ones, and products for the elementary grades precede those for middle school. If more than one product is published the same year, reviews are ordered alphabetically by the last name of the lead author.

Like Core Technology products, these curriculum materials also are intended for classroom use, but they address technology *and* some other subject area(s). Most often, technology receives a treatment in these products that is comparable to or less than the treatment given to the other subjects. Some cross-curricular materials present multiple content areas in such a way that they "get at" one area through focusing first on one of the other disciplines (e.g., students learn technology content during the course of science inquiry activities, social studies investigations, etc.). Some others of these integrated products blend the subjects so seamlessly or holistically that they do not explicitly indicate when various subjects are being taught. A few cross-curricular products cover much of the Standards for Technological Literacy (STL). However, most of these products differ from the Core Technology products because they are not intended to provide the same comprehensive, in-depth coverage of the STL.

While all five Core Technology products are textbooks, the structures or components of the Cross-Curricular Products vary. They range from an elementary series, having one volume per grade level for Grades K–5 (*T.R.A.C.S.*), or a set of modules, each of which can span several elementary grades (*Children Designing and Engineering, Stuff That Works!*), to a single large module that contains long-term projects (*A World in Motion*). Because these curricula integrate at least three subjects, technology is not their sole, or even primary, focus. The three reviewed products for the middle grades also have quite different structures. Before providing the seven reviews, we briefly describe a few other cross-curricular products.

We chose cross-curricular products that had a clearly identifiable technology component or substantial amounts of technology content infused throughout the product. Science teachers should be aware that there are other science products that include some technology content. A recent example is the Kendall-Hunt series *Challenges in Physical Science* (www.kendallhunt.com), created by Phil Sadler of the Science Education Department at the Harvard-Smithsonian Center for Astrophysics (www.cfa.harvard.edu). This National Science Foundation (NSF) funded curriculum for Grades 5–8 includes technology in such units as Bridges, Gravity Wheel, and Solar House.

■ LATE-BREAKING PRODUCTS

Project Lead the Way (www.pltw.org) has been better known as a high school project, but its middle school curriculum is also becoming popular. Seven middle-grades units are available or in development, each of which requires ten weeks of class time: Design and Modeling, The Magic of Electrons, The Science of Technology, Automation and Robotics, Aerospace Engineering, Environmental Engineering, and Energy and the Environment. A laudable feature of this curriculum for science, mathematics, and technology is the extensive professional development provided prior to teachers' first use of the product. However, because this professional development is a required provision for obtaining the curriculum, we did not consider it to be readily accessible to any reader, a selection criterion that we specified for this book.

A couple of NSF-funded projects at the Georgia Institute for Technology aim to teach technology within a science context. *Learning by Design* by Janet Kolodner (www.cc.gatech.edu/edutech/projects/lbdview.html) is a series of middle-grades modules that use design challenges as catalysts for learning science and mathematics content more deeply. Although the developers are exploring commercial publication, the products currently can only be obtained by contacting the developers directly. David Crismond is adapting *Learning by Design* and other technology curriculum materials into a professional development system (www.gatech.edu/projects/lbd/davidCrismond.html). These products are not formally reviewed because they currently do not meet the readily available selection criterion for this book.

Children Designing and Engineering

Developer/Author:	Patricia Hutchinson and others
Distributor/Publisher:	Design and Technology Press
Publication date:	2004
Funders/Contributors:	National Science Foundation (NSF), The College of New Jersey, New Jersey Chamber of Commerce, Institute of Electrical and Electronics Engineers (IEEE)
Ordering information:	Design and Technology Press, Belmar, NJ
Distributed through:	http://Childrendesigning.org
Target audience:	Elementary school (Grades K–5)

BRIEF DESCRIPTION

This curriculum contains twelve *Teacher Guides* (six for Grades K–2 and six for Grades 3–5) that challenge students to solve practical problems related to real work-world settings. Developed in partnership with several New Jersey businesses, the product lets students experience the planning, designing, development, and operation of their own classroom businesses and services. The twelve *Teacher Guides* and accompanying multimedia supports offer teachers strong help in implementing this creative problem-solving curriculum.

As young businesspeople, students learn techniques and apply concepts from mathematics, science, technology, and several other fields. They must carry out investigations, generate ideas, plan a course of action, make and test things, and reflect on what they learned. Units begin with the posing of a Big Challenge (usually related to product or service development), and the ensuing four to six weeks of lessons focus on achieving a solution to that challenge. As active investigators and designers, students become the owners of knowledge rather than passive recipients of information.

Students have a very good chance at achieving technological literacy from these units. Nineteen of the twenty Standards for Technological Literacy (STL) are addressed in *Children Designing and Engineering* (*CD&E*). The careful planning of standards-based learning goals across many subject areas is obvious in the lessons. A blended approach to topic and subject integration allows students to gain simultaneously new understanding and skills in many content areas.

CURRICULUM COMPONENTS

The twelve units in *CD&E* may be used in any order. The following table shows the units, their costs, and, because this curriculum was in development at press time, when they will be available.

Each unit is accompanied by the following materials, which are included in the costs listed in Table 9.1.1.

- Scene Setter (video, CD-ROM interactive story, big book, or other focusing device)
- *Teacher's Guide* (daily lesson plans, transparency masters, teacher technical references, student portfolio reference pages)
- Assessment instruments (either on paper or in interactive CD-ROM format)
- Classroom kit for twenty-five students
- Student guided portfolio masters
- Printed portfolios are available as an option for $5.00 per student

Unit-specific teacher training videos are in the planning stages, as well as an online module, *Introduction to Integrated Mathematics, Science, and Technology*, which is being adapted from a *CD&E* trainer course.

Table 9.1.1 *Children Designing & Engineering* units, their costs, and release dates

Unit title K–2	Release date	Cost	Unit title 3–5	Release date	Cost
Bright Ideas Playhouse	Spring 2004	$400.00	Camp Koala	Spring 2004	$840.00
Opening Day at the Safari Park	Spring 2004	$840.00	Say It With Light, Inc.	Spring 2004	$860.00
Cranberry Harvest Festival	Fall 2004	Not avail.	The Suds Shop	Fall 2004	Not avail.
Earth-Friendly Greetings	Fall 2004	Not avail.	The Juice Caboose	Fall 2004	Not avail.
Germbuster Kit	2005	Not avail.	Paper Products: You Be the Judge	2005	Not avail.
Waterworks for Watertown	2005	Not avail.	Solar-Powered Energy Savers	2005	Not avail.

Materials/Equipment

The classroom kits contain tools and consumables for twenty-five students and include almost all of the materials necessary to complete the activities and lessons. Any remaining materials are commonly found in schools. The Week-at-a-Glance section and margin notes for each daily lesson list the materials required, as well as useful Web sites, additional resources, and technology tools. Some units require word processing, spreadsheet, drawing, desktop publishing, and graphics programs such as PowerPoint.

Special Preparations

The developers of *CD&E* offer optional in-depth professional development and training for teachers using this product. A four-day introductory course recommended for first-time users is planned for summer 2005. Four two-day unit-specific workshops will also be offered by summer 2005.

Additional, larger-scale professional development courses for schools and districts interested in introducing onsite *CD&E* schoolwide or districtwide are also available. Another four-day course for Grades 10–12 teachers introduces design and technology and integration of mathematics, science, and technology. Teachers or schools who do not choose to participate in these professional development opportunities should still be able to implement the *CD&E* curriculum successfully.

CURRICULUM OVERVIEW

Technology Topic Overview

Table 9.1.2 describes the Big Challenges that focus each unit and the major learning goals and skills associated with solving the challenges.

Integration Review

The curriculum moves seamlessly from subject to subject, using a blended integration approach that combines mathematics (including algebra and geometry), physical and life sciences, technology, workplace readiness, geography, language arts, art, and social sciences. Each lesson and activity presents content from multiple subject areas rather than having a series of separate lessons on math, science, language arts, and so on. A list at the beginning of each unit specifies the content goals for each subject area, and a list of the specific standards or benchmarks addressed is given at the beginning of each week's lesson plan. Table 9.1.3 presents examples of typical integrated topics covered in the Grades K–2 and Grades 3–5 *CD&E* units.

Instructional Model

A simplified, developmentally appropriate design process forms the foundation for the instructional model promoted in *CD&E*. Students explicitly learn the steps to this process and put them into practice for every activity:

1. Get to know the problem

2. Explore ideas

3. Plan and make a solution

4. Test your work

5. Share your week

The focus of student learning is on the problem-solving activities that are derived from the Big Challenge. The Big Challenge is a design brief found at the beginning of

Table 9.1.2   Descriptions of *CD&E* units

Unit title, Grades K–2	
Bright Ideas Playhouse	Students explore properties of light, then apply what they've learned to design and make shadow-puppet plays based on familiar nursery rhymes. Students learn about and experience nursery rhymes and stories, storyboards and plays, color, materials and tools, running a box office, and properties of light and shadow. The final product is a performance of their plays to which they charge admission.
Opening Day at the Safari Park	Following a video tour of a real safari park, students collaborate on a plan to build their own classroom park. Experiences include building animal safari park homes, designing clothing and tools for workers, making rules for visitors, modeling safari vehicles, and celebrating opening day with parents and friends.
Cranberry Harvest Festival	Students plan and stage a cranberry festival based on information they have gathered while acting as scientists (studying buoyancy and bounce in cranberries) and designers. Students learn about and experience properties of cranberries, materials and tools, sorting and grading fruit quality, wet and dry harvesting, assembly-line mass production, and reading and writing recipes and invitations.
Earth-Friendly Greetings	Students study the waste stream and recycle paper products into new paper, which they use to design and make original greeting cards. Students learn about and experience ways to care for the environment, conduct surveys, recycle paper, design and make paper, understand color and texture, use design process, and work cooperatively. The greeting cards are sold at a holiday boutique.
Germbusters & Co.	After learning about germs and hygiene, students design a performance to share their knowledge and promote/sell their health-related products. They learn about germs and health, hygiene technology, soap making, designing a product, packaging, and communicating a message.
Waterworks for Watertown	Students design and build a water distribution system for Watertown, USA. They become experts in moving and controlling water efficiently as they learn about sources of water, properties of water and the water cycle, water conservation, and the uses and importance of water.

Unit title, Grades 3–5	
Camp Koala	After learning about koala bears and other endangered species, students design and make a visitors' center for Camp Koala, a new home for an endangered species that is being planned for a local safari park. Topics include conservation and endangered species; impacts of technology on animals; characteristics, needs, and habitats of koalas; structures, movements, and controls; fundraising; and making displays. Students stage a "Koala Gala" to publicize and raise funds for wildlife preservation.
Say It With Light, Inc.	Students are employees of a communication company where they learn about the roles of scientists, designers, engineers, and marketing professionals in product development. They investigate light and communication, then work as interdisciplinary teams to propose new products that use light for communication. Students experience and learn about light, communication and codes, electric circuits, persuasive presentations, material properties, and planning and making techniques. The final product is a presentation to the company's directors.
The Suds Shop	Based on their health and manufacturing research, students design, manufacture, and sell a new soap at their own Suds Shop. They learn about germs, design and manufacturing, packaging and promotion, operating a retail shop, setting prices and profits, and basic chemical properties of soap.
The Juice Caboose	This unit challenges students to develop new combination juice drinks as they learn how companies gauge consumer preferences and explore the physiology of taste. They mass produce, package, promote, and launch their products. Students learn about data collection and analysis, packaging, materials and structures, the design process, graphic communications, making technologies, and investigating tastes.
Paper Products: You Be the Judge	Students design and produce a news broadcast that reports their findings on the quality of commercial paper towels. In the process, they learn how to create and administer a consumer survey, use the scientific method, create and explain visual representations of data, collect and analyze data, employ planning and making techniques, carry out objective testing, redesign a testing device, and work cooperatively.
Solar-Powered Energy Savers	Students are challenged to design and manufacture the prototype for an inexpensive solar-powered device to be given away at a community "energy awareness day." They learn energy facts, properties of solar energy, planning and making techniques, persuasive presentation making, properties of shapes and materials, electrical circuitry, and the financial considerations and constraints associated with giveaway items.

Table 9.1.3   Sample topic integration for Grades K–2 and 3–5 *CD&E* units

Technology		Science	
• Build structures to hold a light signal • Build a system to create rotary motion • Model a historic lighthouse • Understand that new technologies are developed to improve on older ones • Assemble a product from instructions • Draw an object from three views • Analyze systems: interpret and use codes • Build and diagram an electrical circuit • Understand the design process • Understand that successful products solve a practical problem • Recognize that all problems have constraints and specifications	• Generate ideas to solve a problem: appreciate human creativity • Use criteria to evaluate ideas • List and manage resources needed to make a product • Understand that drawing is the language of human design • Identify different types of technological drawings • Choose and use appropriate materials and tools effectively • Design and make a product presentation using technology, graphic design techniques, and other tools • Determine audience needs and wants • Design and feedback to evaluate success	• Understand that light travels in straight lines from a source • Learn that different materials affect light differently • Investigate optical qualities of materials • Demonstrate light transmission, reflection, and absorption	• Observe energy changing form • Learn how the eyes determine the colors we see • Understand that all colors we see are contained in white light • Experiment with electric circuits

Language arts
• Understand the importance of written communication • Write reports using communication approaches appropriate for team roles

Art
• Understand that primary colors of paint are different from the primary colors of light • Name the three pigment primary colors • Name the three pigment secondary colors

Social studies
• Research state, costal, etc., lighthouses

Mathematics		Workplace readiness
• Measure lengths, widths, angles, and dimensions • Create a pattern that conveys information • Interpret and use codes • Estimate time and resources • Use spatial reasoning • Use math skills to design a board game	• Present mathematical data using charts and graphs **Supplemental** • Graph ratio of height to surface distance • Graph diameter versus distance • Analyze functions • Manipulate objects in space	• Work cooperatively in groups to solve problems and meet goals • Follow directions • Use tools and resources safely and effectively • Explore careers such as designers, engineers, scientists, and marketing specialists • Take specific responsibilities in a team • Demonstrate effective communication, critical thinking, decision-making, problem-solving, and self-management skills • Provide and accept constructive criticism

each chapter that is accompanied by a set of questions students need to answer in order to accomplish it. Most challenges are authentic to elementary students' experiences and should be of high interest to them. In addition to hands-on activities, students complete worksheets and other handouts and collect work samples for their portfolios.

At the end of each daily lesson plan (or session), the summary section directs teachers to ask students questions about what they just did or learned and to remind them to relate their experiences to each step of the design process using a class set of design process cards. This summary exercise keeps students aware of the central role of the design process in everything they do.

Because the twelve curricular units are collections of lesson plans written for teachers, they do not contain many photos, graphics, drawings, and so on. These kinds of visual aids for elementary-age students are used, however, in the student portfolio/workbook pages and in blackline masters and other student handouts from the teacher pages. For Grades K–2, these graphics are mostly very simple cartoons that help beginning or lower-level readers understand the limited text or provide them with storyboards for directions. For Grades 3–5 portfolio/workbook pages, the simple cartoons are replaced with text and occasional diagrams, but no photographs or drawings are used. The reading level required for the student pages is grade-level appropriate. The teacher pages include some photographs and drawings of materials or actual projects in various stages of completion.

The video and CD-ROM components feature either entertaining, age-appropriate live footage from various locations or colorful, lively animations. The worksheets and handouts are simple, clear, and, like the CD-ROM and videos, relate directly to the content of the lessons and activities. These components greatly enhance students' problem-solving experiences and their ability to successfully complete and understand the lessons.

Because the Big Challenges are inspired by real New Jersey businesses, and the units are developed in partnership with them, students have opportunities to relate the work they are doing with "real jobs" in the work world. A few of the units include specific information and activities related to careers.

Duration

Each of the twelve units requires four to six weeks to complete (between 15 and 22 hours per unit). The units are carefully structured, with specific activities and lessons occurring on all five days of the school week. Each daily session lasts between 30 and 60 minutes.

Nature of Technology Activities

Technology activities in the *CD&E* curriculum are largely guided explorations, meaning that student choice about how to complete the activities is balanced with teacher- or curriculum-determined procedures. Almost equal, though lesser amounts of directed and supporting activities round out the offerings. These activities generally appear at the beginning of the weekly sessions or as a means of dividing more complex activities into bite-sized chunks. Often the directed activities concentrate on assembly of kits supplied by *CD&E*. Students work in teams and use their portfolio sheets to document the progress, results, and self- or peer-assessment of their activities and projects. Figure 9.1.1 shows the distribution of the technology activities by type of activity.

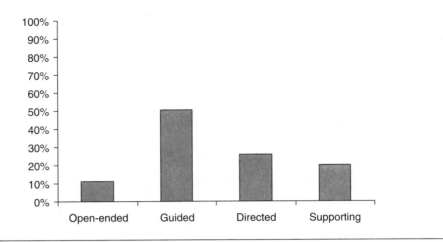

Figure 9.1.1   Activity type distribution in *CD&E*

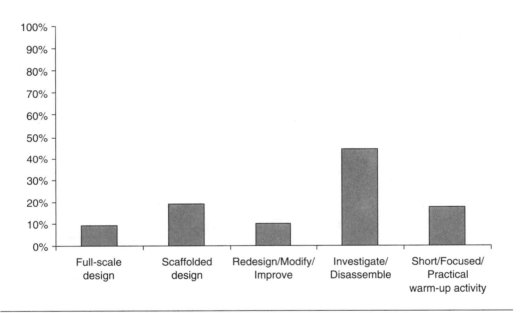

Figure 9.1.2   Design approach distribution in *CD&E*

The most common design approach found in the activities is investigate/disassemble/evaluate, followed by scaffolded design and short/focused/practical warm-up activities (see Figure 9.1.2). These more rudimentary approaches are primarily accounted for by kit assembly or whole class planning and research activities. Use of the scaffolded design approach is most often paired with guided activities.

The activity types and designs show that the developers were careful to give students achievable, well-supported design challenges and activities that are developmentally appropriate for elementary students. Even though the students create quite complex final products, the rollout of activities leading to those products is carefully staged to give even the youngest students success along the way.

Table 9.1.4   Student assessment tools and their presence in *CD&E*

Assessment approach	Presence in the curriculum
Paper-and-pencil tests—multiple-choice, short answer, true/false, vocabulary, completion	◆ ◆
Projects/Products/Media—individual and group activities, projects, products, media	◆ ◆ ◆ ◆
Performance-based assessments—demonstrations, presentations, multimedia, performances	◆ ◆ ◆ ◆
Portfolios—student papers, notes, project reports, research, work samples	◆ ◆ ◆
Student work—workbook or lab journal pages, handouts, graphs, charts, etc.	◆ ◆ ◆ ◆
Open-ended questioning—essays, extended writing exercises, critical thinking questions, etc.	◆ ◆ ◆ ◆
Computerized assessment—online simulations, tests, etc.	◆ ◆ ◆
Evaluations—peer assessments, self-reflections, self-evaluations	◆ ◆ ◆
Rubrics/Checklists	◆ ◆
Informal observations/ Discussions—teacher observations	◆ ◆ ◆

◆◆◆◆   Dominant—There are a large number of assessments of this type in the curriculum.

◆◆◆   Substantial—There are a substantial number of assessments of this type in the curriculum

◆◆   Some/Moderate—There are a moderate number of assessments of this type in the curriculum.

◆   Marginal/Missing—There are very few or no assessments of this type in the curriculum.

Assessment

This product offers an unusually rich array of assessments (see Table 9.1.4). Within each unit, each of the five sessions concludes with an Evidence section. Typically this section asks the teacher about the student performance pertinent to the learning goals and skill building in the session. This includes content questions, observation of student progress, review of student portfolios and team logs, and occasional assessment rubrics. The curriculum also stresses student self-assessment, using both individual and peer assessment. Each unit is also accompanied by a student-paced, interactive CD-ROM that provides learning reinforcement and self-assessment.

Table 9.1.5   Results of analyses of STL coverage in the overall curriculum for *CD&E*

STL theme	Coverage rating	Primary standards covered for each theme
Theme 1	◆ ◆ ◆ ◆	Standard 1—The characteristics and scope of technology Standard 2—The core concepts of technology Standard 3—The connections between technology and other fields
Theme 2	◆ ◆	Standard 5—The effects of technology on the environment Standard 6—Technology and society
Theme 3	◆ ◆ ◆ ◆	Standard 8—The attributes of design Standard 9—Engineering design Standard 10—Problem solving
Theme 4	◆ ◆ ◆	Standard 11—Applying the design process Standard 12—Using and maintaining technological products and systems
Theme 5	◆	*

◆ ◆ ◆ ◆   Dominant—A large portion of this theme is covered.

◆ ◆ ◆   Substantial—There is substantial coverage of this theme.

◆ ◆   Some/Moderate—There is moderate coverage of this theme.

◆   Marginal/Missing—There is little or no coverage of this theme.

Primary standards coverage = standard has dominant or substantial coverage within the theme.

* Standards are not reported for marginal/missing themes.

STL STANDARDS-LEVEL ANALYSIS

CD&E addresses 19 of the 20 STL. As Table 9.1.5 demonstrates, the standards from Themes 1, 3, and 4 are particularly well covered. This product was published after the STL, and the careful planning and deliberate use of the STL as the technology education framework is obvious. The lessons and activities consistently address the standards at the benchmark level and provide many opportunities for students to achieve technological literacy—one of the few cross-curricular resources to do this.

TEACHER MATERIALS REVIEW

Overview of Teacher Materials Components

The twelve *CD&E* units contain lesson plans, teacher pages (special instructions and resources for completing the sessions and activities), student portfolio/workbook pages, and matrices of weekly lessons and their connections to specific national standards and benchmarks (science, technology, mathematics, and workplace readiness).

Each unit starts with five introductory pages that provide general background information about the Big Challenge, the learning context, the subjects that are integrated in the unit (including specific skills and understandings to be gained), a list of design decisions that students will need to grapple with, and a list of the unit's weekly learning goals. Plus, each of the five or six weeks within the unit is prefaced with a Week-at-a-Glance section that highlights learning expectations, multisubject objectives and standards addressed in the sessions, resources, and vocabulary.

Each daily lesson plan is one to three pages long and is organized into five subsections:

- Prep Notes—additional guidance for the teacher to assist in lesson preparation
- Introduction—questions to ask the children to prepare for the upcoming lesson
- Procedure—step-by-step descriptions of activities and lessons
- Summary—review and discussion of concepts and skills and their relationship to the Big Challenge
- Evidence—questions and strategies for assessing student progress

Margin notes in the daily lesson plans remind teachers about objectives, resources, portfolio pages, new vocabulary, and, sometimes, career connections. A section called Notes to the Teacher sometimes provides additional teaching tips and guidance.

Following all of the lesson plans are a glossary, a standards-alignment matrix, teacher pages, reproducible student portfolio pages (including other student handout materials), and supplemental math handouts and worksheets. The standards that provide the framework for the technology, math, science, and workplace readiness content are

- Technology education—Standards for Technological Literacy: Content for the Study of Technology (ITEA)
- Mathematics—Principles and Standards for School Mathematics (NCTM)
- Science—National Science Education Standards (NRC)
- Workplace readiness—Cross Content Workplace Readiness Skills (NJ Core Curriculum Content)

The *CD&E* curriculum includes dominant or substantial support for teaching the curriculum, assessment, technology standards, and twenty-first-century workplace skills (see Table 9.1.6). At this point in its development, *CD&E* offers limited support, however, for teaching design as pedagogy (the instructional approach claimed by the developers). Although teachers are given fairly detailed procedural guidance for lessons and activities, this guidance assumes that they already know how to ask open-ended questions, organize and manage student teams, facilitate student choices in planning their designs, and so on. A teacher who is new to design- or project-based learning would most likely have no difficulty implementing the activities per se, but they could have problems actually teaching standards-based content and concepts through them. The optional teacher training that *CD&E* offers could enhance teachers' abilities to teach design as pedagogy. Given the high quality of this product and its thorough treatment of design as an instructional strategy for even young children, the additional focus on teacher training will make this excellent resource even better.

Table 9.1.6 Categories of teacher support materials and adequacy ratings for *CD&E*

Categories of support found in teacher support materials	Adequacy of teacher support
Support for teaching the curriculum	◆ ◆ ◆ ◆
Support for pedagogy	◆ ◆
Support for assessment	◆ ◆ ◆ ◆
Support for teaching technology standards	◆ ◆ ◆
Support for teaching twenty-first-century workplace skills	◆ ◆ ◆

◆◆◆◆   Dominant—Almost all of the criteria for support in this category are present.

◆◆◆   Substantial—Most of the criteria for support in this category are present.

◆◆   Some/Moderate—Some of the criteria for support in this category are present.

◆   Marginal/Missing—Very few or none of the criteria for support in this category are present

---

Table of Contents: Say It With Light (3–5)
(Typical of all 3–5 units)
(Number of pages indicated in parentheses)

The Learning Context (1)
The Big Challenge (4)
Weekly Learning Goals (1)

Week 1: Communicating with Lighthouses (5)

- Session 1—Introduction to light (2)
- Session 2—Lighthouses (2)
- Session 3—Making light brighter: Reflectors and lenses (3)
- Session 4—A rotating signal (3)
- Session 5—Modeling a NJ lighthouse: Designing and planning (2)
- Session 6—Modeling a NJ lighthouse: Making, testing and evaluating (2)

Week 2: Electricity and Light (5)

- Session 1—A credit card flashlight (1)
- Session 2—Analyzing a product by drawing: 3-view drawing (1)
- Session 3—Parts of a system: An electrical circuit (2)

- Session 4—Communication and codes (3)
- Session 5—Angles of incidence and reflection: Mirror investigations (2)
- Session 6—Sending a message around the corner (3)

Week 3: Light, Materials, and Color (4)

- Session 1—Light and sight: Lens-holder glasses (2)
- Session 2—Colors from white light (2)
- Session 3—Changing light with filters (2)
- Session 4—Mixing colors of pigment (2)
- Session 5—Hidden answers game (3)

Week 4: Designing a Communication Product (4)

- Session 1—Investigating roles of scientists, engineers, designers and business people in product development (3)
- Session 2—The design process (1)

- Session 3—Identifying possible devices (2)
- Session 4—Exploring ideas (2)
- Session 5—Research, development and planning in team roles (2)
- Session 6—Managing resources (2)

Week 5: Making a Communication Product (3)

- Session 1—Developing the idea with drawings (2)
- Session 2—Safety and quality (2)
- Sessions 3 & 4—Making, testing, and improving (1)
- Sessions 5 & 6—Team role reports (2)

Week 6: Product Presentation (3)

- Session 1—A product presentation (3)
- Session 2—Using and presenting data (2)
- Session 3—Presentation tools and techniques (2)
- Session 4—Preparing your message (1)
- Session 5—Rehearsal (2)
- Session 6—The presentation (1)
  Glossary (7)
  Standards (32)
  Teacher Pages (51)
  Guided Portfolio Pages (26)
  Team Log Sheets (15)
  Supplemental Math (42)

SAMPLE PAGES

The sample pages selected for *CD&E* include a sample daily lesson plan for Grades 3–5. The session follows the standard Note, Introduction, Procedure, Summary, and Evidence format, and the margin notes demonstrate typical teacher supports.

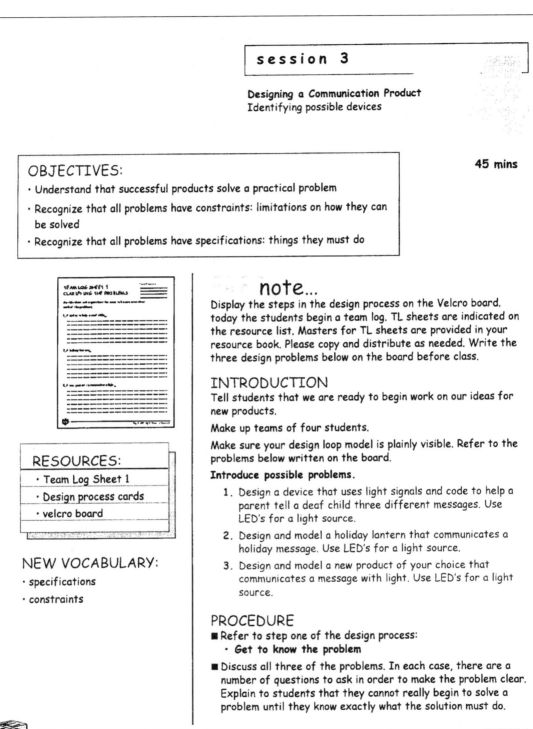

session 3

Designing a Communication Product
Identifying possible devices

45 mins

OBJECTIVES:
- Understand that successful products solve a practical problem
- Recognize that all problems have constraints: limitations on how they can be solved
- Recognize that all problems have specifications: things they must do

note...

Display the steps in the design process on the Velcro board. today the students begin a team log. TL sheets are indicated on the resource list. Masters for TL sheets are provided in your resource book. Please copy and distribute as needed. Write the three design problems below on the board before class.

INTRODUCTION

Tell students that we are ready to begin work on our ideas for new products.

Make up teams of four students.

Make sure your design loop model is plainly visible. Refer to the problems below written on the board.

Introduce possible problems.

1. Design a device that uses light signals and code to help a parent tell a deaf child three different messages. Use LED's for a light source.

2. Design and model a holiday lantern that communicates a holiday message. Use LED's for a light source.

3. Design and model a new product of your choice that communicates a message with light. Use LED's for a light source.

PROCEDURE

- Refer to step one of the design process:
  - **Get to know the problem**
- Discuss all three of the problems. In each case, there are a number of questions to ask in order to make the problem clear. Explain to students that they cannot really begin to solve a problem until they know exactly what the solution must do.

RESOURCES:
- Team Log Sheet 1
- Design process cards
- velcro board

NEW VOCABULARY:
- specifications
- constraints

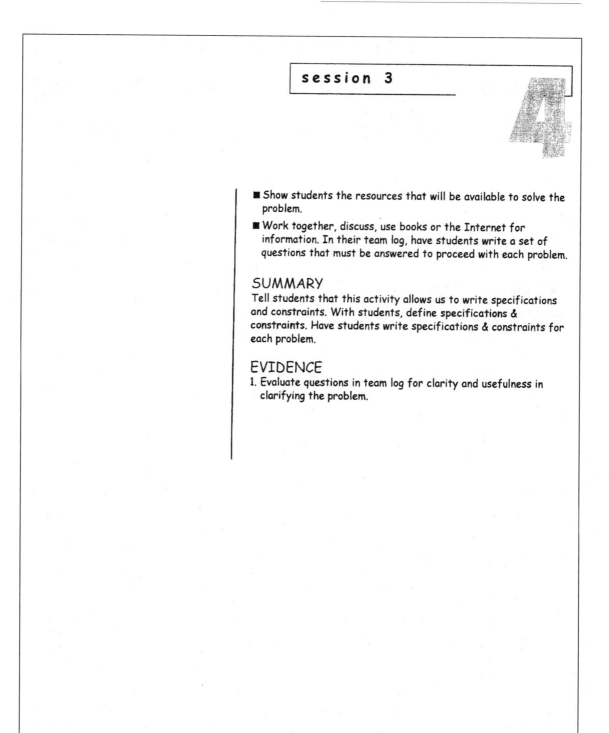

session 3

- Show students the resources that will be available to solve the problem.
- Work together, discuss, use books or the Internet for information. In their team log, have students write a set of questions that must be answered to proceed with each problem.

SUMMARY
Tell students that this activity allows us to write specifications and constraints. With students, define specifications & constraints. Have students write specifications & constraints for each problem.

EVIDENCE
1. Evaluate questions in team log for clarity and usefulness in clarifying the problem.

Stuff That Works!
A Technology Curriculum for the Elementary Grades

Developer/Author:	Gary Benenson and James Neujahr, City College of New York
Distributor/Publisher:	Heinemann
Publication date:	2002
Funders/Contributors:	National Science Foundation
Ordering information:	Heinemann, 1-800-225-5800, www.heinemann.com
Target audience:	Elementary school (Grades K–6)

BRIEF DESCRIPTION

Stuff That Works! (STW) is a five-unit, cross-curricular resource developed to teach technology through the technology design process. Each unit is a teacher's guide that contains richly detailed background, content, and implementation information, plus a set of seven to twenty-three activities for students. Each guide uses a single technology topic—designed environments, mechanisms, signs and symbols, packaging and structures, or mapping—as the focal point for teaching math, science, English language arts, social sciences, and, of course, technology. Every activity involves applying at least four of these subject areas simultaneously.

This product has several unique features. It provides an unusual amount of detail, context, and content in the teacher instruction chapters; it engages teachers in the same technology design process they will be using with their students; it has many pages of classroom vignettes and journals written by teachers who implemented the activities during field testing; it offers several excellent pages on theory and best practices in assessment; and, in addition to identifying standards alignments for the major subject areas, it presents a very thorough history and explanation of how the standards came to be, their place in the curriculum, how to use them, and the unifying content and concepts found in each set.

STW addresses 14 of the 20 Standards for Technological Literacy (STL), with particular emphasis on standards from Themes 1, 3, and 4. However, only one guide, *Designed Environments*, provides activities that are aligned to the STL at the standards and benchmark levels. The other four guides address the STL more generally, requiring teachers to familiarize themselves with those standards and identify opportunities to teach them on their own.

CURRICULUM COMPONENTS

This curriculum contains five softcover volumes, or guides, that may be used in any order. This curriculum is available in English only.

- *Packaging & Other Structures*, 192 pp., $17
- *Mechanisms & Other Systems*, 192 pp., $17
- *Designed Environments: Places, Practices & Plans*, 160 pp., $17
- *Mapping*, 192 pp., $17
- *Signs, Symbols & Codes*, 168 pp., $17

Materials/Equipment

Each activity lists the necessary materials. Most materials are typical classroom supplies or can be easily obtained from home or the neighborhood store. A small number of activities require more specialized items (e.g., petri dishes, geoboards, bell wire).

Special Preparations

A three-page section at the back of each guide emphasizes the importance of securing the support of other people such as the custodian (who can provide discarded materials and is knowledgeable about the school building), parents, other teachers, and school administrators. Some of the activities involve field trips, so preparation for those outings would need to be handled well in advance. In addition, many activities in *Mechanics & Other Systems* require special knowledge about making and using electrical circuits, simple machines, construction, tools, and so on. Although these skills are taught as part of the teacher materials at the beginning of the units, someone who is not familiar with them would need time to master the skills and be comfortable teaching them to students.

A professional development model is being developed and tested for this curriculum and should be available soon. This model will offer an online component as well as teacher workshops.

CURRICULUM OVERVIEW

Technology Topic Overview

Stuff That Works! contains five guides. Each guide contains from seven to twenty-three activities. Some, but not all, of the activities have grade-level designations.

Packaging & Other Structures teaches how and why bags, boxes, cartons, and bottles work to contain, protect, dispense, and display products. Students discover how different types of packaging materials are examples of structures and how structures are technologies designed to support mechanical loads. It includes thirteen student activities.

Mechanisms & Other Systems shows students how and why basic technologies work. Students discover how to transform motion, convert energy, and/or process information to get the task done. It includes fourteen student activities.

Designed Environments: Places, Practices & Plans gives students an understanding of how the process of design makes environments work. Students explore the organization of space and time in daily life, work with others on solving problems, then create and evaluate their own designs. This guide is the only one to structure its activities around a specific design loop. It includes seven student activities.

Mapping teaches students how space is organized and used and how maps express meaning about space. Students explore the possibilities of mapping, from drawing their desktops or representing their bedrooms and the important things in them to using coordinates, grids, and scale as tools for redesign. It includes twenty-three student activities.

Signs, Symbols & Codes teaches students different methods for representing information. The activities in this book involve signs, symbols, or codes of some sort, and all draw on a broad range of places and situations that are part of everyday experience. It includes seven student activities.

Integration Review

The product uses a blended integration style, such that most activities require students to use ideas and skills from at least two or three content areas as they grapple with technological concepts and skill building. *STW* teaches technological content in the following cross-curricular contexts:

- Mathematics
- Science and technology
- Language arts
- Social sciences
- Physical science

Standards and/or benchmark alignment for these subject areas is provided for each activity. The introductory pages in each guide include information and background knowledge to help teachers understand some of the cross-curricular content that appears in the activities.

Instructional Model

The five *STW* guides involve students in "doing technology" in order to teach them how to identify and solve problems, create understanding, and gain skills and knowledge across multiple subject areas and processes. Table 9.2.1 shows the broad categories of competence and specific skills students will gain from this curriculum.

In addition to the general competencies and skills noted earlier, teachers who have used this product report that it helped their students to

- Observe and describe phenomena in detail
- Explore real objects and situations by creating models and other representations
- Identify salient aspects of problems
- Solve authentic problems
- Use evidence-based reasoning
- Apply the scientific method
- Ask thoughtful questions
- Communicate in oral, written, and graphic forms
- Collaborate effectively with others

The guides are written for teachers and therefore contain very few graphics, photos, charts, drawings, and the like in the activities themselves. The Introduction, Appetizers,

Table 9.2.1 Competencies and skills taught in *Stuff That Works!*

General competencies	*Specific skills*
Collect examples	Brainstorm Scavenger hunts
Sort the examples	Develop categories Classify
Analyze selected examples	Infer purpose Divide into components
Design process	Identify problem Formulate criteria & constraints Develop alternative designs Evaluate alternative designs Make tradeoffs Review criteria & constraints
Start from an existing design	Modeling Redesign Repair Reuse

and Stories chapters, however, contain many photos, drawings, and samples of student work. These graphics are extremely helpful in getting across the ideas and procedures presented in the text. The generous use of student work samples also helps shed light on the directions and discussions and makes the stories and teacher journals more pertinent and real. The activities represent real-world situations and problems that are relevant to children's daily lives, thus helping to "demystify" technology, the designed world, and the design process for students and teachers.

Duration

Activities vary widely in duration, from as little as one forty-five-minute session up to as many as fourteen sessions. Many of the activities are in the four to eight session range. Each activity introduction provides information on the amount of time needed to complete it.

Nature of Technology Activities

Students work cooperatively in teams for the majority of the activities in this product. Each activity is supported by classroom discussions and preliminary exercises aimed at gaining the prerequisite skills and knowledge needed for students to complete the activity. Every activity ends with a summary classroom discussion about what the students just learned or did. All of the activities are structured as follows, and some also include strategies for amending the activities for special needs students:

- Activity title
- Grade level
- Prerequisites
- Activity overview

- Standards and benchmarks
- Time needed
- Materials
- Procedure

- Activity concepts
- Vocabulary
- Skills

- Extensions
- Teacher tips
- Worksheets

Designed Environments: Places, Practices & Plans deserves special comment in terms of activities. Because the topic of this guide is design, the seven activities are structured around a five-step technology design process. Even though parts of the design process are taught and used in all of the guides, *Designed Environments* gives both students and teachers the most systematic and consistent experience with it. The steps, or phases, of the design process are

1. Problem identification

2. Data collection and analysis

3. Design and implementation

4. Evaluation

5. Assessments and extensions

The majority of the activity types found in *STW* are supporting or guided, with directed and open-ended types occurring much less frequently (see Figure 9.2.1). Throughout the curriculum, students are involved in numerous supporting activities that are actually small tasks and exercises designed to give them prerequisite knowledge or skills for completing the larger guided explorations. Students also participate in a fair percentage of directed activities, which help to scaffold their learning for the open-ended explorations.

Figure 9.2.2 shows the distribution of design approaches employed in *STW*. A large percentage of the activities involve students in researching topics, evaluating technology artifacts and processes, and collecting data, usually as part of supporting or directed activities. Short/focused/practical and full-scale design and make approaches are each represented in about 20 percent of the activities. Scaffolded and redesign/modify/improve approaches are represented in fewer of the activities.

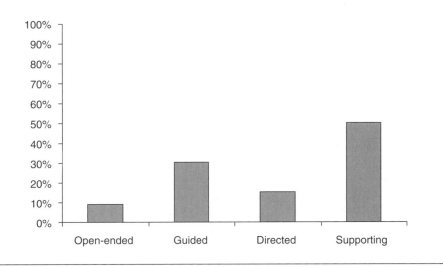

Figure 9.2.1 Activity type distribution in *Stuff That Works!*

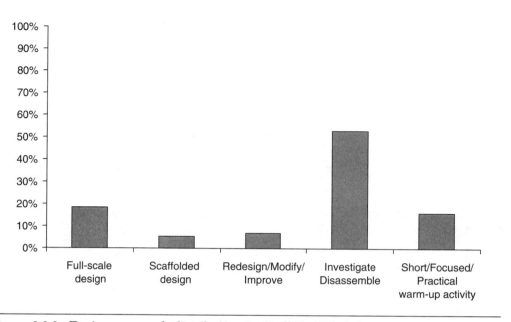

Figure 9.2.2 Design approach distribution in *Stuff That Works!*

Assessment

Each of the guides contains a three-page section on assessment in Chapter 5. These sections vary only slightly from unit to unit and are divided into six key areas:

- Assessment (an introduction)
- Educational Goals
- Information from a Variety of Sources
- Curriculum as a Major Source of Assessment Data
- Students Assess Their Own Learning
- Assessing the Learning Environment

The introduction provides a brief and very clear background on what is meant by assessment, why it is important, and its relationship to the curriculum and the learning environment. The ensuing five assessment topics are explored with a fair amount of detail, using classroom examples of how other teachers used the activities to assess their students. However, these examples, and some of the vignettes in the Stories section, are the only concrete treatment of assessment in the curriculum in four of the five guides. Although the authors encourage teachers to take a broad view of the issues surrounding assessment and of what constitutes an assessment (basically, any student work or activity), only paper-and-pencil assessments in the form of student worksheets and open-ended questions and discussion topics appear in the activities themselves. The authors do discuss that remaining flexible is important and that many times the best assessment opportunities occur unexpectedly, but teachers who are new to thinking broadly about assessment will likely need more support for actually turning student work and classroom discussions into methodical assessments.

The exception to this pattern is the *Designed Environments: Places, Practices & Plans* guide. As discussed previously, this guide focuses on teaching the design process, and its activities are structured around a five-step design loop. As part of this loop, all of the activities include an evaluation phase where students are given specific

Table 9.2.2 Student assessment tools and their presence in *Stuff That Works!*

Assessment approach	Presence in the curriculum
Paper-and-pencil tests—multiple-choice, short answer, true/false, vocabulary, completion	◆ ◆
Projects/Products/Media—individual and group activities, projects, products, media	◆ ◆ ◆ ◆
Performance-based assessments—demonstrations, presentations, multimedia, performances	◆ ◆ ◆
Portfolios—student papers, notes, project reports, research, work samples	◆ ◆ ◆
Student work—workbook or lab journal pages, handouts, graphs, charts, etc.	◆ ◆
Open-ended questioning—essays, extended writing exercises, critical thinking questions, etc.	◆ ◆ ◆ ◆
Computerized assessment—online simulations, tests, etc.	◆
Evaluations—peer assessments, self-reflections, self-evaluations	◆ ◆
Rubrics/Checklists	◆
Informal observations/ Discussions—teacher observations	◆ ◆ ◆

◆ ◆ ◆ ◆ Dominant—There are a large number of assessments of this type in the curriculum.

◆ ◆ ◆ Substantial—There are a substantial number of assessments of this type in the curriculum.

◆ ◆ Some/Moderate—There are a moderate number of assessments of this type in the curriculum.

◆ Marginal/Missing—There are very few or no assessments of this type in the curriculum.

instructions for assessing their own designs and processes. The design loop ends with a closing step called Assessment/Extensions where specific suggestions are given for several different ways to assess what students learned from the activity.

Table 9.2.2 shows ten categories of assessment tools and how often they are found in the curriculum. When reviewing this table, bear in mind that only the paper-and-pencil tests and some open-ended questions and discussion topics are actually provided in the majority of the curriculum. The remaining categories are clearly described and strongly suggested, but it is up to the teacher to recognize opportunities to implement assessments while teaching the activities.

STL STANDARDS-LEVEL ANALYSIS

Fourteen of the twenty STL are addressed in *Stuff That Works!* The text and activities give particular attention to Themes 1, 3, and 4, not an unusual pattern for the cross-curricular

Table 9.2.3 Results of analyses of STL coverage in the overall curriculum for *Stuff That Works!*

STL theme	Coverage rating	Primary standards covered for each theme
Theme 1	◆ ◆ ◆	Standard 2—The core concepts of technology Standard 3—The connections between technology and other fields
Theme 2	◆	*
Theme 3	◆ ◆ ◆ ◆	Standard 8—The attributes of design Standard 9—Engineering design Standard 10—Problem solving
Theme 4	◆ ◆ ◆	Standard 11—Applying the design process Standard 12—Using and maintaining technological products and systems
Theme 5	◆ ◆	Standard 16—Energy and power technologies Standard 17—Information and communication technologies

◆◆◆◆ Dominant—A large proportion of this theme is covered.

◆◆◆ Substantial—There is substantial coverage of this theme.

◆◆ Some/Moderate—There is moderate coverage of this theme.

◆ Marginal/Missing—There is little or no coverage of this theme.

Primary standards coverage = standard has dominant or substantial coverage within the theme.

* Standards are not reported for marginal/missing themes.

technology products reviewed in this book. Table 9.2.3 shows the coverage ratings for each theme as well as the specific standards within those themes that receive dominant or substantial treatment in the overall curriculum.

Designed Environments: Places, Practices & Plans is the only guide that aligns specific STL standards and benchmarks to its activities. The other guides provide general information on the STL, but do not include them in the activity alignments.

TEACHER MATERIALS REVIEW

Overview of Teacher Materials Components

The instructional support materials for each guide are located at the front and back of the book, sandwiching the student activities. The organization, number of chapters, and chapter sections are consistent throughout most of the five guides (see Table 9.2.4).

STW offers dominant and substantial support for teaching the curriculum, pedagogy, and assessment (see Table 9.2.5). Support for teaching technology and twenty-first-century workplace skills is not as strong.

The introduction is the same for each guide, with the exception of two sections. Appetizers and Concepts (Chapters 1 and 2) provide the meat of the teacher support

Table 9.2.4   Organization of the *Stuff That Works!* Guides

Chapter title	Description
Introduction	Background information for teachers about technology as a discipline, the educational goals of the guide, how to use the guide, and a brief history of the guide and its topic
Chapter 1—Appetizers	Suggestions for activities teachers can do to familiarize themselves with the guide's main technology topic
Chapter 2—Concepts	Content background, exercises, tasks, and activities to prepare the teacher for the student lessons
Chapter 3—Activities	Activities—student activities, including prerequisites, overview, concepts, vocabulary, skills taught, standards and benchmark alignment, procedures, extensions, teacher tips, and worksheets
Chapter 4—Stories	Collection of real-life classroom vignettes and teacher journals developed while using the activities
Chapter 5—Resources	Support for implementing the activities, connections to children's literature, and ideas for assessments
Chapter 6—About Standards	Lists of the national science, technology, math, English language arts, and social studies standards addressed in the activities and lessons

Table 9.2.5   Categories of teacher support materials and adequacy ratings for *Stuff That Works!*

Categories of support found in teacher support materials	Adequacy of teacher support
Support for teaching the curriculum	◆ ◆ ◆
Support for pedagogy	◆ ◆ ◆ ◆
Support for assessment	◆ ◆ ◆
Support for teaching technology standards	◆ ◆
Support for teaching twenty-first-century workplace skills	◆ ◆

◆◆◆◆   Dominant—Almost all of the criteria for support in this category are present.

◆◆◆   Substantial—Most of the criteria for support in this category are present.

◆◆   Some/Moderate—Some of the criteria for support in this category are present.

◆   Marginal/Missing—Very few or none of the criteria for support in this category are present.

materials by preparing teachers to teach the curriculum and providing information and discussions about pedagogy. These are very detailed, comprehensive treatments (from 24 to 61 pages) that help teachers understand the technology topic and content of the volume, teach them how to use and teach the technology design process by having them experience it firsthand, provide them with clear explanations of technology artifacts and systems and how they work, and provide pedagogical discussions of what students need to know to successfully identify and solve problems. The student activities and a table that provides standards alignments for all the activities in the guide make up Chapter 3.

Chapter 4, Stories, contains further support for teaching the curriculum, pedagogy, and assessment. This chapter presents classroom vignettes, teacher journals, and extension exercises written by teachers who have used the curriculum. These very accessible stories are easy for teachers to identify with and contain numerous embedded tips and suggestions that, if applied, can make the activities a much more meaningful experience for both students and teachers. Although suggestions and lessons learned from the stories are not referenced in any of the activities, teachers should have no problem identifying and implementing the suggestions that are relevant to their own classrooms.

In addition to the blended integration of technology with other subjects in the activities, Chapter 5 offers additional literature and English language arts connections to the activities. This chapter also includes a section called The Institutional Context, in which teachers are given advice for how to mobilize support for teaching technology in the school and community environments. This chapter contains the main assessment support materials.

Standards are the focus of Chapter 6, appropriately titled About Standards. This chapter contains an overview of which standards were used as the framework for the cross-curricular content (see following list), a history of standards in general and what they mean, and a synopsis of the content of the standards and how some of that content is realized in *STW*. The text for Chapter 6 varies only slightly from guide to guide.

- Standards for Technological Literacy: Content for the Study of Technology (ITEA)
- Benchmarks for Science Literacy (AAAS)
- National Science Education Standards (NSTA and NRC)
- Principles and Standards for School Mathematics (NCTM)
- Standards for English Language Arts (NCTE and IRA)
- National Standards for Teaching Social Studies (NCSS)

The treatment of the standards in Chapter 6 provides a very solid foundation for teachers to understand their basic principles and see how those principles come to play in the activities. This, coupled with the standards alignments in the activities and at the end of Chapter 3, should be more than adequate support for most teachers to identify where there are opportunities in the activities to teach the standards. All five guides discuss the STL and explain what is meant by technological literacy in Chapter 6; however, only *Designed Environments* aligns its activities with specific STL standards and benchmarks.

STW does not directly address workplace skills; however, many of the activities involve students in such processes as forming teams and taking on team roles, project management and planning, brainstorming, and so on.

Table of Contents: Designed Environments: Places, Practices, & Plans
(Number of pages indicated in parentheses)

Introduction (6)
Chapter 1: Appetizers

What Is a Designed Environmental Problem? (5)
Designed Environments and You (1)
Getting Started: Redesign Your Desk (5)
Designed Environments in the Classroom (1)
Design of Space in the Classroom (4)
Redesign of Time in the Cafeteria (5)
Rules and Procedures in the Classroom (3)
Designed Environments: Projects and Life in the Classroom (2)

Chapter 2: Concepts

Technology Design Process (11)
What Children Need to Know for Designed Environment Projects (3)
Systems Thinking and Environments (1)
Learning and Child Development in Designed Environments Activities

Chapter 3: Activities

Activities at a Glance (1)
Let Us Count the Ways: An Introduction to Data Collection (2)
Activity # 1: Interruptions (3)
Activity # 2: Examining Classroom Procedures (3)
Activity # 3: The Broken Rules Project (7)
Activity # 4: The Games Project (5)
Activity # 5: Classroom Environmental Design (4)
Activity # 6: Environmental Design of Larger Spaces (6)

Activity # 7: Critter Habitats (3)
Standards for Activities (4)

Chapter 4: Stories
Part I: Rules and Procedures
Classroom Procedures (3)
Classroom Rules (5)
Recording Behavior (2)
Rules of Games (1)
Modifying Games (1)
Inventing Games (1)
Evaluating Student Designed Games
Part II: Analysis and Redesign of Spatial Environments
Redesign of a Classroom (2)
Redesign of a Cafeteria (7)
Designing Environments and Solving Problems for Classroom Pets (1)
Cricket Suicide (1)
Designed Environments for Mealworms (4)

Chapter 5: Resources

Making Connections with Literature (6)
Assessment (3)
The Institutional Context (5)

Chapter 6: About Standards

Overview (1)
Where the Standards Came From (1)
What the Standards Actually Mean (1)
What Use Are Standards? (2)
What the Standards Really Say (11)

References (6)

SAMPLE PAGES

A Grades 5–6 activity from *Packaging & Other Structures* is shown in the sample page spread. Note the detailed Procedures section that includes open-ended questions for discussion, teaching prerequisite knowledge, and skill building. Because this three- to five-period activity includes so many procedures, the following regular features of the activities could not be included in the spread: Overview, Prerequisites, Vocabulary, Concepts, Skills, Standards, Grade Level, Time Needed, and Activity Sequence.

Activity №8

How Does the Shape of a Column Affect Its Strength?

Overview

In this activity, students investigate the relative strength of columns of different shapes and discover the importance of controlling variables in a test or experiment.

Materials

- Paper of assorted sizes and shapes (for preliminary construction)
- Shape templates (pages 69–72)
- Tape or glue
- Weights for load testing (tiles, washers, or marbles)
- Bucket or coffee can
- Square pieces of cardboard large enough to support a can or bucket
- Worksheet #8

Procedure

1. A column is a vertical piece whose purpose is to support parts of a structure, such as a building, a platform, or a bookshelf. The legs of tables and chairs also work as columns. Find a structure in the classroom or nearby in the school that has support columns. This could be part of the room or building, a raised platform, a large table, or a bookshelf. Ask students to observe the columns carefully, and answer questions like these:

  - What purpose do these columns serve in this structure? What are they holding up?
  - What would happen if one or more of the columns were removed?
  - What would happen if the columns weren't strong enough to do their job of supporting the structure?
  - What makes a column strong? Is it the length, the diameter, the material, the shape, or a combination of those?
  - How would we measure the length of a column?
  - How would we measure the circumference or perimeter of a column?
  - What kinds of materials can columns be made of?
  - What shapes can columns be?

  Regarding the latter question, show columns that are in the shape of a circle, a square, a rectangle, and a triangle. You can find some of these in furniture or in the structure of a building, or make them out of paper or cardboard for demonstration purposes.

  Record students' answers so they can return to them later after they've done some tests to learn more about this topic.

2. Draw four shapes on the chalkboard: square, triangle, rectangle, and circle. Take a vote among students on which of these shapes they think would make the strongest column. Ask them to give their reasons for their choices. Don't label answers as right or wrong. Instead, record their ideas and tally up the votes for each shape for future reference.

3. Ask students to work in pairs to construct the four different-shaped columns out of paper and use them to test their hypotheses. Don't specify any rules or guidelines for the sizes of the columns or the construction techniques. Make paper of different weights and sizes available, but don't suggest which one should be used. Let students make all the decisions regarding the columns. The only requirement is that one must be round, one must be square, one must be rectangular, and one must be triangular.

4. Distribute copies of Worksheet #8 to each team. On the worksheet, have them identify this as "Test #1." Once students have constructed their columns, have them measure the length and enter the measurements on Worksheet #8. They should also enter the construction material used for each column.

5. The next step is for students to test the columns for strength and record the results. The test consists of centering a square platform of cardboard on top of the column, holding the column securely and making sure it is exactly vertical, placing the can on top of this platform, and adding weights (identical washers, tiles, or marbles) to the can until the column buckles. One student can hold the column upright at its base while the other places the cardboard platform on top, places the empty can on the platform, then adds the weights to the can, one at a time. Students should count the number of weights added in each test to determine the point at which the column buckles.

6. Make a simple chart on the board or chart paper to compare the results of all student teams. Tally how many columns of each shape were found to be the strongest in the preliminary tests. If a clear winner emerges, ask student teams who identified that shape as the strongest to share their data with the class:

  - Length of column
  - Material used
  - Point of failure

  Ask students to compare and discuss similarities and differences among these variables.

7. Discuss the meaning of these preliminary tests, starting with these questions:
  - Why didn't every team get the same result?
  - Do these tests really reveal which shape makes the strongest column?
  - Were these fair tests—that is, were the variables (such as length, width, type of paper) the same for each test?

8. Review the principles of fair testing with students. Have them identify what would be necessary to make these fair tests for the strongest shape—that is, controlling all variables so that the only difference among the columns being tested is the shape. This requires using the same materials, making columns of the same length, and using the same platform, can, and weights to test for strength.

9. Once the principles of a fair test have been established, set aside class time for students to perform their tests again. Distribute more copies of Worksheet #8 to student teams and have them identify this as "Test #2." Make copies of the templates on pages 69–72 and distribute them to students. Point out that it's important to follow the template directions carefully so that all columns are folded and taped in the same way.

10. Have students make the columns and perform the tests again. Remind them to follow the principles of fair testing in all cases—all variables must be the same except the shape of the column.

11. Students once again fill out the worksheet and present their findings to the class. Compare and discuss the findings, which should reveal the round column to be the strongest. If there are results that don't agree with this finding, have students analyze their test procedures and conditions to look for evidence that fair test guidelines were not followed.

Extensions

- Challenge students to create a graph of their test data and to rank the four shapes from strongest to weakest.
- As homework, have students look for examples of columns they see in their homes and community, and also find pictures of columns in newspapers and magazines and bring them to class. Set aside class time to discuss the shapes, materials, and functions of the columns students identify.

A World in Motion: The Design Experience, Challenge 1

Developer/Author:	Education Development Center, Inc.
Distributor/Publisher:	Society of Automotive Engineers (SAE) Foundation
Publication date:	2000
Funders/Contributors:	National Science Foundation, SAE International
Ordering information:	SAE Foundation, 1-800-457-2946, www.sae.org/foundation/awim/
Target audience:	Late elementary (Grades 4–6)

BRIEF DESCRIPTION

A World in Motion: The Design Experience, Challenge 1 (AWIM, Challenge 1) consists of three three-week units: Skimmer Challenge (Grade 4), JetToys Challenge (Grade 5), and Steel Can Rover Challenge (Grade 6). The publisher, a nonprofit organization, provides a *Teacher Manual* with reproducible student handouts and a student materials kit for free to the first classroom in a school.

Each unit is a blended, three-week curriculum, designed to be taught by a single teacher. For its instructional model, the curriculum modifies the Engineering Design Experience (EDE) used by engineers and engineering schools. The curriculum makes strong real-life connections, especially by involving industry volunteers (real-life engineers and professionals) intimately in the design. Students go through a simulated real-world design process (from product request to presentation of ideas to the company board) and are mentored by these industry volunteers who have firsthand, authentic experience participating in design teams.

The units most strongly and transparently address the International Technology Education Association (ITEA) Standards for Technological Literacy (STL) Theme 3 (design) and Theme 4 (abilities for a technological world) through the use of the EDE. The first part of a unit typically provides investigatory activities to prepare students to do more complex full-scale and scaffolded design activities later. Most of the activities are guided.

The teacher support materials—especially the scientific and technological information—are so thorough and clearly written that any elementary teacher could teach all the lessons, even the topics previously unfamiliar to them. Further, the support for ongoing embedded assessment strongly supports and complements its pedagogy.

The *AWIM* product line spans Grades 4–10. *Challenge 1,* for Grades 4–6, is reviewed here. *Challenges 2* and *3,* for Grades 7–8, are discussed in a separate review. *Challenge 4,* designed for Grades 4–10, is not reviewed in this book, although we provide some basic information.

CURRICULUM COMPONENTS

AWIM, Challenge 1. The *Teacher Manual* contains three instructional units, or challenges. For each unit, the publisher offers an optional *Classroom Materials Kit.* Available in English only, the curriculum has the following pricing structure:

- For the first classroom in each school, the *Teacher Manual* (357 pp.) and *Classroom Materials Kits* for the three instructional units are free.
- Subsequent full sets containing the *Teacher Manual* and three *Classroom Materials Kits,* $170
- Subsequent *Teacher Manuals* ($20) and *Classroom Materials Kits* ($50/unit) can be purchased separately:
  Replacement Kits: $20

- Scholarships are available.

AWIM, Challenge 4. The components and pricing structure are similar. Separate *Classroom Materials Kits* for elementary, middle school, and high school will be available at the end of 2004.

Materials/Equipment

The *Classroom Materials Kit* contains most of the materials needed for nine classroom teams—optimally for teams of three students each (total of twenty-seven students) but can accommodate teams of four students (up to thirty-six students). Items in the kits are consumable and nonconsumable. Replacement kits can be ordered. Additional materials are listed in the introduction to each unit and can be found in the technology laboratory or purchased locally at reasonable costs.

Special Preparations

The introduction to the *Teacher Manual* provides extensive, explicit guidance to help teachers prepare to teach the three units, including identifying, scheduling, preparing, and motivating industry volunteers to participate with the class as much as possible. No computer usage is required, although students and teachers can use such tools as available. The publisher offers workshops, inservice trainings, and other professional development services.

CURRICULUM OVERVIEW

Technology Topic Overview

Skimmer Challenge (Grade 4). Students make paper sailboats that cross the floor powered by fans. They test the effects of different sail shapes, sizes, and construction methods on the performance of their skimmers. The goal is to design a set of skimmers that reliably meet specific performance criteria. Students encounter friction, forces, and the effect of surface area.

JetToys Challenge (Grade 5). Students make balloon-powered toy cars. Their challenge is to design an appealing toy that performs in a specific way, such as travels far, carries weight, or goes fast. Students experiment with different chassis designs and nozzle sizes to determine their effect on the JetToy's performance. Students explore jet propulsion, friction, and air resistance.

Steel Can Rover Challenge (Grade 6). Students make rolling toys from coffee cans, powered by rubber bands and weights. The challenge is for the class to design a fleet of toy vehicles that meet a range of performance criteria including speed, travel distance, and manner of stopping. Students experiment systematically to explore relationships between rubber band thickness, number of wind-up turns, amount of weight, and wheel size. Students work with inertia, friction, and energy transformations.

Challenge 4, Electricity and Electronics (Grades 4–10). A separate curriculum not reviewed in this book, it consists of 35 individual, hands-on activities and experiments that range from simple applications of electricity and electronics concepts to advanced projects.

Integration Review

The blended integration approach of the *AWIM, Challenge 1* curriculum weaves together technological concepts in language arts, mathematics, science, social studies, and art. The integration is so blended that the curriculum does not isolate or separate out which topic the lesson is addressing. Even if a teacher is not comfortable teaching one of these subjects, she could still easily teach this curriculum with the help of the support materials.

Instructional Model

The program uses a modified version of the EDE model, an actual problem-solving process. Students examine what must be accomplished and determine the target market; gather and synthesize information; predict a plausible solution; design, develop, and test a prototype or potential design; and prepare a presentation of their design ideas. The curriculum is organized by the design phases in the EDE:

1. Set goals
2. Build knowledge
3. Design
4. Build and test
5. Finalize the model
6. Present

Unique to the *AWIM, Challenges 1–3* is the participation of engineer volunteers in the classroom who enhance students' learning by sharing their professional experiences. The volunteers can serve as technical resources to the teacher or play the roles of independent technical reviewers to further challenge the students' understanding of their designs.

The *Teacher Manual* is clearly designed and has a very clear lesson organization and section headers. Its lesson plans describe the lessons the student completes in the following order: introduction, classroom activity, assessment, homework, and handouts. Table 9.3.1 lists the basic format and features for the lesson plans.

Table 9.3.1 Outline of *Teacher Manual* lesson plans, *AWIM, Challenge 1*

Introduction	Identification of EDE phase What Students Do in This Activity Rationale Time Materials Preparation for the Activity
Classroom activity	Activity Description, which may include discussion guidance, topic information, background notes, etc. Facilitating Student Exploration Sharing and Interpreting
Assessment	See Assessment section
Homework	Typically, writing opportunities that reinforce and extend students' thinking
Reproducible handouts	Student Pages
Sidebar boxes interspersed	Volunteer Opportunity Teacher Tip

This curriculum, designed for teachers to present to students, is very text heavy. The only student materials are the student handouts. There are no photographs, only hand-drawn graphics that do not include people. Student worksheets, handouts, and sketches are simple, clear, uncluttered, and relate to the lessons and activities. They directly support the activities and lessons in the teacher text and move the lessons forward.

Although this curriculum does not explicitly address careers in technology, its structure and philosophy provide students with direct experience that implicitly suggests to them that they can have such careers. The curriculum simulates the real-world design process (from product request to presentation of ideas to the company)—the same process real designers would use to solve the same problem. Further, through exposure to actual technology industry volunteers in the classroom, a student can witness firsthand, imagine, and explore the possibility of a career with technology.

Duration

Each unit, or challenge, takes approximately three weeks. The *Teacher Manual* provides a Challenge Activity Calendar at the beginning of each unit and specifies the number of forty-minute classroom sessions required for each lesson.

Nature of Technology Activities

For each grade, the activities build sequentially, culminating with a final product that is unique for each design team. Grade 4 has ten activities and Grades 5 and 6 have eleven activities each. Students typically work in three-member design teams, and each member has a specific role (project engineer, facilities engineer, and test engineer). Students change roles every few days to assure they develop and practice the variety of skills needed on a design team.

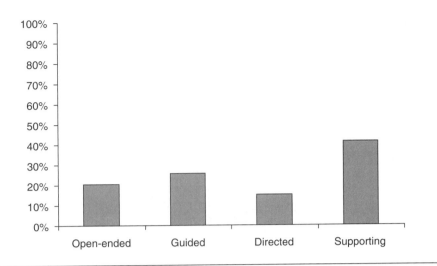

Figure 9.3.1 Activity type distribution in *AWIM, Challenge 1*

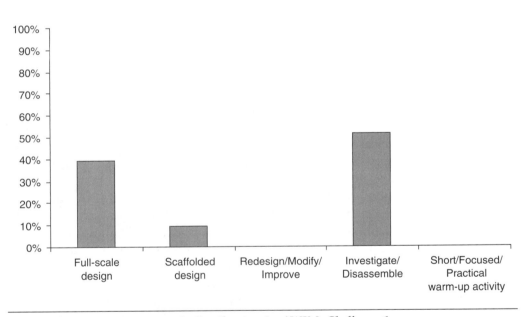

Figure 9.3.2 Design approach distribution in *AWIM, Challenge 1*

Most of the activities are guided (Figure 9.3.1). The investigate/disassemble/evaluate design approach is heavily featured in the first two-thirds of each unit, particularly in the Set Goals and Build Knowledge EDE phases. The more active full-scale (and to a lesser degree, scaffolded) design approaches appear mostly for the culminating unit activities (Figure 9.3.2).

Assessment

This curriculum strongly promotes ongoing assessment (Table 9.3.2). It recommends that teachers use portfolio review and embedded assessment tasks such as observation, discussion, and writing to gain information for making ongoing instructional decisions. It also suggests that, at the end of each unit, students write letters to their parents or

Table 9.3.2   Student assessment tools and their presence in *AWIM, Challenge* 1

Assessment approach	Presence in the curriculum
Paper-and-pencil tests—multiple-choice, short answer, true/false, vocabulary, completion	◆
Projects/Products/Media—individual and group activities, projects, products, media	◆ ◆ ◆ ◆
Performance-based assessments—demonstrations, presentations, multimedia, performances	◆ ◆ ◆
Portfolios—student papers, notes, project reports, research, work samples	◆ ◆ ◆ ◆
Student work—workbook or lab journal pages, handouts, graphs, charts, etc.	◆ ◆ ◆ ◆
Open-ended questioning—essays, extended writing exercises, critical thinking questions, etc.	◆ ◆ ◆
Computerized assessment—electronic (online or CD-ROM) simulations, tests, etc.	◆
Evaluations—peer assessments, self-reflections, self-evaluations	◆ ◆
Rubrics/Checklists	◆ ◆
Informal observations/Discussions—teacher observations	◆ ◆ ◆ ◆

◆ ◆ ◆ ◆   Dominant—There are a large number of assessments of this type in the curriculum.

◆ ◆ ◆   Substantial—There are a substantial number of assessments of this type in the curriculum.

◆ ◆   Some/Moderate—There are a moderate number of assessments of this type in the curriculum.

◆   Marginal/Missing—There are very few or no assessments of this type in the curriculum.

guardians about what they did and what they could have done to make their experience better. A pretest and posttest are included for each challenge.

Teachers and students decide together what should go in the portfolios and the criteria on which to assess the contents. The curriculum also provides rubrics for assessing teamwork, final models, the design log, and team presentations. The students' design log rubric evaluates four areas: content, organization, test log sheets, and design sheets. The presentation rubric has a four-point grading system—1: needs improvement through 4: distinguished—which evaluates the following:

- Presentation well planned and carried out
- Presentation easily seen and heard
- Visual information easy to understand
- Design decisions explained clearly
- Problems and solutions explained clearly
- Questions answered clearly

More than half of the lesson plans include an assessment section. Typically the assessment sections provide a series of questions to guide teachers as they assess student understanding using the various assessment tools.

STL STANDARDS-LEVEL ANALYSES

AWIM, Challenge 1 is designed to meet Content Standard E (Science and Technology) of the National Research Council's National Science Education Standards (NSES), not the ITEA STL, which were published later. The main technology education objectives this product addresses are

- Applying scientific understanding to a design problem
- Designing to optimize one of more variables
- Creating design specifications, drawings, and models
- Testing and evaluating a design
- Exploring properties of materials

Even though it was written before the STL, the curriculum still provides substantial or dominant coverage for three of the STL themes (Table 9.3.3). The EDE Instructional Model and the units' organization around it create a focus on Theme 3 (design) and Theme 4 (abilities for a technological world).

Table 9.3.3   Results of analyses of STL coverage in the overall curriculum for *AWIM, Challenge 1*

	Coverage rating	*Primary standards covered for each theme*
Theme 1	◆ ◆	3—The connections between technology & other fields
Theme 2	◆	*
Theme 3	◆ ◆ ◆ ◆	8—The attributes of design 9—Engineering design 10—Problem solving
Theme 4	◆ ◆ ◆ ◆	11—Applying the design process 13—Assessing the impacts of products and systems
Theme 5	◆	*

◆◆◆◆   Dominant—A large proportion of this theme is covered in the curriculum.

◆◆◆   Substantial—There is substantial coverage of this theme in the curriculum.

◆◆   Some/Moderate—There is moderate coverage of this theme in the curriculum.

◆   Marginal/Missing—There is little or no coverage of this theme in the curriculum.

Primary standards coverage = standard has dominant or substantial coverage within the theme.

* Standards are not reported for marginal/missing themes.

- The application of the EDE Instructional Model is a closely aligned application of Standard 9 (engineering design process).
- The lessons engage students in Theme 4 (abilities for a technological world), and particularly in Standard 11 (applying the design process), for which students go through every step of the process, and Standard 13 (assessing the impacts of products and systems), for which students do much sorting, comparing, and classifying of collected information in order to identify patterns.
- Standard 3 (connections between technology and other fields) represents nearly all of the occurrences of Theme 1 in this blended, cross-curricular product.

TEACHER MATERIALS REVIEW

This curriculum consists of a *Teacher Manual* and *Classroom Materials Kit.* The introduction to the product provides the bulk of the pedagogical support (Table 9.3.4).

The introductions to each of the three units include teaching supports such as Overview, Objectives, Correlation with National Science Benchmarks and Standards, Materials, Calendar, Glossary, and Science Notes.

As Table 9.3.5 shows, the level and range of teacher support materials are impressive. In addition to the teaching, pedagogical, and assessment supports in the introductions, each lesson plan provides comprehensive support (more than 100 pages per unit).

The quality and comprehensiveness of the background knowledge and grade-level content knowledge provided for teachers are outstanding. Even a teacher new

Table 9.3.4   Outline of the *Teacher Manual* Introduction, *AWIM, Challenge 1*

Introduction section titles	Subsections
Curriculum Content, National Standards, and Local Frameworks	Curriculum Content National Standards Local Frameworks
Teaching the Design Challenges	Student Design Teams (Forming, Building, Managing) Team Design Logs (Role, Managing) Student Assessment Industry Volunteers in the Classroom Implementation Ideas (Interdisciplinary Team Teaching Opportunities, Materials Management, Classroom Management, Classroom Discussions)
Industry Volunteer Guide	Rationale and Goals of Curriculum Design Challenges and EDE Volunteering in a Classroom (Suggestions for sharing your work and for supporting students' work) Logistics for Successful Volunteering

Table 9.3.5   Categories of teacher support materials and level ratings, for *AWIM, Challenge 1*

Categories of support found in teacher support materials	Level of teacher support
Support for teaching the curriculum	◆ ◆ ◆
Support for pedagogy	◆ ◆ ◆ ◆
Support for assessment	◆ ◆ ◆ ◆
Support for teaching technology standards	◆ ◆
Support for teaching twenty-first-century knowledge and abilities	◆ ◆

◆◆◆◆   Dominant—Almost all of the criteria for support in this category are present.

◆◆◆   Substantial—Most of the criteria for support in this category are present.

◆◆   Some/Moderate—Some of the criteria for support in this category are present.

◆   Marginal/Missing—Very few or none of the criteria for support in this category are present.

to science content could teach these lessons with just the help of the teacher support materials.

Further, the curriculum closely relates the pedagogy to the assessment. It effectively uses multiple, ongoing, and embedded assessments to support the pedagogical principles the curriculum espouses. It advocates creating independent, self-directed learners; tailoring learning opportunities to address student needs; facilitating inquiry, critical thinking, problem solving, and decision making; and encouraging collaboration, respect for diverse ideas, and other technological problem-solving values.

The product effectively supports the communication and collaboration skills advocated for twenty-first-century workplace readiness. In particular, it provides support for collaboration, teamwork and team building, team roles and responsibilities and places an emphasis on recording and reporting data.

Table of Contents—*A World in Motion: The Design Experience, Challenge 1*
(Number of pages indicated in parentheses)

Introduction

Educating Children for Tomorrow's World (1)

Overview of the Curriculum (2)

The Engineering Design Experience (2)

Curriculum Content, National Standards, and Local Frameworks (2)

Teaching the Design Challenges (11)

Materials Order Form (1)

Industry Volunteer Guide (5)

Skimmer Design Challenge

Introduction

Overview (2)

Objectives (1)

Correlation with National Science Benchmarks and Standards (3)

Materials (1)

Calendar (1)

Glossary (1)

Science Notes (8)
1. Receiving the Skimmer Letter (6)
2. Building the Skimmer (18)
3. Our First Sail Designs (18)
4. Sharing Our First Results (4)
5. Deciding What to Test (8)
6. Testing Sails (4)
7. What We've Learned About Sails (6)
8. Designing a Skimmer (6)
9. Building and Testing a Skimmer (10)
10. Skimmer Presentations (4)

JetToy Design Challenge

Introduction

Overview (3)

Objectives (1)

Correlation with National Science Benchmarks and Standards (3)

Materials (2)

Calendar (1)

Glossary (1)

Science Notes (8)
1. Introducing the JetToy Challenge (6)
2. Building and Testing a JetToy Chassis (22)
3. Adding a Balloon Motor (12)
4. Sharing First Results (4)
5. Revising the Vehicle (8)
6. Designing Experiments (12)
7. Formal Testing (4)
8. Reviewing Experimental Data (4)
9. Designing a JetToy (6)
10. Building and Testing a JetToy (12)
11. Presenting JetToy Designs (7)

Steel Can Rover Design Challenge

Introduction

Overview (2)

Objectives (1)

Correlation with National Science Benchmarks and Standards (3)

Materials (2)

Resources on Steel and Steel Recycling (1)

Calendar (1)

Glossary (1)

Science Notes (8)
1. Introducing the Rover (10)
2. Assembling a Rover (12)
3. Preliminary Testing (8)
4. Forming Hypotheses (4)
5. Testing the Effect of Ballast (14)
6. Testing the Effect of the Rubber Band (4)
7. Testing Large Wheels (12)
8. Analyzing Test Results (10)
9. Designing the Rover Fleet (8)
10. Building and Testing Rovers (12)
11. Presenting the Rover Fleet (9)

Appendices

Lloyd Ruess Award Application (6)

Teacher Survey (2)

SAMPLE PAGES

AWIM, Challenges 1–3 all follow the same format, opening with a lesson to discuss a product request letter from a fictitious company. Refer to the sample pages at the end of the *AWIM, Challenges 2* and *3* review to view the high level of support given to teachers to teach a lesson.

VOLUNTEER OPPORTUNITY:

The industry volunteer may relate experiences of creating a design in response to an assignment. Ask the volunteer to bring any visual aids such as actual products or photographs of products he or she has designed or sketches and models of products in development. The volunteer can also talk about the importance of working as a team.

The Letter from EarthToy Designs

Introduce the letter from a fictitious toy company, EarthToy Designs, which invites students to produce designs for a toy skimmer. Pass out copies of the letter. Ask a student volunteer to read it aloud.

Discuss the letter with the class. Make sure students understand that EarthToy Designs is not a real company.
• What do you think the letter means?
• What is EarthToy Designs looking for?
• What requirements does EarthToy Designs have for the toy?

Demonstrate the Skimmer

Show the skimmer prototype to the class. Explain that the prototype sample which students will begin to work with in the next class sessi

Turn on the fan so students can see how the skimmer moves. Set the on the highest speed. The skimmer will not move very far. Explain to students that over the next few weeks they will learn how sails work : that they will be able to design sails that perform better than this on

Homework

Ask students to select a toy or object they frequently use and conside what went into its design. Have them write about the use of the obje What purpose does it serve? How is it used? Who uses it? What mater is it made of? How expensive do they think these materials are? How much do they think it cost to manufacture? What impact does it have on the environment? After thinking about all of these issues, do they consider the object to be well designed for its purpose?

EarthToy
Designs, Inc.

Dear Student Designers:

We need your help! The mission of EarthToy Designs, Inc. is to develop and promote toys that use recycled or recyclable materials. As you know, recycling is a very important part of taking care of our environment.

We are working on a design for our new toy called a skimmer. This is a toy vehicle that "skims" across a table or floor when blown by a fan. Please see the sample we have sent to your class.

Our designer completed a bottom, or hull, for the skimmer but, unfortunately, did not design a set of sails before she left the company. We invite your class to design a set of sails that children can attach to our toy skimmer.

It is important that each sail your class designs allows the skimmer to travel at least 60 centimeters in a straight line. Some of your sails will probably go farther than this.

In addition to this minimum requirement, here are other things we would like to see in your class set of sails:
• a variety of interesting sail shapes that children, our customers, would like
• some sail designs that make the skimmer turn
• some sails that customers can adjust to give the skimmer different paths

Your class will present its skimmer sail designs in a few weeks. Be prepared to demonstrate your skimmer and sails, present your test data, and explain why different sails give the skimmer different paths.

Good luck with your designs, and happy skimming!

I. M. Green
President

BSCS Science T.R.A.C.S.: An Elementary School Science Program

Developer/Author:	Rodger Bybee, Nancy Landes, Harold Pratt, et al.
Distributor/Publisher:	Kendall/Hunt
Publication date:	1999
Funders/Contributors:	National Science Foundation
Ordering information:	Kendall/Hunt Publishing Company, 1-800-770-3544, www.kendallhunt.com
Target audience:	Kindergarten and Elementary (Grades 1–5)

BRIEF DESCRIPTION

T.R.A.C.S. (Teaching Relevant Activities for Concepts and Skills) segments the primarily science curriculum for each grade into four instructional units, or modules (Physical Science, Earth & Space Science, Life Science, and Science & Technology). However, the Kindergarten unit is a blended science and technology curriculum. We review only the Science & Technology units for Grades 1–5 and the Kindergarten curriculum.

These units support the National Science Education Content Standards' (NSES) recommendation that "children's abilities in technological problem solving can be developed by firsthand experience in tackling tasks with a technological purpose" (NRC, 1996, p. 135). They also address the Benchmarks for Science Literacy that deal with technology.

Students develop concepts, inquiry, and problem-solving skills by "doing science" and "doing technology" through a sequence of developmentally appropriate activities. Each module provides hands-on experiences that emphasize development of concepts over coverage of vocabulary and facts. The curriculum has extensive embedded supports for teachers to conduct ongoing assessment using a variety of assessment methods. It also provides teachers with developmentally appropriate background information for each unit's scientific and technological concepts.

CURRICULUM COMPONENTS

Each grade level (1–5) has four units, each with a *Student Guide*, a *Teacher's Edition*, a Materials Kit, and Consumable Kits. Similar products and pricing are available for Levels 1 through 5 Science & Technology Modules:

- *Teacher's Edition*, 122 pp., $39.99
- *Student Guide*, $9.99
- A *Teacher's How-To Handbook* (common for levels 1–5), $19.99
- Student Guides and Blackline Masters are available in Spanish
- Complete Materials Kit, $69.99
- Complete Consumable Kit, $29.99

The Kindergarten curriculum, *Investigating My World,* has a different configuration:

- *Teacher's Guide,* 366 pp., $169.99
- Complete Consumable Kit, $129.99
- Complete Materials Kit, $399.99
- Spanish Blackline Masters and Stories, $39.99

Materials/Equipment

Materials kits, integral to the *T.R.A.C.S.* program, provide most of the materials needed to implement this curriculum. Materials come in two kit types: consumable and nonconsumable. Kits are designed for a classroom of thirty students. A master materials list helps teachers collect and prepare materials in advance of activities. Any items needed in addition to the kits can be easily obtained locally or found in a typical classroom (glue, scissors, markers, construction paper, etc.).

Special Preparations

The *Teacher's Edition* provides a section called Before You Begin at the start of each lesson, which typically discusses special classroom and team organization required, trying activities in advance, requirements for storage, and safety.

CURRICULUM OVERVIEW

Technology Topic Overview

The *BSCS Science T.R.A.C.S.* curriculum contains six levels (K–5). Level K has one unit with four chapters, each of which stands alone and does not need to be taught sequentially.

Each of levels 1–5 has four units, or modules: three science units (Physical Science, Earth & Space Science, Life Science) and a Science & Technology unit, meant to be taught sequentially. This review analyzes *only* the Science & Technology unit. Each unit emphasizes technological design, providing students with structured and independent design opportunities. This curriculum stresses two types of design outcomes of the NSES standards: students developing abilities necessary to perform technological design and students understanding technological design. The Science & Technology modules address 16 of the International Technology Education Association (ITEA) Standards for Technological Literacy (STL) topics with varying degrees of thoroughness.

Table 9.4.1 summarizes the entire *T.R.A.C.S.* instructional unit (curriculum) framework.

Table 9.4.1   T.R.A.C.S. curriculum framework

Level	Physical Science	Earth & Space Science	Life Science	Science & Technology
K (Teacher's Edition Only)	Investigating My World			
1	Investigating Properties	Investigating Earth Materials	Investigating Animals and Their Needs	Testing Materials
2	Investigating Position and Motion	Investigating Weather	Investigating Plants	Designing Sound Systems
3	Investigating Electrical Systems	Investigating Objects in the Sky	Investigating Life Cycles	Designing Structures
4	Investigating Changing Properties	Investigating the Changing Earth	Investigating Ecosystems	Solving Pollution Problems
5	Investigating Heat and Changes in Materials	Investigating Weather Systems	Investigating Human Systems	Designing Environmental Solutions

Highlighted units are addressed in this review.

Investigating My World (Kindergarten) concentrates on understanding and "doing" science; however, students engage in some technological activities centered on exploring differences in materials, using tools, and experimenting with fasteners. The unit culminates in building a simple plumbing system.

In *Testing Materials* (Level 1), students discover that all materials have properties, such as color, hardness, transparency, and absorbency, and that people select a material for a certain purpose according to the properties of the material. Students compare structures made from different materials and explain why certain structures are made of specific materials.

In *Designing Sound Systems* (Level 2), students explore how sound systems produce sounds. Students search for sounds at home and in the neighborhood and describe and compare how these sounds are produced. In later lessons, students develop a musical system using simple equipment and tools and describe how their systems make music.

Designing Structures (Level 3) emphasizes the processes of technological design as students investigate the size, shape, and strength of various structures. Students determine what shapes make a structure strong and identify the design elements of structures in their local environment.

In *Solving Pollution Problems* (Level 4), students investigate causes of air pollution in the environment, explore its harmful effects on the respiratory system, and propose ways our society might reduce air pollution, improve air quality, and promote a healthy environment.

In *Designing Environmental Solutions* (Level 5), students examine possible solutions to environmental problems, such as water pollution from oil spills, solid waste, and destruction of wildlife habitat. Students evaluate proposed solutions and begin to understand the constraints and trade-offs involved as they investigate a local environmental problem and propose possible solutions.

Integration Review

As Table 9.4.1 shows, the Kindergarten curriculum, *Investigating My World*, provides a blended, integrated approach to science and technology; that is, there is no separation of technology from other subjects within it. The curriculum for Levels 1–5 divides the curriculum into subject areas at the instructional unit level. Within each Science & Technology unit, however, the major ideas from many areas of science, such as earth and life sciences, and technology are blended to teach a theme. In addition to earth, life, physical, and space science contexts, the *T.R.A.C.S.* Science & Technology curriculum also teaches technological concepts in mathematics, social science, and language arts contexts.

Instructional Model

The *T.R.A.C.S.* instructional model incorporates five steps (the five E's): Engage, Explore, Explain, Elaborate, Evaluate. This approach sequences learning experiences so that students have the opportunity to construct their understanding of a concept over time. First, students are *engaged* by an event or question related to the concept that the teacher plans to introduce. The students then participate in one or more activities to *explore* the concept. This exploration provides students with a common set of experiences from which they can initiate the development of their understanding of the concept. In the *explain* phase, the teacher clarifies the concept and defines relevant vocabulary terms. Students *elaborate* and build on their understanding of the concept by applying it to new situations. Finally, students complete an activity that will help them and the teacher *evaluate* their understanding of the concept.

The hands-on activities, called investigations, are the primary vehicle for student learning. The activities engage students both physically and mentally and are high interest, developmentally appropriate, and relevant to a student's life. Collaboration and teamwork infuse the curriculum.

Each lesson follows approximately the same format:

- A text introduction
- One or more activities. Each activity has the following components: introduction, team task, team skill, team jobs, team supplies, and directions. Some activities close with a set of questions, Ideas to Think About.
- Other occasional features, such as scientist vignettes, a mystery, or other information
- Checking Understanding questions close the lesson.

In addition to traditional textual information delivery, *T.R.A.C.S.* uses stories, cartoon characters, and other vehicles to introduce and explain science and technology information. Two cartoon characters, I.O. (investigates and observes) and C.Q. (curious and questions), demonstrate the collaborative social skills being taught through the use of speech bubbles.

The black-and-white drawings and pictures effectively move the lessons along. They provide visual cues for understanding the concepts and often, especially in the

Table 9.4.2   Number of suggested sessions and session lengths by level in *T.R.A.C.S.*

Level	Number of sessions	Session length (minutes)
1	22	25
2	28	30–40
3	22	30+
4	43	45–60
5	29	45–60

lower grades, are the primary method of communication. They feature children of the appropriate age for each grade and represent a balance of gender and racial groups. In the activities, the drawings and pictures typically show sample student work and demonstrate what needs to be done at key moments. They rarely have captions.

The *Student Guide* text is written at approximately grade level, but the readability at Grade 1 may be difficult for some children. The authors did not intend first graders to use the *Student Guides* independently, but with teachers who use guided reading and other early reading instruction strategies to help beginning readers understand the content on the page.

Duration

Each level, including Kindergarten, requires one school year to complete. Table 9.4.2 lists the amount of time suggested for each Science & Technology unit (one of four units per year) for Levels 1–5.

Nature of Technology Activities

As students' understanding grows, the focus of the Science & Technology units transitions from concrete to more abstract. Grades 1–3 use problems that involve selecting materials and designing and building structures and devices. Grades 4 and 5 use problems that require application of ideas and procedures rather than construction with actual materials. About two-thirds of the lessons are science lessons or investigations that provide students with the necessary background knowledge to complete successfully later technology lessons.

Overall, the most frequently occurring activity type is supporting, and the most common design approach is short/focused/practical. In fact, half of the activities are that combination—supporting, short/focused/practical activities. See Figures 9.4.1 and 9.4.2.

In keeping with the structure of the units, the supporting activities tend to occur earlier in the units, and the guided and open-ended activities tend to be culminating or assessment activities later in the unit. Similarly, the investigate/disassemble/evaluate and short/focused/practical activities tend to appear more frequently and earlier in the units. Although fewer, the open-ended and guided activities and the full-scale and scaffolded design approach activities typically take longer, require application of concepts learned, and are used to assess student understanding.

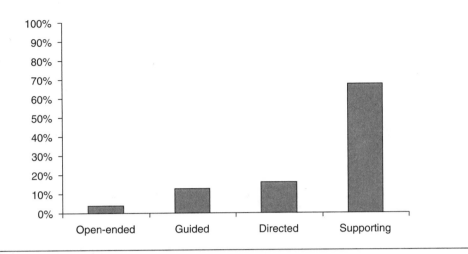

Figure 9.4.1 Activity type distribution in *T.R.A.C.S.*

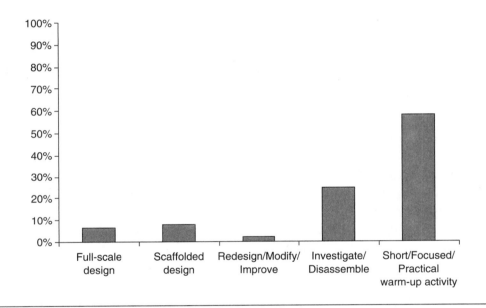

Figure 9.4.2 Design approach distribution in *T.R.A.C.S.*

Teamwork is emphasized throughout the curriculum. Students work cooperatively together in two- (Kindergarten and Level 1) or three-member teams. The curriculum requires that team members have specific roles.

Assessment

T.R.A.C.S., which stresses ongoing assessment, incorporates a rich and varied assortment of assessment strategies into the curriculum (Table 9.4.3). Each lesson opens with a table of learning outcomes and assessment indicators. Each lesson closes with a Checking Understanding section, which has children answer questions in their technology journals. Each unit has an Evaluate lesson at the end. Technology assessment in the Kindergarten level unit requires teacher observation to evaluate student progress through the use of teacher's notes, student observations, and questions directed to individual students.

Table 9.4.3   Student assessment tools and their presence in *T.R.A.C.S.*

Assessment approach	Presence in the curriculum
Paper-and-pencil tests—multiple-choice, short answer, true/false, vocabulary, completion	◆
Projects/Products/Media—individual and group activities, projects, products, media	◆ ◆ ◆ ◆
Performance-based assessments—demonstrations, presentations, multimedia, performances	◆ ◆ ◆
Portfolios—student papers, notes, project reports, research, work samples	◆ ◆ ◆ ◆
Student work—workbook or lab journal pages, handouts, graphs, charts, etc.	◆ ◆ ◆ ◆
Open-ended questioning—essays, extended writing exercises, critical thinking questions, etc.	◆ ◆ ◆ ◆
Computerized assessment—Online simulations, tests, etc.	◆
Evaluations—peer assessments, self-reflections, self-evaluations	◆ ◆
Rubrics/Checklists	◆ ◆ ◆
Informal observations/Discussions—teacher observations	◆ ◆ ◆ ◆

◆◆◆◆   Dominant—There are a large number of assessments of this type in the curriculum.

◆◆◆   Substantial—There are a substantial number of assessments of this type in the curriculum.

◆◆   Some/Moderate—There are a moderate number of assessments of this type in the curriculum.

◆   Marginal/Missing—There are very few or no assessments of this type in the curriculum.

The *Teacher's Editions* for Levels 1–5 provide two reproducible masters: Notes for Assessing Understanding and Ability and an assessment checklist for each unit, which teachers can use for as many activities as needed. Instructions for their use are provided in the *Teacher's How-To Handbook*. In addition, the *Teacher's Editions* provide embedded assessment strategies for each lesson. Teachers are instructed to collect students' work and review it for student understanding almost daily. The first activity in each Science & Technology unit is to make a technology journal in which to place student work.

STL STANDARDS-LEVEL ANALYSES

Written before the STL were published, this curriculum covers three of the STL themes in a dominant or substantial way: Theme 4 (abilities for a technological world), followed by Theme 3 (design) and Theme 1 (nature of technology; see Table 9.4.4).

Table 9.4.4   Results of analyses of STL coverage in the overall curriculum for *T.R.A.C.S.*

	Coverage rating	*Primary standards covered for each theme*
Theme 1	◆ ◆ ◆	2—Understanding the core concepts of technology 3—The connections between technology & other fields
Theme 2	◆ ◆	4—The cultural, social, economic, & political effects of technology 5—The effects of technology on the environment
Theme 3	◆ ◆ ◆	8—The attributes of design 9—Engineering design 10—Problem solving
Theme 4	◆ ◆ ◆ ◆	11—Applying the design process 12—Using and maintaining technological products and systems 13—Assessing the impacts of products and systems
Theme 5	◆	*

◆◆◆◆   Dominant—A large proportion of this theme is covered in the curriculum.

◆◆◆   Substantial—There is substantial coverage of this theme in the curriculum.

◆◆   Some/Moderate—There is moderate coverage of this theme in the curriculum.

◆   Marginal/Missing—There is little or no coverage of this theme in the curriculum.

Primary standards coverage = standard has dominant or substantial coverage within the theme.

* Standards not reported for marginal/missing themes.

Theme 4 (abilities for a technological world): This curriculum excels in providing technological literacy for Standard 13 (assessing the impacts of products and systems). This technology standard for the elementary grades stresses science-related skills—collecting information by asking questions, comparing and classifying information, and finding patterns—and so makes sense for this science curriculum. Standard 11 (applying the design process) is covered far less frequently, typically in culminating activities near the end of modules or in assessment activities.

Theme 3 (design): Also strongly covered, the first chapter of each Science & Technology unit, "Doing Technology," introduces the technology design process as well as team and collaboration skills.

Theme 1 (nature of technology): Almost half of these instances are for Standard 3 (connections between technology and other fields), which seems appropriate for an integrated science and technology curriculum.

This is primarily a science curriculum that addresses the Benchmarks for Science Literacy and the NSES mandate for students to be technological problem solvers. It does not address the STL. This can explain why the coverage of Theme 5 (the designed world) is marginal. It can also explain why, over the course of six years (K–5), the Science & Technology units address only 12 STL standards and to varying degrees—a third of these standards are barely covered. Last, *T.R.A.C.S.* frequently does touch upon the concepts in the STL narratives for the 20 standards, especially when providing the scientific information behind a technology. In most cases, however, the curriculum does not make explicit enough connections to the "meat" of the standard to be considered truly addressing the standard.

TEACHER MATERIALS REVIEW

The two main teacher support materials are the *Teacher's How-To Handbook,* a common resource for Levels 1–5, and the *Teacher's Editions* for each unit, which provide teaching and assessment strategies for each lesson.

The *Teacher's How-To Handbook* contains the following articles:

- Complete Program Overview
- How to Manage Hands-on Instruction
- How to Promote Safety Indoors and Out-of-Doors
- How to Create a Collaborative Classroom
- How to Assess Student Understanding
- How to Use Journals to Promote Understanding

- How to Do Scientific Inquiry and Technological Design
- How Students Construct Science Concepts
- How to Promote Scientific Conversations
- How to Foster Independent Investigations
- How to Address Equity Issues
- How to Use Vignettes of Scientists and Engineers

Table 9.4.5 lists the major components of the Kindergarten teacher's materials.

Although similar to the Kindergarten *Teacher's Edition,* the *Teacher's Editions* for Levels 1–5 are organized slightly differently (Table 9.4.6).

Overall, substantial teacher support is provided (Table 9.4.7). In the *Teacher's Editions* for every unit, teachers receive support for teaching every page of the student guide—every student page is displayed and surrounded by detailed planning, teaching, and assessment suggestions for implementing the lessons. Support for pedagogy can be found at the beginning of each *Teacher's Edition* and in the *Teacher's How-To Handbook.* Assessment support is infused throughout the *Teacher's Edition*—in the introductory chapters and in the assessment strategies for each lesson—and in the *Teacher's How-To Handbook.* The teacher's support materials make a case for teaching the technology NSES rather than the STL. Last, the *Teacher's Editions* stress the importance of collaboration and technological problem solving.

Table 9.4.5   Outline of kindergarten *Teacher's Edition, T.R.A.C.S.*

Program Overview	Introduction
	Curriculum framework
	T.R.A.C.S. features
	Relationship to National Science and Education Standards and Benchmarks for Science Literacy
Kindergarten Overview	Children in Science
	Introduction to *Investigating My World*
	Introduction to Doing Science
	Introduction to Units 1–4
	The 5 Es Instructional Model
	Assessing Understanding and Skills
	Introducing the Characters C.Q. and I.O.
	Collaborative Learning
	Communicating with Parents and Guardians
	References
	Sample Letter to Parents and Guardians
	Kindergarten Program at a Glance
Lesson Plans— teaching strategies	Concept Introduction
	Purpose
	Skills
	Language of Science
	Supplies
	Before You Begin
	Teaching Strategies
Additional Resources	Reproducible Blackline Masters

Table 9.4.6 Outline of Levels 1–5 *Teacher's Editions*, *T.R.A.C.S.*

Program Overview	General philosophy, goals, and features
	Relationship to National Science and Education Standards and Benchmarks for Science Literacy
	Curriculum framework
	BSCS approach to conceptual development and inquiry
	Structure of the *Student Guide* and *Teacher's Edition*
Module Overview	Children and Science
	Introduction to the Module Topic
	Module at a Glance
	Advanced Preparations
	Guidelines for Using the Student Guide
	Learning Outcomes and Related Standards and Benchmarks
	Communication with Parents and Guardians
	Master List of Supplies
Lesson Plans—teaching and assessment strategies	Lesson Overview
	Estimated Time
	Purpose(s) of the Lesson
	Outcomes and Assessment Indicators
	Supplies
	Before You Begin
	Teaching Strategies
	References to the *Student Guide* Pages
	Assessment Strategies
	Information for the Teacher
	Lesson Extensions
Additional Resources	Reproducible Blackline Masters
	Related Children's Literature and Multimedia Resources

Table 9.4.7 Categories of teacher support materials and level ratings for *T.R.A.C.S.*

Categories of support found in teacher support materials	Level of teacher support
Support for teaching the curriculum	◆ ◆ ◆
Support for pedagogy	◆ ◆ ◆
Support for assessment	◆ ◆ ◆
Support for teaching technology standards	◆ ◆
Support for teaching twenty-first-century knowledge and abilities	◆ ◆

◆◆◆◆ Dominant—Almost all of the criteria for support in this category are present.

◆◆◆ Substantial—Most of the criteria for support in this category are present.

◆◆ Some/Moderate—Some of the criteria for support in this category are present.

◆ Marginal/Missing—Very few or none of the criteria for support in this category are present.

Table of Contents: *BSCS Science T.R.A.C.S.*
Science & Technology Module
Teacher's Editions
(Number of pages indicated in parentheses)

Level 1

Preface (1)

Program Overview (6)

Module Overview (10)

Master List of Supplies (3)

Teaching and Assessment Strategies

Introduction: *Doing Technology* (14)

Lesson 1 *I'll Huff and I'll Puff* (10)

Lesson 2 *Let It Soak In* (12)

Lesson 3 *Jeepers Creepers–Find the Keepers* (8)

Lesson 4 *Materials Matter* (6)

Lesson 5 *Beds for Bears* (6)

Lesson 6 *Puffy Pig* (8)

Blackline Masters (36)

Related Children's Literature and Multimedia Resources (2)

Level 2

Preface (1)

Program Overview (6)

Module Overview (14)

Master List of Supplies (4)

Teaching and Assessment Strategies

Introduction: *Doing Technology* (16)

Lesson 1 *The Sound Museum* (12)

Lesson 2 *Making Sound* (12)

Lesson 3 *What Makes Sound?* (10)

Lesson 4 *Matching Ideas About Sound* (12)

Lesson 5 *Changing Sound* (8)

Lesson 6 *Patterns and Pitch* (10)

Lesson 7 *Showing What You Know About Sound* (10)

Lesson 8 *Designing Sound Systems* (16)

Lesson 9 *We Are Designing!* (8)

Lesson 10 *The Sound Show* (6)

Blackline Masters (104)

Related Children's Literature and Multimedia Resources (2)

Level 3

Preface (1)

Program Overview (6)

Level 3 (continued)

Module Overview (10)

Master List of Supplies (2)

Teaching and Assessment Strategies

Introduction: *Doing Technology* (16)

Lesson 1 *Straw Towers* (8)

Lesson 2 *Strong or Weak?* (10)

Lesson 3 *Patterns of Strength* (10)

Lesson 4 *Constructing and Testing Bridges* (8)

Lesson 5 *Strong Bridges* (8)

Lesson 6 *Engineers and Testing* (6)

Lesson 7 *Strong Towers* (8)

Blackline Masters (28)

Related Children's Literature and Multimedia Resources (2)

Level 4

Preface (1)

Program Overview (6)

Module Overview (22)

Master List of Supplies (4)

Teaching and Assessment Strategies

Introduction: *Doing Technology* (16)

Lesson 1 *The Perfect Problem* (6)

Lesson 2 *A Breathing System* (16)

Lesson 3 *Personal Pollution* (12)

Lesson 4 *What Pollutes?* (14)

Lesson 5 *Pollution Detectors* (14)

Level 4 (continued)

Lesson 6 *How Much Air Pollution?* (10)

Lesson 7 *Take Another Look* (8)

Lesson 8 *Pollution Problems* (12)

Lesson 9 *Pollution Solutions* (8)

Blackline Masters (20)

Related Children's Literature and Multimedia Resources (2)

Level 5

Preface (1)

Program Overview (6)

Module Overview (16)

Master List of Supplies (2)

Teaching and Assessment Strategies

Introduction: *Doing Technology* (18)

Lesson 1 *How Do Your Choices Affect the Environment?* (12)

Lesson 2 *Rain Forest Detectives* (16)

Lesson 3 *Oil Spill* (20)

Lesson 4 *The Diaper Debate* (16)

Lesson 5 *Designing Environmental Solutions* (16)

Lesson 6 *Debating the Issues* (10)

Lesson 7 *Taking Action* (10)

Blackline Masters (40)

Related Children's Literature and Multimedia Resources (3)

SAMPLE PAGES

Note the age-appropriate drawings of the students, the reading levels, and the length of the activities for this Level 1 unit. In particular, the activity features cartoon characters and students modeling behaviors and a Checking Understanding component. (Note: In this Level 1 unit, the curriculum calls containers "keepers.")

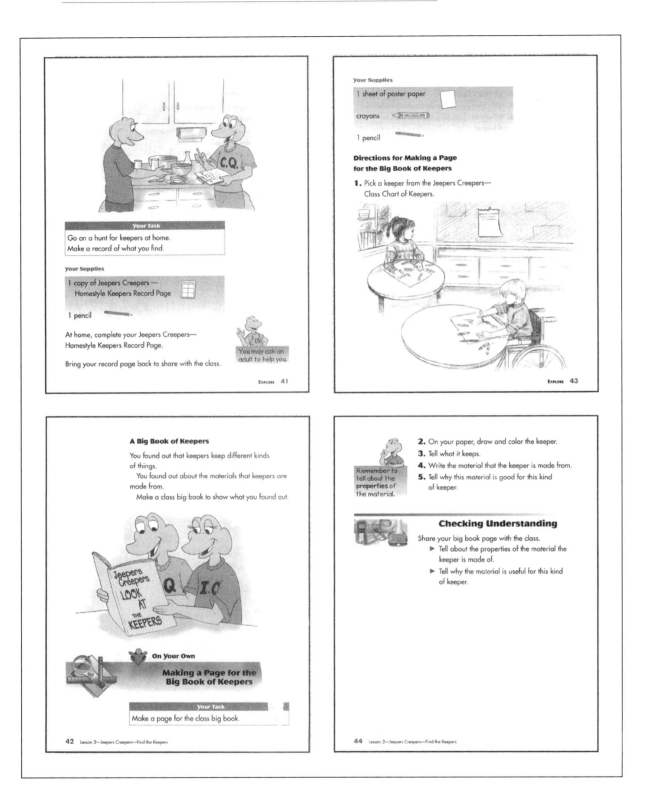

Your Task

Go on a hunt for keepers at home.
Make a record of what you find.

Your Supplies

1 copy of Jeepers Creepers—
    Homestyle Keepers Record Page

1 pencil

At home, complete your Jeepers Creepers—
Homestyle Keepers Record Page.

Bring your record page back to share with the class.

You may ask an adult to help you.

Explore 41

Your Supplies

1 sheet of poster paper

crayons

1 pencil

**Directions for Making a Page
for the Big Book of Keepers**

1. Pick a keeper from the Jeepers Creepers—
   Class Chart of Keepers.

Explore 43

A Big Book of Keepers

You found out that keepers keep different kinds
of things.
    You found out about the materials that keepers are
made from.
    Make a class big book to show what you found out.

On Your Own

**Making a Page for the
Big Book of Keepers**

Your Task

Make a page for the class big book.

42 Lesson 3—Jeepers Creepers—Find the Keepers

2. On your paper, draw and color the keeper.
3. Tell what it keeps.
4. Write the material that the keeper is made from.
5. Tell why this material is good for this kind
   of keeper.

Remember to tell about the **properties** of the material.

Checking Understanding

Share your big book page with the class.
▶ Tell about the properties of the material the
  keeper is made of.
▶ Tell why the material is useful for this kind
  of keeper.

44 Lesson 3—Jeepers Creepers—Find the Keepers

Integrated Mathematics, Science, and Technology (IMaST)

Developer/Author:	Franzie Loepp, Richard Satchwell, and many others
Distributor/Publisher:	RonJon Publishing, Inc.
Publication date:	2002–2004 (different modules)
Funders/Contributors:	National Science Foundation, Eisenhower Funds from the Illinois State Board of Education, and the Center for Mathematics, Science, and Technology at Illinois State University
Ordering information:	RonJon Publishing, 1-800-262-3060, www.ronjonpublishing.com/imast.html
Target audience:	Middle school (Grades 6–8)

BRIEF DESCRIPTION

This "*IMaST*-plus" curriculum significantly revamps and extends the original *IMaST* program published by Kendall-Hunt in the late 1990s. *IMaST* now consists of sixteen separate, theme-based modules for Grades 6–8, designed to replace existing mathematics, science, and technology curricula. In Grade 6, the three subject areas are blended together into integrated lessons, called learning cycles. In Grades 7–8, the learning cycles for each subject are taught separately but are interrelated. All three years require teams of teachers from math, science, and technology to coordinate and plan together. This review covers all of the blended, integrated lessons in the Grade 6 modules and only the technology learning cycles in the Grades 7 and 8 modules.

Each learning cycle is divided into four stages: Exploring, Getting, Applying, and Expanding the Idea. The problem-solving instructional model taught is DAPIC (Define, Assess, Plan, Implement, Communicate). Consistent with its constructivist philosophy, the *Student Texts* often do not build and connect the ideas for students; the *Teacher's Editions*, however, provide the support for teachers to facilitate students' drawing those connections on their own.

Impressively, of the cross-curricular products, *IMaST* covers the International Technology Education Association (ITEA) Standards for Technological Literacy (STL) most consistently. It addresses all five of the STL themes at least moderately, and two in a substantial way (Theme 4 [abilities for a technological world] and Theme 5 [the designed world]). It completely covers Theme 5 (the designed world) and addresses all twenty of the STL, something that even some of the core technology products do not accomplish.

CURRICULUM COMPONENTS

This curriculum contains sixteen units, or modules, with a softcover, spiral-bound *Teacher's Edition* and a softcover *Student Text* for each unit. The price for each *Student Text* ranges from $15.95 to $19.95. There are seven modules for Grade 6, five modules for Grade 7, and four modules for Grade 8. It is available in English only.

Materials/Equipment

The materials and tools used in these activities are commonly found in schools or can be purchased at local stores at a reasonable cost. The program does not require specialized equipment beyond what is typically found in the mathematics, science, and technology laboratories in traditional programs. The *Teacher's Editions* list the materials needed at the beginning of each learning cycle. Some *Teacher's Editions* also list the materials needed for the entire module in a section called the Red Flag Pages.

Special Preparations

The *IMaST* curriculum intends that a science teacher, math teacher, and technology teacher teach this curriculum together, as a coordinated team. The *IMaST* Web site explains, "The decision to use the *IMaST* curriculum involves group effort by teachers from more than one discipline. Implementing this curriculum will likely require changes in aspects of the school-learning environment as well."

The three teachers need to hold daily team planning sessions to carefully coordinate the pace and content of instruction in each class and to track student progress and needs. The expectation is that the "instruction in all disciplines . . . take place on the same day . . . to sequence the class periods so that activities can be done in the right order." In addition, they should use the daily planning sessions to coordinate sharing of equipment and supplies, assignment of students into teams, and scheduling of common events such as field trips, parent open houses, and classroom management strategies.

Some of the materials and activities raise safety considerations. For example, in Grade 6, student teams are supposed to use candles, hot plates, laser pointers, and heat lamps. For another activity, each student team is supposed to look under the hood of a different car, examine the exhaust pipe, and measure fumes.

CURRICULUM OVERVIEW

Technology Topic Overview

The *IMaST* curriculum contains sixteen units, or modules, distributed over three grades (Table 9.5.1). Each theme-based unit is organized into instructional lessons called learning cycles. The objectives for each learning cycle are outlined in the *Teacher's Editions*.

Integration Review

The *IMaST* integration approach provides teachers with an alternative to teaching separate courses for mathematics, science, and technology. In addition to mathematics and science, the *IMaST* modules teach technological concepts in geography, language arts, and the social sciences. The sixth-grade approach differs from the seventh- and eighth-grade approaches. The sixth-grade modules teach the three main subjects lended together. According to the developers, this organization can accommodate both a Grades K–6 and Grades 6–8 paradigm. The *Teacher's Editions* make recommendations as to which type of teacher (mathematics, science, or technology) should teach which lesson, or learning cycle.

The Grades 7 and 8 modules have separate sections for each subject, and the lessons within any subject are sequential (e.g., Science Learning Cycle 1, Science Learning Cycle 2, . . . then the math learning cycles, and then the technology learning cycles). However, the science, mathematics, and technology teachers need to coordinate carefully, because work done in science learning cycles will need to be applied in mathematics and technology learning cycles, and vice versa.

Instructional Model

Each module is divided into carefully sequenced lessons, or learning cycles. The instructional sequence for each learning cycle follows a constructivist-based approach for developing understanding: Exploring the Idea, Getting the Idea, Applying the Idea, and Expanding the Idea. As a result, the activities and text fully support and enhance each other.

- *Exploring the Idea.* Students manipulate objects, test materials or products, observe carefully, collect data and/or make general observations, and sometimes make predictions. These can be indicators of student understanding.
- *Getting the Idea.* In these structured classroom discussions, students share the data collected and the problems encountered during exploring. The discussion should allow as much student interaction as possible and lead the students to arrive at or construct the desired idea or concept for themselves.
- *Applying the Idea.* Students apply the concepts, generalizations, or ideas developed in previous sections to a new situation. Students must supply evidence that they understand the idea and meet the objectives by experimenting with new variables, completing written exercises, developing new designs, making projects, and/or completing reading assignments. Some activities require students to design an experiment or design and construct a project (using the DAPIC model, see following section).

Table 9.5.1   Description of *IMaST* units

6th grade units	Brief description (quoted from Web site)
Tools for Learning	Introduces the tools used throughout the *IMaST* program (e.g., observation, design, data display).
Patterns of Mobility	The objective of this module is to analyze patterns within the structure, function, and behavior of living organisms.
Patterns Within Us	The objective for this module is to compare genetic patterns that determine traits and explore concepts related to genetic engineering.
Patterns Around Us	The objective of this module is to analyze natural patterns of water through data display.
Patterns in Weather	Students use number relationships to study changes in climate and weather with a historical perspective while designing and building weather-related instruments.
Patterns Above Us	Students study the relationship between the atmosphere and life on the planet Earth in this module.
Patterns Below Us	Students analyze and discover patterns among geological systems.
7th grade units	
The Body Works	Students discover and analyze information to make educated decisions to improve their quality of life.
Living on the Edge	Students examine the effects that influence the symbiotic relationships between human-made and natural worlds and between populations and their environment.
Shaping Our World	Students identify and analyze the effects that time, movement, and geometry have on the natural and human-made world.
Manufacturing	Students design, produce, and evaluate a product that meets a need, demonstrates effective use of materials, and conforms to prescribed constraints.
Forecasting	Students develop, graph, and solve linear equations verbally, tabularly, graphically, and symbolically while exploring the context of aviation.
8th grade units	
Human Settlements	Students design a sustainable human settlement that considers the impacts of and the relationship among the built environment, human behavior, and the natural environment.
Animal Habitats	Students plan a balanced ecosystem that considers the impact of and relationship between the physical environment and the behavior of animals.
Systems	Students use a systems model to analyze, design, and model natural and human-made systems.
Communication Pathways	Students analyze, design, and construct communication systems.

- *Expanding the Idea.* Students connect the concepts developed earlier to daily life, to other disciplines, and/or to a global concept. This section may also show new aspects of the concept.

Each stage has multiple hands-on activities and problems. Some modules have multiple instances of the same stage, such as Exploring I, Getting the Idea I, Exploring II, Getting the Idea II, and so on. Sometimes a stage opens with a focusing question. The curriculum teaches the DAPIC model for problem solving:

- **D**efine—students clearly state the problem and define what they need to know
- **A**ssess—evaluate conditions surrounding the problem
- **P**lan—suggest alternative solutions to the problem and then evaluate each alternative
- **I**mplement—implement the plan and modify the plan when required
- **C**ommunicate—after analyzing the results and forming conclusions, share oral and written reports that include predicting consequences or posing new problems

Students use DAPIC for problem solving at each stage of the learning cycle as needed, although it is most frequently invoked in the Applying the Idea stage. DAPIC is not a series of steps that must be followed in a linear order, but a flexible, iterative process with multiple entry points.

The *Teacher's Editions* are essential to teaching this curriculum, especially the activities. The *Student Texts* provide the basic information about what students are supposed to do at each stage, in addition to some basic background reading. However, in keeping with constructivist philosophy, the *Student Texts* often do not provide the connections between activities, discussions, and readings and between different stages of the instructional flow. The *Teacher's Editions* do provide specific instruction for the teachers on relating the different parts of the lessons. Because of this model, students cannot just read the text and do the activities on their own; it is truly a team- and class-based exploratory process.

The modules follow the same basic format. Each unit opens with an explanation of DAPIC, preface, module objective and key concepts, and then an introductory challenge to engage students in the topic of the theme. Grade 6 modules launch into the blended lessons (learning cycles), whereas the Grades 7 and 8 modules present the lessons for mathematics, then for science, and then for technology. Each learning cycle and each module closes with an assessment activity, each of which is found only in the *Teacher's Edition.*

Some learning cycles conclude with a Making Connections reading and discussion questions or with a Career Connections reading. These readings make connections to real-life situations and consider technology applications and ramifications. The Career Connections introduce a mix of blue- and white-collar, technical (drafting), and technological (engineering) jobs, featuring people from Illinois, where the development team is located.

The curriculum tries to make further connections to students' lives in several other ways. The authors use kid-friendly topics, such as popcorn and bicycles, to teach complex concepts such as genetic diversity and simple machines. The activities are designed to connect to students' lives whenever possible (such as looking under the hood of their teacher's car) or to have them simulate every stage of a technology process. The photographs and graphics are up-to-date, crisp, and student friendly and often represent different cultures and different time periods. They also break up the text and make it more inviting to students.

The quality of the photographs and graphics is high. They set a context for the lesson topic and improve the visual appearance of the page but seldom deliver new or supporting information. The product also has graphics containing cartoon characters that are appealing to kids, but do not have an apparent consistent purpose in the layout of the text. However, when graphics do demonstrate concepts or a task in an activity, they are well executed and helpful.

Duration

Table 9.5.2 displays the suggested durations for the units, by grade level:

The *IMaST* Web site explains, "This curriculum is intended to be taught for approximately 120 minutes of total class time each day. The mathematics, science, and technology teachers who teach the same module must share the same students, and instructions in all disciplines must take place on the same day. Students can be scheduled for three separate class periods so that activities can be done in the right order." The length of time to complete each learning cycle is listed in the *Teacher's Editions*. The estimates assume a fifty-minute class period.

Table 9.5.2   Number of weeks per unit for *IMaST*

Grade (number of units)	Number of weeks per unit
Grade 6 (7)	4
Grade 7 (first 3)	6
Grade 7 (last 2)	9
Grade 8 (4)	9

Nature of Technology Activities

The distribution of the activity types and design approaches is relatively even across the curriculum (Figures 9.5.1 and 9.5.2). There are about the same amount of open-ended and guided activities and nearly twice as many supporting activities. Four of the five design approaches appear with just about the same frequency.

Activities appear in nearly every stage (Exploring, Getting, Applying, and Expanding the Idea) of the learning cycles. The activities in the Exploring stage are typically supporting activities as are those in the Expanding the Idea stage. The Exploring stage supporting activities, however, may cover a concept over several separate, consecutive activities, whereas those in the Expanding stage are stand-alone activities. The design approaches for Exploring and Getting activities tend to be short/focused/ practical or investigate/disassemble/evaluate. The Getting the Idea section tends to focus on more discussion than hands-on activities and has the fewest activities in each learning cycle. Applying sections tend to be where the main design activities occur and most frequently feature open-ended and guided activities, although many of the directed activities also occur at this stage. Similarly, the full-scale and scaffolded design approaches are frequently found in the Applying section. They are also prevalent in Expanding the Idea ("Develop an inquiry-based activity using magnets."). The authors tell students explicitly where they expect them to use the DAPIC problem-solving process, although they assume students will apply DAPIC wherever possible.

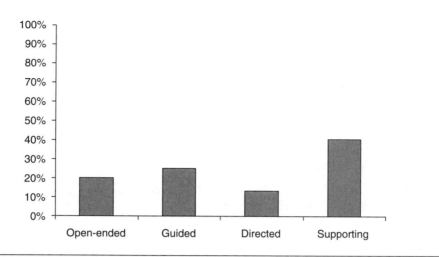

Figure 9.5.1 Activity type distribution in *IMaST*

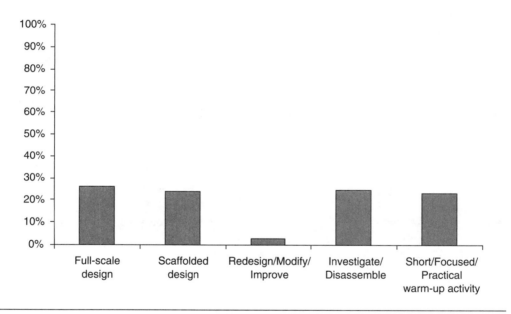

Figure 9.5.2 Design approach distribution in *IMaST*

The *Teacher's Editions* provide suggestions for

- Knowing how to design or do an activity should students not be able to figure it out on their own,
- Helping teachers guide students to discover the connections they need to draw between previous learnings and the current activity, and
- Helping teachers facilitate the drawing of conclusions and hypothesis posing based on the current activity.

Most of the activities are designed for the students to work together as a team. The organization of the teams is left to the teacher.

Table 9.5.3   Student assessment tools and their presence in *IMaST*

Assessment approach	Presence in the curriculum
Paper-and-pencil tests—multiple-choice, short answer, true/false, vocabulary, completion	◆
Projects/Products/Media—individual and group activities, projects, products, media	◆ ◆ ◆
Performance-based assessments—demonstrations, presentations, multimedia, performances	◆ ◆ ◆
Portfolios—student papers, notes, project reports, research, work samples	◆ ◆ ◆ ◆
Student work—workbook or lab journal pages, handouts, graphs, charts, etc.	◆ ◆ ◆ ◆
Open-ended questioning—essays, extended writing exercises, critical thinking questions, etc.	◆ ◆ ◆
Computerized assessment—Online simulations, tests, etc.	◆
Evaluations—peer assessments, self-reflections, self-evaluations	◆ ◆ ◆
Rubrics/Checklists	◆ ◆ ◆ ◆
Informal observations/Discussions—Teacher observations	◆ ◆ ◆

◆◆◆◆   Dominant—There are a large number of assessments of this type in the curriculum.

◆◆◆   Substantial—There are a substantial number of assessments of this type in the curriculum.

◆◆   Some/Moderate—There are a moderate number of assessments of this type in the curriculum.

◆   Marginal/Missing—There are very few or no assessments of this type in the curriculum.

Assessment

The assessment in *IMaST* is authentic, embedded, and ongoing. Although not explicitly stated or supported in the *Teacher's Editions,* this curriculum expects teachers to use all student output—whether performances, products, evaluations, observations, or discussions—as evidence for assessing students' current understanding and adjusting instruction appropriately. Because this hands-on curriculum requires copious amounts of student work, projects, performances, writing, and discussion, teachers have ample opportunities for assessment (Table 9.5.3).

The *Teacher's Editions* specifically support the assessment activities that occur at the end of each learning cycle and of each module. For these, the *Teacher's Editions* provide a reproducible master that provides activity requirements and an assessment rubric. Sometimes a learning cycle uses the Apply the Idea activity for assessment, rather than providing an additional assessment activity.

In addition to the module assessment activity, most of the *Teacher's Editions* provide the following assessment materials:

- Team growth rubric—assesses students cooperative teamwork skills
- Key Concept Essay—a student assignment with an accompanying rubric. Scoring criteria include key concepts, structure, and punctuation.
- DAPIC assessments—Criteria for assessing how well student groups executed each stage of the DAPIC process. Separate versions for students and teachers.
- Portfolio Assignment and Rubric—Assignment suggests that the student portfolio include DAPIC Student Self-Assessment sheets; student sketches, tables, charts, photographs, journal sheets, and outside resources; and the module key concept essay. Scoring criteria include a variety of samples, organization, and rationale for sample selection.

All of the rubrics are open-ended and assume that the students will either create the criteria or have input into the criteria for grading.

Teachers who are not already accustomed to teaching in a constructivist classroom, where all student output is constantly assessed for understanding, may not find enough support in the teacher materials to implement this curriculum.

STL STANDARDS-LEVEL ANALYSES

Intended to replace existing mathematics, science, and technology education curricula, *IMaST* is written to meet national standards in each of these disciplines. The program Web site provides an alignment of *IMaST* to the standards for each discipline.

Published after the STL were widely available, *IMaST* does the best job of all the cross-curricular products in addressing them. It provides consistent coverage of all 20 STL themes, with substantial coverage of Themes 4 (abilities for a technological world) and 5 (the designed world; see Table 9.5.4). Two of the three levels provide coverage of all twenty standards, and Grade 8 covers 19 of the 20. In fact, the minimum number of standards any module touches upon is eleven.

The top four standards addressed are Standards 11 (applying the design process) and 12 (using and maintaining technological products and systems), followed by Standards 17 (information and communication technologies) and 3 (connections between technology and other fields).

TEACHER MATERIALS REVIEW

The *Teacher's Editions* are essential for successfully implementing this curriculum. The team of teachers must use them for planning teaching responsibilities and for effectively teaching the lessons. They provide the glue that teachers need to facilitate students' making connections between the activities, discussions, and concepts to be learned. Table 9.5.5 describes the organization of each *Teacher's Edition*.

The bulk of the day-to-day instructional support is found in the *Teacher's Editions'* instructions for the first three stages (Exploring, Getting the Idea, and Applying the Idea) of any module. Many of these stages in the *Teacher's Editions* open with a helpful Focus on This question. Each numbered item in the *Student Text* usually has a corresponding numbered teacher explanation in the *Teacher's Edition*. The teacher information for any item varies widely and could involve, for example,

- Background information
- Possible misconceptions

Table 9.5.4   Results of analyses of STL coverage in the overall curriculum for *IMaST*

	Coverage rating	*Primary standards covered for each theme*
Theme 1	◆ ◆	2—Understanding the core concepts of technology 3—The connections between technology & other fields
Theme 2	◆ ◆	4—The cultural, social, economic, & political effects of technology 5—The effects of technology on the environment
Theme 3	◆ ◆	8—The attributes of design 9—Engineering design 10—Problem solving
Theme 4	◆ ◆	11—Applying the design process 12—Using and maintaining technological products and systems
Theme 5	◆ ◆	17—Information and communication technologies

◆◆◆◆   Dominant—A large proportion of this theme is covered in the curriculum.

◆◆◆   Substantial—There is substantial coverage of this theme in the curriculum.

◆◆   Some/Moderate—There is moderate coverage of this theme in the curriculum.

◆   Marginal/Missing—There is little or no coverage of this theme in the curriculum.

Primary standards coverage = standard has dominant or substantial coverage within the theme

- Expectations of what students should think or connections they should make at this stage
- Detailed instructions on how to make something for an activity or demonstration
- Suggestions for doing an activity
- Recommendations to give students for completing an activity
- Information about what students should do

The support for teaching the curriculum is strongest in terms of providing the background information for teachers, the clear goals for each learning cycle, and the focusing questions.

Because this strong curriculum is just coming to market, the *Teacher's Editions* have some bugs and gaps. It is not always clear what the item in the *Teacher's Editions* is referring to in the *Student Text,* and it is not always explicit which learning cycles in other subjects need to be completed before the current one. For teachers not used to teaching in a constructivist classroom, the lack of explicit connections in several areas may cause difficulties: for example, between the *Teacher's Editions* and the *Student Text;* between the activity the student is doing and the conclusions the student should come to; and between what is assessed and how to use that assessment in the teaching. Even though technology is infused throughout the curriculum, the product could provide more guidance and background in teaching the technology standards, the importance of technology education, technological literacy, and a technology scope and sequence. The *Teacher's Editions* contain many organizational inconsistencies, typos, and other errors such as the wrong module name.

Table 9.5.5   Outline of the *Teacher's Editions, IMaST*

Part of Teacher's Edition	Topics
First 10 pages of most of the *Teacher's Editions*	Provide an overview of the *IMaST* program characteristics and rationale: Discuss the role of problem solving and DAPIC Explain the constructivist structure of the learning cycle Define teacher and student roles during the learning cycle Discuss the importance of group work and authentic assessment Provide basic implementation information (scheduling, team planning, facilities, and materials)
Learning Cycle Introductions	Help the teacher organize instruction for every learning cycle: Summarize what students will be doing Provide a detailed, itemized equipment and materials list Suggest time frames Provide background information and suggestions for preliminary or accompanying activities Include a list of careers related to the activity's subject
Learning Cycle Closing	Cyberspace Connections provide key search terms for further Internet research Learning cycle assessment activity and accompanying rubrics
Module Closing	Module assessment activity Additional assessment rubrics

Table 9.5.6   Categories of teacher support materials and level ratings for *IMaST*

Categories of support found in teacher support materials	Level of teacher support
Support for teaching the curriculum	◆ ◆
Support for pedagogy	◆ ◆ ◆
Support for assessment	◆ ◆ ◆ ◆
Support for teaching technology standards	◆ ◆
Support for teaching twenty-first-century knowledge and abilities	◆ ◆ ◆

◆◆◆◆   Dominant—Almost all of the criteria for support in this category are present.

◆◆◆   Substantial—Most of the criteria for support in this category are present.

◆◆   Some/Moderate—Some of the criteria for support in this category are present.

◆   Marginal/Missing—Very few or none of the criteria for support in this category are present.

Table of Contents–*IMaST*–1 Sample Module/Grade
(Number of pages indicated in parentheses)

PATTERNS AROUND US (Grade 6)

Preface (2)

Problem Solving (2)

Challenge: Operation Purification (2)

LC1: Testing, Testing, 1, 2, Water? (12)

LC2: Now You See It, Now You Don't (12)

LC3: Go With the Flow (12)

LC4: What Did You Do with All That Water? (14)

MANUFACTURING (Grade 7)

Problem Solving (2)

Preface (2)

Challenge (2)

Challenge (2)

Math

LC1: Blue Stick Estimation (8)

LC2: Measures with Fractions (4)

LC3: Measuring for Geoboards (4)

LC4: Playing the Nails (6)

LC5: The Importance of Planning Ahead (12)

LC6: Similarity (12)

LC7: Levels of Acceptable Standards (4)

LC8: Program Evaluation and Review Technique (PERT) (4)

LC9: Statistical Process Control (6)

Science

LC1: Materials of Manufacturing (4)

LC2: The Nature of Polymers (10)

LC3: Physical Properties of Materials (8)

LC4: Chemical Properties of Materials (6)

LC5: Other Physical Properties (8)

LC6: Choices for a Product (4)

LC7: Dowel Rod Strength Versus Diameter and Weathering (6)

LC8: Joining and Fastening (6)

LC9: Color Separation (8)

LC10: Wood Finish Testing (6)

LC11: Impact Study on Protozoa (4)

LC12: Product Testing (6)

LC13 Materials Impact Study (10)

MANUFACTURING (Contined)

Technology

LC1: Materials and Processes (6)

LC2: Manufacturing Geoboards by Processing Materials (6)

LC3: Combining and Interchangeable Parts (6)

LC4: Product Design and Development (8)

LC5: Conducting Market Research (4)

LC6: Manufacturing Systems (18)

LC7: Production Training (4)

LC8: Pilot Run (4)

LC9: Production Run (6)

HUMAN SETTLEMENTS (Grade 8)

Preface (2)

Challenge (2)

Math

LC1: H_2O + ? (10)

LC2: The Capacity of Water-Carrying Structures (6)

LC3: Shapes, Angles, and Structures (22)

LC4: Tessellate a Structural Design (14)

Science	*Technology*
LC1: Why Here? (6)	LC1: Essentials of a Settlement (8)
LC2: What Goes Up Must Come Down (6)	LC2: Human Structures (12)
LC3: Getting to Know H_2O (20)	LC3: Design a City (10)
LC4: Heating and Cooling (8)	LC4: Essential City (16)
LC5: Investigating Potential and Kinetic Energy (8)	LC5: Building a Sustainable Human Settlement (4)
LC6: Energy Detectives (6)	
LC7: Generating Electricity with an Eye on Sustainability (12)	

SAMPLE PAGES

Because each learning cycle follows the same format, we selected sample pages from different grade levels to illustrate the features of a learning cycle. In the Grade 6 Patterns Around Us spread, observe a typical lesson opening: Introduction, Objectives, Exploring I, and Getting the Idea I. As shown in the Grade 8 Human Settlements pages, a Making Connections feature follows a learning cycle.

Go with the Flow

Introduction

Even though you may know it is wasteful, you turn on the water, and then wait for it to warm up. To get a drink, you turn on the cold water at the sink and wait for it to get cold. Right? This is fairly common. After all, you do not want to take a cold bath or have to drink lukewarm water. How long does it take for the water to get hot or cold? What are some factors that influence the time it takes for the water to reach the desired temperature?

How much water do you use? Well, to figure that out, you would need some unit of measurement. Cups, gallons, pints, and quarts—you have heard these words before. They are all U.S. Customary Units of measurement for liquids. How does a cup compare to a gallon? In this activity, you will use some containers and lots of water to find out. This activity does not stop there. Measuring water volume is only one part of determining water use. The rate at which the volume of water is used is also very important.

Flow rate is important information for many applications. For example, a pilot of an airplane must know that the flow rate of fuel differs depending on the speed of the airplane, wind speed and direction, altitude, and other factors. This knowledge will help determine how long it will be before the fuel tank is empty. A firefighter will

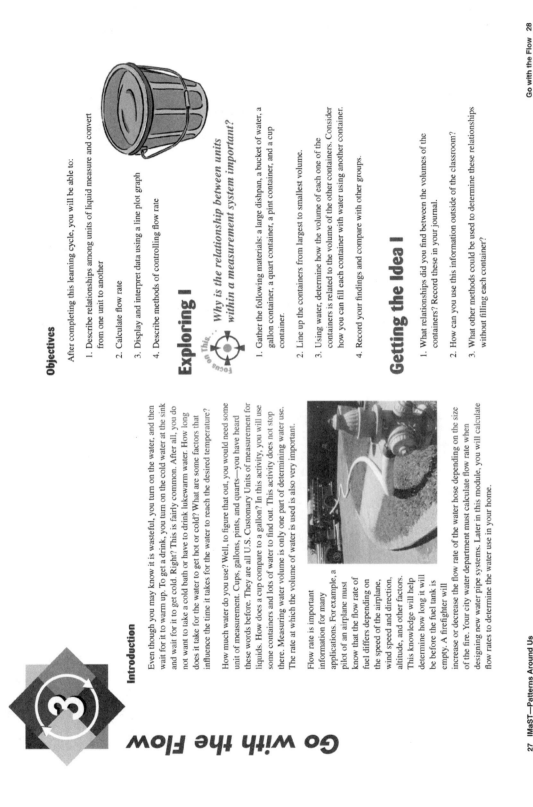

increase or decrease the flow rate of the water hose depending on the size of the fire. Your city water department must calculate flow rate when designing new water pipe systems. Later in this module, you will calculate flow rates to determine the water use in your home.

Objectives

After completing this learning cycle, you will be able to:

1. Describe relationships among units of liquid measure and convert from one unit to another
2. Calculate flow rate
3. Display and interpret data using a line plot graph
4. Describe methods of controlling flow rate

Exploring I

Focus on This... *Why is the relationship between units within a measurement system important?*

1. Gather the following materials: a large dishpan, a bucket of water, a gallon container, a quart container, a pint container, and a cup container.

2. Line up the containers from largest to smallest volume.

3. Using water, determine how the volume of each one of the containers is related to the volume of the other containers. Consider how you can fill each container with water using another container.

4. Record your findings and compare with other groups.

Getting the Idea I

1. What relationships did you find between the volumes of the containers? Record these in your journal.

2. How can you use this information outside of the classroom?

3. What other methods could be used to determine these relationships without filling each container?

making CONNECTIONS

A number of great civilizations sprang up in central Mexico many years ago. This occurred between 3000 and 500 years ago. These included the Teotihuacan, Toltec, and Aztec empires. They became centers of power in the **Mesoamerican** region.

Tenochtitlan was the capital city of the Aztec. The city is of interest because of its unusual water control system.

Tenochtitlan developed its agricultural system around water. It developed a series of dams and irrigation and drainage canals. Crops were grown **intensively** all year. They were grown on mounds that were built up for gardening. These **chinampas** were highly productive.

At its peak size, Tenochtitlan perhaps had 100,000 inhabitants. As the population of the city increased, the environment **deteriorated**. The **production system** began to decline.

Tenochtitlan was still a grand city in 1519 A.D. This is the year that the Spanish invader, Hernando Cortez, first saw the city. Cortez was greatly impressed. He noted the city's many engineering wonders. He admired its beauty.

TENOCHTITLAN
A MANAGED CITY

The city maintained an **elaborate** physical infrastructure. It had a network of canals, gardens, pyramids, and temples. The chinampas system was complex. The water level needed to be regulated. It had to be kept within narrow limits. The Aztec state managed the water system.

Think About it!

1. Why was water control and management important in ancient Tenochtitlan?

2. Why is water control and management important in your community today?

 Decoder Alert

Mesoamerican: middle-American; Central America and Mexico

intensively: highly concentrated

chinampas: an intensive irrigated agricultural system developed by the Aztecs

productive: producing in abundance

deteriorated: inferior in quality

production system: coordinated method of producing goods

elaborate: detailed or complex

BSCS Middle School Science and Technology, Second Edition

Developer/Author:	Rodger Bybee, Janet Carlson Powell, Pamela Van Scotter et al.
Distributor/Publisher:	Kendall/Hunt
Publication date:	1999
Funder:	National Science Foundation
Ordering information:	Kendall/Hunt Publishing Company, 1-800-770-3544, www.kendallhunt.com
Target audience:	Middle school (Grades 6–8)

BRIEF DESCRIPTION

BSCS Middle School Science and Technology (BSCS MSST) is a three-year, Grades 6–8, primarily science curriculum with technology infused throughout. Each of the three years, or levels, has a unifying theme that blends major ideas from all areas of science with technology. Each level is organized into four units, three of which explicitly address technological literacy. The technology in this curriculum is so blended that it would be difficult to separate the technology education from the science-focused curriculum. This curriculum has the least technology of any of the cross-curricular products.

The product uses the five E's (Engage, Explore, Explain, Elaborate, and Evaluate) as its instructional model, extensively uses cooperative learning strategies, and incorporates teaching to different learning styles. It makes great effort to connect to children's lives in terms of how the content is presented, the transition of instructional focus from the personal to the global, and the selection of graphics and photographs. This product provides among the most expansive range of embedded assessment opportunities, particularly portfolio assessment, projects, student work, open-ended questioning, rubrics, and observation. The teacher materials offer exceptionally strong support for assessment and other pedagogical strategies.

Published before the *Standards for Technological Literacy* (STL), *BSCS MSST* was created to support the National Science Education Standards and the Benchmarks for Scientific Literacy. Only one of the STL themes is addressed in a dominant or substantial way—Theme 1 (nature of technology). The four other STL themes are addressed in at least a moderate way. The activities, which average three to four per chapter, like the text, are primarily science based with technology infused throughout.

CURRICULUM COMPONENTS

Each of the three levels, available only in English, includes a hardcover *Student Edition,* spiral-bound softcover *Teacher's Edition* and *Teacher's Resource Book (TRB),* Materials Kits, and video.

- Level A—*Patterns of Change* (Parallel products are available for Levels B and C)
- *Teacher's Edition,* 454 pp., $99.99
- *Teacher's Resource Book,* 468 pp., $99.99
- *Student Edition,* 466 pp., $48.99
- Weather Video, $29.99
- Deluxe Nonconsumable Kit, $1,052.99
- Deluxe Consumable Kit, $218.99
- Level A—Minds On Science Videos (3-pack), $269.99
- MicroTest CD: Levels A–C (multiplatform), $189.99

Materials/Equipment

The Materials Kits are available in two formats—consumable and non-consumable—are designed for classrooms of thirty students, and contain most of the recommended materials needed to implement this curriculum. A master materials list helps teachers collect and prepare materials in advance of activities. The list includes manufactured items found in the kits, as well as other materials needed to implement the program. These additional items (e.g., cardboard box, poster board, broom) can be easily obtained locally.

Special Preparations

The most time-consuming preparation activities are collecting materials, setting up learning stations, and making copies. The *Teacher's Edition* provides an exhaustive treatment of how teachers new to the program can prepare, including setting up a peer support network or teaming up with another teacher who is also teaching the program.

The publisher offers several teacher training and professional development options including an on-site inservice for schools and districts and a weeklong, intensive session to "train the trainer." The *TRB* describes what should be covered to implement the curriculum in a two-day professional development overview workshop and in follow-up workshops.

CURRICULUM OVERVIEW

Technology Topic Overview

BSCS MSST is primarily a science curriculum that includes an emphasis on technology. Rather than teaching individual topics in Earth, life, and physical sciences, the curriculum uses a theme approach to unify major ideas from all areas of science with technology.

- Level A—*Patterns of Change.* Students learn about patterns in the natural world and the relationship between patterns and prediction. Students look at patterns associated with the increasing size of human populations, such as garbage generation.

- Level B—*Diversity and Limits.* Students learn about the distribution of characteristics in humans and other organisms. They study limits, diversity of materials, genetic diversity, and genetic engineering and explore how technology can address these concepts.
- Level C—*Systems and Change.* Students examine systems that are in and out of balance and develop a conceptual understanding of systems. They look at evolution, energy, and population systems and how technology can help solve problems in each.

The curriculum targets the following technological concepts: design process, efficiency, costs, benefits, criteria, constraints, and decision making. It features technological problem solving as a process for adapting to and solving problems and stresses that technology, science, and society are intertwined.

Integration Review

As the product suggests, the curriculum blends technology primarily with science. The theme for each level unifies major ideas from many areas of science (Earth, life, physical, and general), from technology, and from other subjects (mathematics, geography, social sciences, and language arts). In at least three of the four units for each level, technology topics are woven throughout such that it would be difficult to separate them from the science (Table 9.6.1).

Instructional Model

BSCS MSST explicitly uses the five E's as its instructional model: Engage, Explore, Explain, Elaborate, Evaluate. First, an event or question **engages** students in the concept to be introduced. Then students **explore** the concept in one or more activities. From this common set of experiences, students can develop their own understanding of the concept. In the **explain** phase, the teacher clarifies the concept and defines relevant vocabulary terms. Students **elaborate** and build on their understanding of the concept by applying it to new situations. Finally, students complete an activity that will help them and the teacher **evaluate** their understanding of the concept.

The curriculum is more than 60 percent hands-on and minds-on investigations. In addition to typical science and technology activities, simulations, debates, plays, outdoor activities, research projects, and creative writing are also included. Each level presents a major project. The *BSCS MSST* curriculum incorporates cooperative learning strategies, but students are individually accountable for the work of their team and for their own learning. Specific social skills are targeted for most investigations and become progressively more advanced throughout the school year. The product also strongly features a series of three inquiry-based physical science videos and accompanying activities, developed by the Agency for Instructional Technology, for each level.

Four cartoon characters, each based on a Gregorc style inventory type (concrete random, concrete sequential, abstract random, abstract sequential), appear periodically and make comments typical of their designated learning styles. In addition to providing a role model for students of each learning style, they demonstrate good communication and collaboration skills.

The five E's organize the content within each chapter, which presents a combination of the following instructional activities:

Table 9.6.1   BSCS Scope and Sequence

Level A: Patterns of Change				
	1	**2**	**3**	**4**
Curriculum emphasis	Personal dimensions of science and technology	The nature of scientific explanations	Technological problem solving	Science and technology in society
Focus question	How does my world change?	How do we explain patterns of change?	How do we adjust to patterns of change?	How can we change certain patterns?

Level B: Diversity and Limits				
Curriculum emphasis	Personal dimensions of science and technology	The nature of scientific explanations	Science and technology in society	Technological problem solving and society
Focus question	How much diversity is there?	Why are things different?	Why are we different?	How does technology affect people and society?

Level C: Systems and Change				
Curriculum emphasis	Personal dimensions of science and technology	The nature of scientific explanations	Technological problem solving	Science and technology in society
Focus question	How much can things change and still stay the same?	How do things change through time?	How can we adapt our use of energy?	What are the limits to growth?

- Readings—provide explanations of concepts, science content, and connections between ideas and investigations; may also confront possible misconceptions
- Investigations—have students use materials to answer a question or solve a problem
- Wrap-Up—concludes each investigation by having students share their results
- Connections—has students reflect upon and talk about that they have been doing and make connections between key concepts
- Sidelights—present interesting materials related to concepts, topics, and themes in the unit, including Sidelights on Nature, Technology, Careers (Level C only), History, and Inquiry
- How To—guides students step-by-step on how to do a particular skill
- Glossary—defines unfamiliar and key terms
- Cooperative learning sidebars—promotes teamwork and valuing each student's contribution
- Safety highlights

Written at a middle school (Grades 6–8) reading level, the *Student Edition* is clearly laid out, well organized, and visually appealing and informative, conveying a sense of kid appeal. The layout clearly reflects which of the five E's is being presented and the instructional focus of any page.

The graphics are crisp and contemporary. They reinforce concepts in the text or present new information and have good captions that provide tie-ins to the text and sometimes pose thought-provoking questions. The photos and pictures provide a balanced gender, multicultural, and historical representation. They often model student performance by showing children demonstrating what students will do in the investigations and by giving examples of "real" student results. When appropriate, children are always used in pictures about a technology or science topic. To teach social skills such as teamwork and collaboration, the four learning style cartoon characters convey proper social behavior through speech bubbles.

This curriculum successfully connects to children's lives both on the surface and in depth. In addition to having photos of real kids involved in real activities, it employs student-friendly topics such as popcorn, bicycles, dinosaurs, and family photos to teach concepts. The structure of the four units for each grade inherently provides connections to the student that gradually transition students through a focus on personal issues to a focus on global issues. Note that the first unit is always "Personal dimensions of science and technology," and the third or fourth unit is "Science and technology in society."

Duration

Each level requires one school year to complete.

Nature of Technology Activities

Each of the eighteen chapters per grade level has between one and seven activities, or investigations, with an average of about three. Learning activities are designed for students to work cooperatively in four-person teams. Each team member assumes a specific role, and they rotate roles throughout each unit. About a quarter of the activities are purely science focused. The remaining activities blend science and technology. They form the basis of this analysis.

There are few open-ended type activities and few full-scale, scaffolded, or redesign/modify/improve design approach activities. The most frequent design approach is investigate/disassemble/evaluate followed by short/ focused/practical, and the most common activity type is supporting. Because each activity acts as a foundation for the subsequent activity, this curriculum supports a large number of supporting-type activities and investigate/disassemble/evaluate and short/focused/practical design approaches (Figures 9.6.1 and 9.6.2). The distribution of activity type and design approach across a school year does not follow a strong pattern.

Assessment

This product has among the widest range of, and deepest support for, assessment of all the products reviewed in this book. The assessments take many forms and are embedded throughout the curriculum. Assessment is feature in the *TRB* and within the

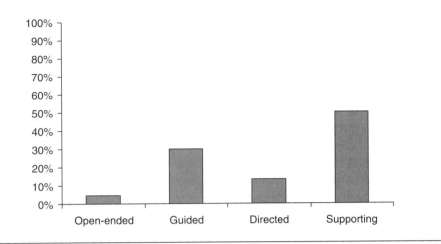

Figure 9.6.1   Activity type distribution in *BSCS*

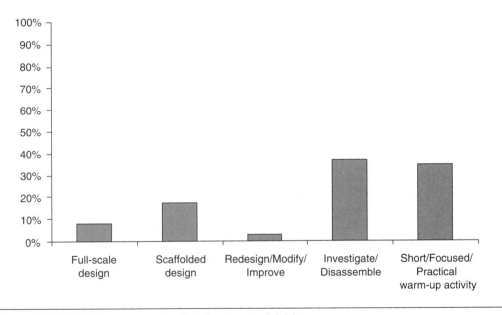

Figure 9.6.2   Design approach distribution in *BSCS*

lesson plans in the *Teacher's Editions* (Table 9.6.2). Because of the detailed, in-depth assessment support, a new teacher could implement the various types of assessment, even if one has not implemented them before.

The *TRB* provides clear explanations about each type of assessment, directions and suggestions for implementation, and assessment handouts. For example:

• The Assessing and Evaluating Student Learning section provides the following topics: distinguishing between and aligning types of assessments and assessment tools; evaluating the Science Notebook; assessing cooperative learning; organizing, managing,

Table 9.6.2   Student assessment tools and their presence in *BSCS*

Assessment approach	Presence in the curriculum
Paper-and-pencil tests—multiple-choice, short answer, true/false, vocabulary, completion	◆
Projects/Products/Media—individual and group activities, projects, products, media	◆ ◆ ◆ ◆
Performance-based assessments—demonstrations, presentations, multimedia, performances	◆ ◆ ◆
Portfolios—student papers, notes, project reports, research, work samples	◆ ◆ ◆ ◆
Student work—workbook or lab journal pages, handouts, graphs, charts, etc.	◆ ◆ ◆ ◆
Open-ended questioning—essays, extended writing exercises, critical thinking questions, etc.	◆ ◆ ◆ ◆
Computerized assessment—Online simulations, tests, etc.	◆
Evaluations—peer assessments, self-reflections, self-evaluations	◆ ◆ ◆
Rubrics/Checklists	◆ ◆ ◆ ◆
Informal observations/Discussions—Teacher observations	◆ ◆ ◆ ◆

◆◆◆◆   Dominant—There are a large number of assessments of this type in the curriculum.

◆◆◆   Substantial—There are a substantial number of assessments of this type in the curriculum.

◆◆   Some/Moderate—There are a moderate number of assessments of this type in the curriculum.

◆   Marginal/Missing—There are very few or no assessments of this type in the curriculum.

and evaluating portfolios; and doing performance assessments and evaluating performance tasks.

• It contains strategies and scoring criteria for using most chapters' Evaluate activities as assessment items and even instructs teachers to share the scoring criteria with students before they begin.

• Assessment blackline masters (AS-BLMs) include BLMs for some Evaluate activities and BLMs for most units' hands-on performance assessments.

• It contains extensive reproducible rubrics and guidelines for portfolio development, projects and presentations, hands-on performance assessments, cooperative learning assessments, and social skills checklists. It also provides guidelines for teachers to help students develop criteria for what should be in the portfolios and what types of work will demonstrate the criteria.

STL STANDARDS-LEVEL ANALYSES

Primarily a science program, this curriculum covers only one of the STL themes in a dominant or substantial way: Theme 1 (nature of technology; see Table 9.6.3). Written before the STL were published, this curriculum is designed to support the National Science Education Standards (NSES) and the Benchmarks for Scientific Literacy. The *TRB* provides a correlation showing how the curriculum supports the NSES Technology Standard E.

All 20 of the STL are addressed at least once over the three grade levels, but some just barely. Fourteen of the twenty standards are addressed at least once every year. Frequently, the curriculum discusses a concept from the science perspective, but does not expand its discussion or approach so that it addresses technology as defined by the STL. For example, Level B focuses on scientific models and not on technological models (Standard 8). Although the concepts are very similar, *BSCS MSST* always approaches the "model" as a way to explain or demonstrate a scientific concept (science emphasis) and not as a way to solve a problem (technology emphasis). Thus we could not say that *BSCS MSST* really addresses Standard 8.

Table 9.6.3   Results of analyses of STL coverage in the overall curriculum for *BSCS*

	Coverage rating	*Primary standards covered for each theme*
Theme 1	◆ ◆ ◆ ◆	2—Understanding the core concepts of technology 3—The connections between technology & other fields
Theme 2	◆ ◆	4—The cultural, social, economic, & political effects of technology 6—The role of society in the development and use of technology
Theme 3	◆ ◆	8—The attributes of design 10—Problem solving
Theme 4	◆ ◆	11—Applying the design process 12—Using and maintaining technological products and systems 13—Assessing the impacts of products and systems
Theme 5	◆ ◆	14—Medical technologies 17—Information and communication technologies

◆◆◆◆   Dominant—A large proportion of this theme is covered in the curriculum.

◆◆◆   Substantial—There is substantial coverage of this theme in the curriculum.

◆◆   Some/Moderate—There is moderate coverage of this theme in the curriculum.

◆   Marginal/Missing—There is little or no coverage of this theme in the curriculum.

Primary standards coverage = standard has dominant or substantial coverage within the theme.

Table 9.6.4 Outline of the *Teacher's Editions, BSCS*

Part of Teacher's Edition	Section titles
Front matter	Introduction to the *Teacher's Edition*
	Program Overview and Goals
	What the Students Will Learn
	Organizing Principles of the Program
	Major Components of the Program
	Teaching with *Middle School Science & Technology*
	Keeping Parents Informed
	References for the Front Matter
Introduction to each unit	Cooperative Learning Overview
	Unit Overview
	Unit Goals
	Unit Advance Preparation
	Educational Technology Resources
Introduction to each chapter	Overview
	Background Information
	Websites of Interest
	Advance Preparation for the Chapter
	Materials Chart
Lesson information provided with reproductions of student pages	Outcomes and Indicators of Success
	Opportunity for Assessment
	Advance Preparation
	Materials
	Cautions
	Strategies (for each section of the lesson)
	Further Opportunities for Learning

TEACHER MATERIALS REVIEW

Each level has its own *Teacher's Edition* and *TRB* that provide a rich array of support materials. Each *Teacher's Edition* uses a wraparound format and provides introductions to the level, unit, and chapter.

The *TRB* has a range of in-depth supports. Some are essential for teachers new to the curriculum while others are more valuable to the experienced *BSCS MSST* teacher.

This curriculum excels in its support for pedagogy and assessment. It gives noteworthy support for teaching the curriculum, especially in terms of the quality and amount of background knowledge provided. It provides less support for teaching technology standards and twenty-first-century knowledge and skills (Table 9.6.6). This is

Table 9.6.5   Outline of the *Teacher's Resource Books, BSCS*

Teacher's Resource Book	Topics
Adopting and Implementing the Program	Making a Well-Reasoned Adoption Decision That Leads to Successful Implementation Professional Development: 2-day Workshop & Follow-up Workshops Ongoing Assessment of Implementation of Program
Background Resources & NSES Correlation	What Are the NSES and What Do They Mean For Me? Assessing and Evaluating Student Learning Cooperative Learning Importance of Learning Styles Importance of Multiple Intelligences Concept Mapping—Visually Understanding Safety Background Correlation to NSES
Extended Learning Opportunities (Extensions)	Using Educational Technologies in the Classroom Ideas for Integrating Science with Math, Social Studies, Music, and Art Extension Activities
Assessment Tools	Strategies and Scoring Criteria (for using each chapter's Evaluate activities as assessment items)
Blackline Masters (BLMS)	Implementation and Adoption BLMS Extended Learning Opportunities BLMS Assessment BLMs Student Edition BLMS

not surprising given that it was written before the STL were published. The assessment strategies complement and reinforce the pedagogical philosophy and vice versa.

The teacher materials provide an impressive array of research on, and implementation suggestions for, student learning styles (e.g., Gregorc, McCarthy, Jung, and Meyers and Briggs) and multiple intelligences.

Although this product does not strongly support the teaching of twenty-first-century knowledge and abilities overall, it does provide strong support of the effective communication and collaboration skills component. The *TRB* devotes more than twenty-five pages to defining cooperative learning and explaining where and how to teach it in *BSCS MSST*; how to create, sustain, manage, assess, and reward teams in the classroom; and how to troubleshoot situations.

This product provides limited support for teaching the STL technology standards. As described earlier, it is primarily a science curriculum and was published before the STL. However, the product does support NSES Technology Standard E, which was the technology standard available at the time of publication.

Table 9.6.6   Categories of teacher support materials and level ratings for *BSCS*

Categories of support found in teacher support materials	Level of teacher support
Support for teaching the curriculum	◆ ◆ ◆
Support for pedagogy	◆ ◆ ◆ ◆
Support for assessment	◆ ◆ ◆ ◆
Support for teaching technology standards	◆ ◆
Support for teaching twenty-first-century knowledge and abilities	◆ ◆

◆◆◆◆   Dominant—Almost all of the criteria for support in this category are present.

◆◆◆   Substantial—Most of the criteria for support in this category are present.

◆◆   Some/Moderate—Some of the criteria for support in this category are present.

◆   Marginal/Missing—Very few or none of the criteria for support in this category are present.

Table of Contents—*BSCS Middle School Science and Technology* (Number of pages indicated in parentheses)

Level A—Patterns of Change
Program Overview (5)

Introduction—What Will This Program Be Like? (2)

Chapter 1—A Learning Journey (24)

Chapter 2—For Safety Sake (10)

Unit 1—Patterns of Change—Overview (4)

Chapter 3—Uncovering Patterns (32)

Chapter 4—Patterns That Grow (18)

Chapter 5—Predictions Are More Than Just a Guess (22)

Chapter 6—The Moon and Scientific Explanations (14)

Chapter 7—Recognizing Patterns of Change (10)

Unit 2—Explanations for the Patterns of Change on Earth and Beyond (4)

Chapter 8—Scientific Explanations Begin With a Question (16)

Chapter 9—Volcanoes, Earthquakes, and Explanations (38)

Chapter 10—Connecting the Evidence (28)

Chapter 11—Using Scientific Explanations (14)

Unit 3—Responding to Patterns of Change (4)

Chapter 12—What Causes Weather Patterns? (28)

Chapter 13—When Natural Events Become Disasters (40)

Chapter 14—Making Decisions to Solve Problems (22)

Chapter 15—Big and Little Decisions (22)

Unit 4—Patterns and People (4)

Chapter 16—It's Everywhere (34)

Chapter 17—Solving Problems (15)

How to . . . ? (44)

Glossary (8)

Level B—Diversity and Limits
Program Overview (5)

Introduction—What Will This Program Be Like? (2)

Chapter 1—A Learning Journey Continues (22)

Chapter 2—Safety in the Science Classroom (10)

Unit 1—Exploring Ranges of Limits and Diversity (4)

Chapter 3—Identifying Limits and Diversity (24)

Chapter 4—Ranges of Limits and Diversity (20)

Chapter 5—Using Limits to Set Standards (30)

Chapter 6—Using Diversity to Set Standards (36)

Chapter 7—Evaluating Your Understanding of Limits and Diversity (10)

Unit 2—Why Are Things Different? (4)

Chapter 8—Properties of the Material World (16)

Chapter 9—Scientific Explanations Are Ancient History (12)

Chapter 10—Using Scientific Models to Answer Questions (24)

Chapter 11—Using Models to Test and Predict (28)

Unit 3—Why Are We Diverse? (4)

Chapter 12—The Trail of Your Traits (34)

Chapter 13—Genes and Society (18)

Unit 4—How Does Technology Address Diversity and Influence Limits? (4)

Chapter 14—Consumer Concerns (24)

Chapter 15—Your Designing Ways (36)

Chapter 16—Why Are There So Many Products That Do the Same Thing? (18)

Chapter 17—Masters of Design (11)

How to . . . ? (19)

Glossary (8)

Level C—Systems and Change

Program Overview (5)

Introduction—What Will This Program Be Like? (2)

Chapter 1—Continuing a Learning Journey (22)

Chapter 2—Safety in the Science Classroom (10)

Unit 1—Systems in Balance (4)

Chapter 3—Keeping Systems in Balance (24)

Chapter 4—What Happens at the Balance Point? (22)

Chapter 5—Dynamic Body Systems (24)

Chapter 6—Drugs and Your Balance (22)

Chapter 7—Looking Back Over Balance (22)

Unit 2—Change Through Time (4)

Chapter 8—Evidence of Change (26)

Chapter 9—Making Sense of Evidence (26)

Chapter 10—How Do Living Systems Change? (34)

Chapter 11—How Much Has Your Understanding Evolved? (12)

Unit 3—Energy in Systems (4)

Chapter 12—Exploring Energy in Systems (18)

Chapter 13—Solar Sources: Energy From the Sun (24)

Chapter 14—Energy Benefits and Costs (54)

Chapter 15—The Power to Choose (28)

Unit 4—Population Systems (4)

Chapter 16—What Is Exponential Growth? (16)

Chapter 17—What Limits Growth in Populations? (32)

Chapter 18—What Are the Limits to Growth in Human Populations? (34)

How to . . . ? (73)

Glossary (20)

SAMPLE PAGES

The Sample Pages demonstrate a short investigation during the Engage phase, a Working Cooperatively suggestion, a picture of students doing an activity and of sample student work, a Stop and Think feature, the beginning of a Connections activity used for evaluation during the Elaborate phase, and how *BSCS MSST* addresses cooperative learning skills. Levels A–C are represented.

Working Cooperatively

Work cooperatively in your teams of three, moving your desks together or sitting together at a table. Practice the social skill *Share your thoughts and ideas.* Use the roles of Communicator and Manager as well as Team Member roles.

Investigation:
Small-Scale Boats

Sometimes as you begin to explore concepts in design, it is helpful to first explore on a small scale. This is definitely the case with boats. In this chapter, you will design and build miniature boats. Before you do that, however, it will help if you know something about how boats move through the water. This investigation and the one that follows will help you explore boat propulsion.

Materials for the Entire Class:

▶ several tubs or sinks for holding water
▶ a water source
▶ "boat fuel" (for small-scale boats) in a small cup
▶ 10 medicine droppers

Materials for Each Team of Three:

▶ 1 pair of scissors
▶ 1 sheet of unlined, white paper
▶ 1 metric ruler
▶ 1 medicine dropper

Process and Procedure

1. Watch closely as your teacher performs a demonstration.
   Notebook entry: Record any observations you make during the demonstration.

2. Obtain the materials for your team.

3. Design your version of a miniature boat.
   You have only five minutes in which to design your boat. Make your boat as similar to or as different from your teacher's as you would like, but you will have to use the same fuel to propel your boat that your teacher used. Your boat also should perform as well as or better than your teacher's boat. Do not put your boat in the water yet.
   Use this opportunity to be open to the ideas of both your teammates.

4. Measure your boat.
   Notebook entry: Record its length and width.

5. Prepare a data table in which you will record the size, a description of the shape, a description of the direction

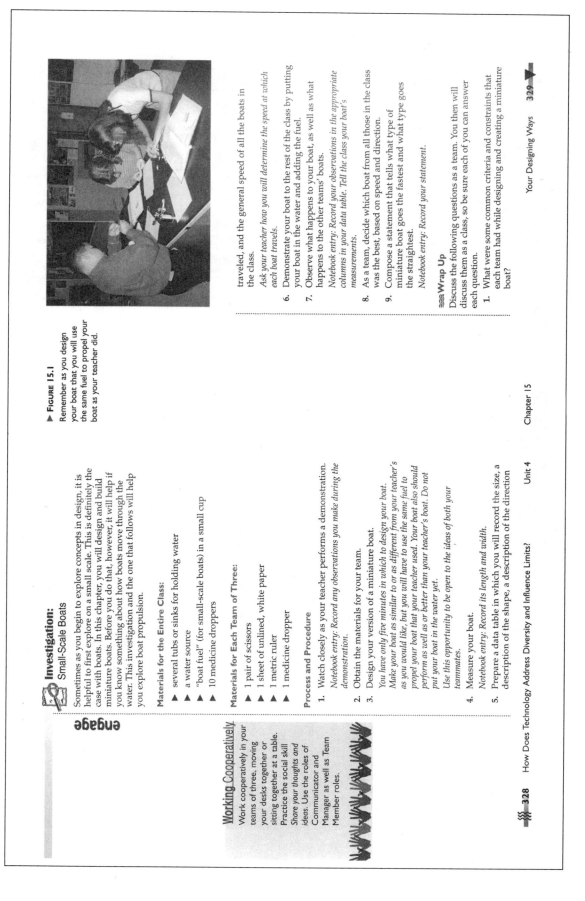

▶ **FIGURE 15.1**

Remember as you design your boat that you will use the same fuel to propel your boat as your teacher did.

traveled, and the general speed of all the boats in the class.
Ask your teacher how you will determine the speed at which each boat travels.

6. Demonstrate your boat to the rest of the class by putting your boat in the water and adding the fuel.

7. Observe what happens to your boat, as well as what happens to the other teams' boats.
   Notebook entry: Record your observations in the appropriate columns in your data table. Tell the class your boat's measurements.

8. As a team, decide which boat from all those in the class was the best, based on speed and direction.

9. Compose a statement that tells what type of miniature boat goes the fastest and what type goes the straightest.
   Notebook entry: Record your statement.

Wrap Up

Discuss the following questions as a team. You then will discuss them as a class, so be sure each of you can answer each question.

1. What were some common criteria and constraints that each team had while designing and creating a miniature boat?

245

▶ **FIGURE 14.13**
Marie has analyzed the costs and benefits for these two ways of getting to school. According to this data table, which solution do you think Marie would choose?

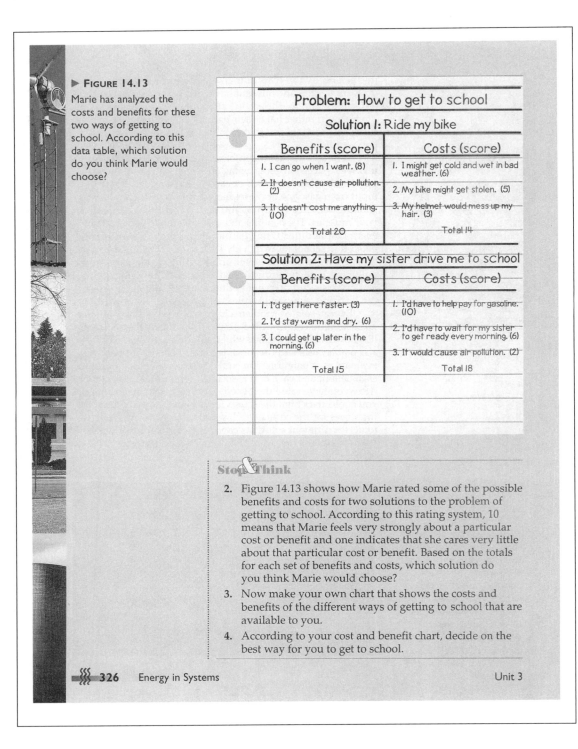

Problem: How to get to school	
Solution 1: Ride my bike	
Benefits (score)	Costs (score)
1. I can go when I want. (8)	1. I might get cold and wet in bad weather. (6)
2. It doesn't cause air pollution. (2)	2. My bike might get stolen. (5)
3. It doesn't cost me anything. (10)	3. My helmet would mess up my hair. (3)
Total 20	Total 14

Solution 2: Have my sister drive me to school	
Benefits (score)	Costs (score)
1. I'd get there faster. (3)	1. I'd have to help pay for gasoline. (10)
2. I'd stay warm and dry. (6)	2. I'd have to wait for my sister to get ready every morning. (6)
3. I could get up later in the morning. (6)	3. It would cause air pollution. (2)
Total 15	Total 18

Stop & Think

2. Figure 14.13 shows how Marie rated some of the possible benefits and costs for two solutions to the problem of getting to school. According to this rating system, 10 means that Marie feels very strongly about a particular cost or benefit and one indicates that she cares very little about that particular cost or benefit. Based on the totals for each set of benefits and costs, which solution do you think Marie would choose?

3. Now make your own chart that shows the costs and benefits of the different ways of getting to school that are available to you.

4. According to your cost and benefit chart, decide on the best way for you to get to school.

elaborate

Connections:
Wind Farms

In 1981, wind energy produced enough electricity in the United States to power two homes. By 1989, wind energy produced enough electricity in the United States to power all the homes in a city as large as Washington, D.C. or San Francisco. By 1996, the capacity of installed wind energy systems in the United States was 1794 megawatts. In 1981, this capacity was only 10 megawatts. One large system that contributed to this increase in wind energy is located in Altamont Pass in California. This system is a collection of 7,500 windmills known as a wind farm. Each windmill contains a turbine on top of a tower. The turbine is attached to a set of blades. When the wind blows, the blades spin and cause the turbine to spin.

The residents of Altamont Pass have mixed opinions of the wind farms in their backyards. A reporter interviewed several of the residents and recorded what they thought about utility companies producing electricity by using energy input from the wind. Read the following interviews and make a list of the benefits and the costs of this solution to the problem of how to generate electricity. Then rate how strongly you feel about each benefit and cost. Finally, use your ratings to decide whether you think wind farms are a good solution for your community's electricity needs. To help you evaluate your decision, answer the following questions. Prepare to share your ratings and answers with the class.

1. What do you consider to be the greatest benefit of wind farms?

2. What do you consider to be the greatest cost of wind farms?

3. Why did you rate the benefits and costs the way that you did?

4. If the local power company planned to install a wind farm in your neighborhood, would you approve of their plan? Explain your point of view.

5. Why are wind farms an appropriate electricity-generating system to use in Altamont Pass, California?

6. Would wind farms be an appropriate electricity-generating system to use in a large city? Explain your answer.

7. Would wind farms be an appropriate electricity-generating system to install in a heavily wooded area, such as in a forest? Explain your answer.

Cooperative Learning Overview

The better you are at working in a team, the better able you are to use challenging skills. Think about it. You started by trying to express your ideas and listen politely. In the next unit, you practiced respect for the ideas that others were expressing. Now that you can express your ideas aloud and can respect the ideas of others, you can learn to encourage others to share their ideas. This will allow you to hear many different opinions. You also can encourage people who do not want to help to be part of the team. You really are becoming a team player!

Now that you have come this far in cooperative learning, you probably have definite opinions about it. Some of you might have found that working cooperatively is not limited to your science classroom. You might not work in teams in other classes, but think of group situations in which you cooperate. The characters have introduced you to your Unit 3 skill of encouraging others to participate. Before you begin Chapter 12, be sure that you have created a T-chart for this skill. Also share your feelings about cooperative learning with your new teammates. Be sure to express both the positive and negative aspects of cooperative learning that you have discovered.

You again will have social skills for each activity. Remember to use your unit skill in each cooperative activity as well as the activity skill. Also try to remember and keep using the social skills you worked on in past units. Finally review the role descriptions with your new teammates so that together you can answer any questions you might have about the duties of each role.

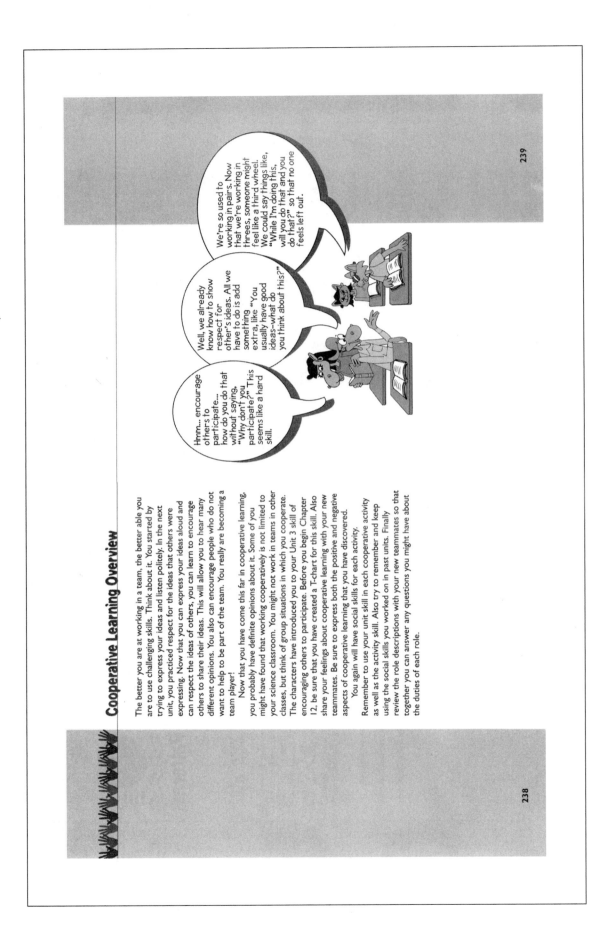

A World in Motion: The Design Experience, Challenges 2 & 3

Developer/Author:	Education Development Center, Inc.
Distributor/Publisher:	Society of Automotive Engineers (SAE) Foundation
Publication date:	1996 (Challenge 2), 1998 (Challenge 3)
Funders/Contributors:	National Science Foundation, SAE International
Ordering information:	SAE Foundation, 1-800-457-2946, www.sae.org/foundation/awim/
Target audience:	Middle school (Grades 7 and 8)

BRIEF DESCRIPTION

This review covers two middle school curriculum units:

- A World in Motion: The Design Experience, Challenge 2 (AWIM, Challenge 2)— Grade 7, Design a Moving Toy
- A World in Motion: The Design Experience, Challenge 3 (AWIM, Challenge 3)— Grade 8, Design a Gliding Toy and Book of Glider Designs.

The publisher, a nonprofit organization, provides a *Teacher Manual* with reproducible student handouts and a *Classroom Materials Kit* for free to the first classroom in a school.

Each Challenge is a blended eight-week cross-curriculum designed to be taught by a core team of science, mathematics, and technology education teachers, with additional support from teachers of social studies, language arts, and art.

For its instructional model, the curriculum modifies the Engineering Design Experience (EDE), used by engineers and engineering schools, for middle school students. The curriculum makes strong real-life connections, especially by intimately involving industry volunteers (career engineers and professionals) in the design. Students go through a simulated authentic design process (from product request to presentation of ideas to the company board) and are mentored by these industry volunteers. The first part of a unit typically provides investigatory activities to prepare students to do more complex design activities later. The units most strongly and transparently address Theme 3 (design) and Theme 4 (abilities for a technological world) through the use of the EDE.

The teacher materials are comprehensive. The scientific and technological information are so thorough and clearly written that almost any teacher could teach all the lessons, even previously unfamiliar topics. Further, the support for ongoing, embedded assessment strongly supports and complements its pedagogy.

The *A World in Motion (AWIM)* product line spans Grades 4–10. *Challenge 1*, for Grades 4–6, is discussed in a separate review. *Challenges 2* and *3*, for Grades 7–8, are reviewed here. *Challenge 4*, designed for Grades 4–10, is not reviewed in this book, although we provide some basic information.

CURRICULUM COMPONENTS

AWIM, Challenges 2 and *3* each consists of an optional *Classroom Materials Kit* and a *Teacher Manual* in a three-ring binder, which includes reproducible handouts. There are no student editions. The *Teacher Manual* contains three instructional units, or challenges. Available in English only, the curriculum has the following pricing structure:

AWIM, Challenge 2

- First *Teacher Manual* (308 pp.) and Classroom Materials Kit are free.
- Subsequent full sets containing the *Teacher Manual* and *Classroom Materials Kit*, $485
- Subsequent *Teacher Manuals* ($20) and *Classroom Materials Kits* ($465) can be purchased separately.

AWIM, Challenge 3

- First *Teacher Manual* (425 pp.) and *Classroom Materials Kit* are free.
- Subsequent full sets containing the *Teacher Manual* and *Classroom Materials Kit*, $170
- Subsequent *Teacher Manuals* ($20) and *Classroom Materials Kits* ($150) can be purchased separately.

AWIM, Challenge 4

The components and pricing structure are similar. Separate *Classroom Materials Kits* for elementary, middle school, and high school will be available at the end of 2004.

Materials/Equipment

The *Classroom Materials Kit* contains most of the materials needed for nine classroom teams of an optimal three students each (total of twenty-seven students). Teams of four students (up to thirty-six students total) can also be accommodated. Items in the kits are consumable and nonconsumable. Individual parts in the *Classroom Materials Kit* can be purchased separately. Additional materials are listed in the introduction to each unit and can be found in the technology laboratory or purchased locally at reasonable costs.

Special Preparations

This integrated learning and teaching curriculum may require adjustments in the middle school curriculum, particularly in terms of team teaching and bringing in industry volunteers. A core team of teachers (science, mathematics, technology education) and a secondary team (social studies and language arts teachers) need to collaborate closely to plan and teach the lessons—the order of lessons, fitting the lessons into the schedule, expectations of student output, teacher roles and responsibilities. The *Teacher Manual* provides extensive explicit guidance to help teachers prepare to teach the challenges, including identifying, scheduling, preparing, and motivating industry volunteers to participate with the class as much as possible.

No computer usage is required, although students and teachers can use such tools as available. The publisher offers workshops, inservice trainings, and other professional development services.

CURRICULUM OVERVIEW

Technology Topic Overview

Almost every activity in this curriculum is a technology activity, meeting at least one of the ITEA Standards for Technological Literacy (STL).

Challenge 2: Design a Moving Toy. A fictitious toy company sends letters to the class requesting that they design new moving toys. Written proposals, sketches, and working models of designs that meet a specific set of requirements are mandatory. Most of the first two-thirds of the activities help students explore and understand the concepts necessary to develop a proposal and a prototype for a toy of their own design. The students work in teams. At the end of the program, students prepare presentations of their working models and a discussion of the design teams' efforts to address the challenge.

Challenge 3: Design a Gliding Toy and Book of Designs. In this challenge, student teams design and prepare two products: a gliding toy and a set of book pages that describe how to build and fly the toy. The instructional approach is similar to the one in *AWIM, Challenge 2.*

Table 9.7.1 presents a selected listing of technology education topics for *AWIM, Challenge 2* activities. The table also provides sample activities for other topics. Although listed here by subject area, the lessons in the curriculum are *not* presented in subject area order, but rather are woven together—a science activity and social studies activity may be running concurrently, followed by separate activities in the science, mathematics, and technology education classrooms.

Table 9.7.2 provides a selected listing of technology education topics for *AWIM, Challenge 3* activities and gives sample activities for other topics.

Integration Review

The curriculum's integration approach recommends a core teaching team that includes a science, mathematics, and technology education teacher, with additional

Table 9.7.1   *AWIM, Challenge 2* topics

Technology Education			
<ul><li>Using Design Logs</li><li>Exploring Body Materials</li><li>Drawing Body Designs</li><li>Building a Prototype</li><li>Performance Testing the Prototype</li></ul>		<ul><li>Interpreting Performance Data</li><li>Redesigning the Body Type</li><li>Constructing the Body</li><li>Assembling, Testing, and Adjusting the Final Design</li></ul>	
Science	*Mathematics*	*Social Studies*	*Language Arts*
<ul><li>Looking at Gears in Bicycles</li><li>Measuring the Rim Forces of Individual Gears</li></ul>	<ul><li>Developing the Gear Ratio Formula</li><li>Torque and Lever Arms</li></ul>	<ul><li>Consumer Research: Conducting Interviews</li><li>Consumer Research: Conducting a Survey</li></ul>	<ul><li>Preparing a Written proposal</li><li>Preparing the Oral Presentation</li></ul>

Table 9.7.2   *AWIM, Challenge 3* topics

Technology Education			
<ul><li>Receiving the Letter from Mobility Press</li><li>Meeting an Engineer</li><li>Making a Design Drawing</li><li>Building a Prototype</li></ul>		<ul><li>Writing Instructions for Building and Flying the Glider</li><li>Producing the Book</li><li>The Book Signing Event</li></ul>	
Science	*Mathematics*	*Social Studies*	*Language Arts*
<ul><li>Investigating Force, Balance, and Center of Gravity</li><li>Testing Wing Properties</li></ul>	<ul><li>Groundwork in Statistics and Graphs</li><li>Graphing the Center of Gravity vs. Nose Weight and Wing Positions</li></ul>	<ul><li>Targeting the Young Consumer</li><li>More Market Research</li></ul>	<ul><li>Planning the Book Content</li><li>Producing the Book</li></ul>

support from social studies, language arts, and art teachers. Although the subject area for each lesson is identified to help teachers coordinate and plan, this curriculum truly blends technological concepts with other subjects.

All learning, no matter the subject area, is immediately incorporated into the design and may need to be revisited when subsequent changes (based on new learning in other subjects) are made. In the blended curriculum for *Challenge 2*, for example, the technology and science lessons include demonstrations and hands-on experience examining force and friction, simple machines, levers and gears, torque, and so on. In mathematics, students apply an understanding of ratio and proportion as they explore the relationship between gear ratios and the radius of a wheel. By gathering information from the client and eventual "customers" and conducting experiments, the students explore data collection and retrieval techniques and apply basic statistical analyses. In addition, students apply their writing and public speaking skills as they prepare a workable proposal and presentation. At least two subject areas are covered in each of the eight weeks for each unit. The overview chart at the beginning of each unit outlines the order of the lessons and the subjects in which they should be presented.

Instructional Model

The program uses a modified-for-middle-school version of the EDE model as its instructional model and organizational metaphor. The EDE, an actual problem-solving process, is used by engineers in design teams and is taught at many engineering schools. The curriculum is organized by the design phases in the EDE:

1. Set goals

2. Build knowledge

3. Design

4. Build and test

5. Finalize the model

6. Present

Through this process, over the course of each unit, students examine what must be accomplished and determine the target market; gather and synthesize information; predict a plausible solution; design, develop, and test a prototype or potential design; and prepare a presentation of their design ideas.

Unique to *AWIM, Challenges 2* and *3* is the participation of volunteers in the classroom who enhance student learning by sharing their professional experiences in engineering, science, math, marketing, oral communications, or consumer research. The volunteers can serve as technical resources to the teacher or play the roles of informed consumers to further challenge the students' understanding of their product.

The *Teacher Manual* has a very clear lesson organization and section heads. Its lesson plans describe the lessons the student is to complete in the following order: introduction, classroom activity, homework idea, and handouts. Although there are small variations between *Challenges 2* and *3*, Table 9.7.3 presents the basic lesson plan organization.

This curriculum, designed for teachers to present to students, is very text-heavy. There are no photographs, only hand-drawn graphics that do not include people. Student worksheets, handouts, and sketches are simple, clear, uncluttered, and relate to the lessons and activities. They directly support the activities and lessons in the teacher text and move the lessons forward.

Although this curriculum does not explicitly address careers in technology, its structure and philosophy provide students with direct experience that implicitly communicates to them that they can have such careers. The curriculum simulates the real-world design process (from product request to presentation of ideas in front of the company board), the same process that real toy and/or book designers would use to solve the same problem. Further, through classroom exposure to actual technology industry volunteers, a student can witness, imagine, and explore the possibility of a technology career. One of the lessons is to create a resume for each member of the team.

Duration

AWIM Challenges 2 and *3* are eight-week programs. The Overview Chart is a week by-week calendar showing the suggested order of each lesson in each subject area. The program assumes each lesson is forty-five to sixty minutes long.

Table 9.7.3 Lesson plan sections and features for *AWIM, Challenges 2 & 3*

Introduction	Identification of EDE phase Identification of subject area What Students Do in This Activity Rationale Time Materials Preparation for the activity
Classroom activity	Introducing the activity Activity description, which may include discussion guidance, topic information, background notes, etc. Facilitating Student Exploration Sharing and Interpreting Assessment (*Challenge 3* only)
Homework ideas	Typically writing opportunities that reinforce and extend students' thinking
Reproducible handouts	Student pages
Sidebar boxes interspersed	Making Connections Volunteer Tip Teaching Tip

Nature of Technology Activities

In both units, the activities build sequentially, culminating in a final product that is unique for each design team. As previously mentioned, almost all of the activities are technology activities, although they are not always attributed as such.

Both units have about the same number of activities (thirty-three and thirty-five). The activities are almost evenly divided between guided and supporting activity types, with occasional directed and open-ended activities. Most supporting activities appear in the first half of each unit (i.e., in the Set Goals and Build Knowledge phases) and provide the building blocks for the later, more complex activities, such as the guided and open-ended activities that usually appear in the second half of the curriculum (Figure 9.7.1).

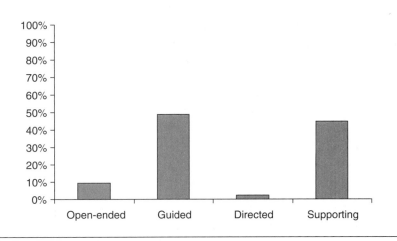

Figure 9.7.1 Activity type distribution in *AWIM, Challenges 2 & 3*

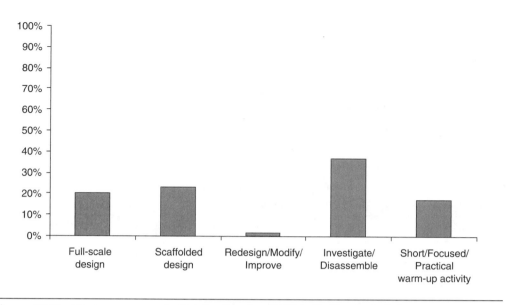

Figure 9.7.2   Design approach distribution in *AWIM, Challenges 2 & 3*

Similarly, the investigate/disassemble/evaluate design approach is heavily featured in the Set Goals and Build Knowledge phases in the first half of each unit, and the more active full-scale (*Challenge 2*) and scaffolded (*Challenge 3*) design approaches appear mostly in the second half (Figure 9.7.2).

Assessment

This curriculum strongly promotes ongoing assessment. It recommends that teachers use embedded assessment tasks and portfolio review to gain information for making ongoing instructional decisions during each eight-week unit (Table 9.7.4).

Each challenge uses portfolio assessment on an ongoing basis. The Assessment Appendix suggests that the class select the types of things that should be included in their portfolio and what criteria should be used to assess them. A list of key items from each learning phase and of selected questions helps the teacher and students have this conversation. The students should find their portfolios helpful when completing each unit's final lesson, "Reflecting on the Engineering Design Experience."

The Assessment Appendix also contains several assessment tasks designed to help teachers collect and interpret data about student understanding of science concepts, data representation and interpretation, and design process skills. These tasks can be completed by individual students, a design team, or the whole class. The program suggests that students present, compare, and discuss their reasoning on the tasks with each other. These interactions are meant to help teachers characterize student understanding, identify misconceptions, and pinpoint areas that require further development of student knowledge and skills. Each assessment activity includes background information about expected student understanding of the concepts and suggestions on how to use the task to assess student comprehension. However, these assessments do not provide grading criteria or rubrics.

The *Challenge 3* unit for Grade 8 frequently provides an assessment section at the end of each activity. This typically suggests what type of skill or understanding can be

Table 9.7.4   Student assessment tools and their presence in *AWIM, Challenges 2 & 3*

Assessment approach	Presence in the curriculum
Paper-and-pencil tests—multiple-choice, short answer, true/false, vocabulary, completion	◆
Projects/Products/Media—individual and group activities, projects, products, media	◆ ◆ ◆ ◆
Performance-based assessments—demonstrations, presentations, multimedia, performances	◆ ◆
Portfolios—student papers, notes, project reports, research, work samples	◆ ◆ ◆ ◆
Student work—workbook or lab journal pages, handouts, graphs, charts, etc.	◆ ◆ ◆ ◆
Open-ended questioning—essays, extended writing exercises, critical thinking questions, etc.	◆ ◆
Computerized assessment—Online simulations, tests, etc.	◆
Evaluations—peer assessments, self-reflections, self-evaluations	◆ ◆
Rubrics/Checklists	◆
Informal observations/Discussions—Teacher observations	◆ ◆ ◆

◆◆◆◆   Dominant   There are a large number of assessments of this type in the curriculum.

◆◆◆   Substantial—There are a substantial number of assessments of this type in the curriculum.

◆◆   Some/Moderate—There are a moderate number of assessments of this type in the curriculum.

◆   Marginal/Missing—There are very few or no assessments of this type in the curriculum.

assessed based on the student's performance in the activity, suggests what specific aspects of the students' discussions or work will indicate understanding, or provides questions to assess understanding.

A few comments about Table 9.7.4:

• Performance-based assessments are not frequent but are a critical component. Each unit culminates with the Present phase, in which student teams present their projects to the fictitious client.

• Students are encouraged to do a lot of writing in their design logs, which were included in the Student Work category.

• There are a few reflection activities scattered throughout the units, designed to have students take stock of their understanding thus far. The final activity, Reflecting on the Engineering Design Experience, asks students to assess how they experienced the EDE process.

STL STANDARDS-LEVEL ANALYSES

Although this curriculum was published before the STL, and each unit is only eight weeks long, it still provides moderate or better coverage for all of the STL themes except Theme 2 (technology and society).

It is obvious from the instructional model used and the units' organization that Theme 3 (design) and Theme 4 (abilities for a technological world) are the foci of the curriculum. The EDE instructional model provides the organization for the hands-on activities and is a transparent application of Standard 9 (engineering design process). Within Theme 4 (abilities for a technological world), the lessons particularly engage students in Standard 11 (applying the design process), for which students apply every middle school benchmark.

Comments on other themes in Table 9.7.5:

- Theme 5 is mostly addressed by the topic of the challenge. By focusing on simple machines, *Challenge 2* introduces students to Standard 16. *Challenge 3* addresses aspects of Standard 18 (transportation technologies). Students focus on Standard 17 (information and communication technologies) when preparing presentations and publishing their work.

Table 9.7.5   Results of analyses of STL coverage in the overall curriculum for *AWIM, Challenges 2 & 3*

	Coverage rating	Primary standards covered for each theme
Theme 1	◆ ◆	3—The connections between technology & other fields
Theme 2	◆	*
Theme 3	◆ ◆ ◆	8—The attributes of design 9—Engineering design 10—Problem solving
Theme 4	◆ ◆ ◆ ◆	11—Applying the design process 12—Using and maintaining technological products and systems
Theme 5	◆ ◆	16—Energy and power technologies 17—Information and communication technologies 18—Transportation technologies

◆◆◆◆   Dominant—A large proportion of this theme is covered in the curriculum.

◆◆◆   Substantial—There is substantial coverage of this theme in the curriculum.

◆◆   Some/Moderate—There is moderate coverage of this theme in the curriculum.

◆   Marginal/Missing—There is little or no coverage of this theme in the curriculum.

Primary standards coverage = standard has dominant or substantial coverage within the theme

* Standards not reported for marginal/missing themes.

- Standard 3 (connections between technology and other fields) is well represented in this blended cross-curricular product. Half of the Theme 1 occurrences in *Challenge 2* are Standard 3, and the other half are Standard 2 (understanding the core concepts of technology). Almost all occurrences of Theme 1 for *Challenge 3* are Standard 3.

TEACHER MATERIALS REVIEW

This curriculum consists of consumable materials kits and a *Teacher Manual*. In addition to the elements of the lessons described in the previous Instructional Model section, the *Teacher Manual* for each unit provides:

The scope of teacher support (Table 9.7.6) for approximately thirty-five activities is comprehensive for each eight-week unit—the total page count for *Challenge 2* is 334 pages and *Challenge 3* is 449 pages.

Table 9.7.6   Outline of *Teacher Manual, AWIM, Challenges 2 & 3*

Chapter title	*Subsections*	*# pages in Challenge 2*	*# pages in Challenge 3*
Introduction to the Challenge	• About the Challenge • The Engineering Design Experience • The Curriculum Content • Integrated Learning and Teaching • Students Working in Teams • Volunteers in the Classroom • The Activity Sequence • Writing and Design Logs • Information about Science Concepts (varies by unit) • About Consumer Research • About Collecting, Analyzing, and Displaying Data	13	14
Overview Chart—Activities by Recommended Discipline	Activities laid out by subject area for Weeks 1–8	9	4
Curriculum (Lessons)	Lessons are organized by phase of the EDE (see Instructional Model section above)	258	354
Appendices	• Contacting Volunteers • The Science of. . . . (varies by unit) • Glossary • Assessment • Resources.	50	71

Table 9.7.7   Categories of teacher support materials and level ratings for *AWIM*,
Challenges 2 & 3

Categories of support found in teacher support materials	Level of teacher support
Support for teaching the curriculum	◆ ◆ ◆
Support for pedagogy	◆ ◆ ◆ ◆
Support for assessment	◆ ◆ ◆ ◆
Support for teaching technology standards	◆ ◆
Support for teaching twenty-first-century knowledge and abilities	◆ ◆

◆◆◆◆   Dominant—Almost all of the criteria for support in this category are present.

◆◆◆   Substantial—Most of the criteria for support in this category are present.

◆◆   Some/Moderate—Some of the criteria for support in this category are present.

◆   Marginal/Missing—Very few or none of the criteria for support in this category are present.

The quality and comprehensive nature of the background information and grade-level content for teachers are outstanding (Table 9.7.7). A teacher new to any of the subject areas targeted could probably teach these lessons just with the help of the teacher support materials.

Further, the curriculum ties the pedagogy to the assessment. It effectively uses multiple, ongoing, and embedded assessments to support the pedagogical principles the curriculum espouses. It suggests creating independent, self-directed learners; tailoring learning opportunities to address student needs; facilitating inquiry, critical thinking, problem solving, and decision making; and encouraging collaboration, respect for diverse ideas, and other technological problem-solving values.

The curriculum makes a strong case for teaching technological literacy, but within the framework of the National Research Council's NSES Content Standard E definition (students should develop abilities of technological design and an understanding about science and technology).

The publisher, SAE, is funded by car manufacturers who have a vested interest in having students acquire twenty-first-century knowledge and abilities, and this curriculum addresses those needs. As previously noted, having industry volunteers in the classroom exposes students to professional and technical careers. It also strongly emphasizes teamwork and collaboration—important skills for the future. Finally, it provides teachers with team-building activities, suggestions, and support such as descriptions of teamwork and team roles.

Table of Contents—*A World in Motion: The Design Experience, Challenge 2*
(Number of pages indicated in parentheses)

Introduction

Introduction to the Challenge (13)

Overview Chart—Activities by Recommended Discipline (8)

Planning Chart (1)

Set Goals (2)

Reading and Evaluating the Request for Proposals—RFP (8)

Meeting an Industry Volunteer (2)

Designing a Team Name, Logo, and Slogan (4)

Using Design Logs (12)

Identifying the Customers (4)

Seeing the Big Picture (6)

Creating a Design Checklist (4)

Building Knowledge (2)

Looking at Gears in Bicycles (6)

What We Know About Gears (4)

Introducing the Gear Materials (6)

Recording Gear Rotations (8)

Developing the Gear Ratio Formula (8)

Using the Gear Ratio Formula (8)

Measurements and Ratios in Wheels and Gears (optional) (4)

Adding a Motor and Wheels (6)

Measuring Performance: Speed and Wheel Rim Force (8)

Compound Gear Trains (6)

Measuring Performance: Compound Gear Trains (4)

Multiplying Fractions to Calculate Gear Ratios (8)

Measuring the Rim Force of Individual Gears (8)

Torque and Lever Arms (8)

What We've Learned About Gears (2)

Exploring Body Materials (6)

Consumer Research: Conducting Interviews (10)

Consumer Research: Conducting a Survey (8)

Consumer Research: What We've Learned About the Consumers (10)

Design (2)

Integrating and Applying What We Know (2)

Writing a Design Brief (4)

Designing a Gear Train for the Prototype (2)

Drawing Body Designs (6)

Build and Test (2)

Building a Prototype (2)

Performance Testing the Prototype (2)

Interpreting Performance Test Data (2)

Redesigning the Prototype (2)

Focus Group Testing of Body Designs (optional) (6)

Finalize the Model (2)

Making a Body Mock-up (4)

Constructing the Body (4)

Assembling, Testing, and Adjusting the Final Design (2)

Planning for the Proposal & Presentation (2)

Preparing the Written Proposal (8)

Writing a Resume (optional) (10)

Preparing the Oral Presentation (8)

Present (2)

The Final Presentations (6)

Reflecting on the Engineering Design Experience (2)

Appendices (2)

Contacting Volunteers (6)

Sample Letter to Potential Volunteers (1)

Mobility Toys, Inc., Request for Proposals (2)

Gears, Torque, and Performance (10)

Designing a Gear Train for the Prototype: Using Calculations (10)

Assessment (6)

Basic Understanding of Gears (4)

Design Log Assessment (2)

Design Log (Sunnyside Toy Co.) (2)

Design Log (Wild West Toys, Inc.) (2)

Resources (3)

SAMPLE PAGES

AWIM, Challenge 1, and *AWIM, Challenges 2 and 3*, follow the same structure. Refer to the sample pages at the end of the *AWIM, Challenge 1* review to see a typical letter introducing the design challenge. Here we display the body of a typical lesson—Activity Description, Facilitating Student Exploration, and Sharing and Interpreting. Note that the outer edge of the right page lists the primary and secondary subjects that the lesson addresses.

CLASSROOM ACTIVITY

ACTIVITY DESCRIPTION

Tell students that in this activity they will evaluate several materials for making a body for their toy.

Students begin this activity by obtaining sample pieces of posterboard, cardboard, newspaper, aluminum foil, plastic wrap, plastic from a two-liter bottle, paper straws, and craft sticks.

Distribute a copy of the Materials Testing Table to each design team. Ask the design teams to cut a sample of each material ½ inch by three inches. Students will perform three tests: a rigidity test, a bending test, and an assembly test.

Before students begin testing, ask several questions to help them think about which materials might be best for creating the toy body:

- What kinds of characteristics might you look for in a body material?
- What material appears to be most rigid?
- What material bends the easiest and seems strong?
- What materials glue together the best?
- What materials tape together the best?
- What materials do you believe have the best appearance?

First the students will test the materials for rigidity. Ask students: Why might rigidity be important in a body material?

Ask the students to hold the materials straight in front of them with one hand. Then they should use the Materials Testing Table to record which materials bent and which did not bend. You should inform students that rigid materials are better for body construction than very flexible materials.

The next test is a bending test. Now the students should attempt to bend each material to form a right angle. As each material is bent, the students should mark the results on the Materials Testing Table. This test will help design teams understand which materials are flexible and which will break when they are bent. Those materials that can be bent and formed in various shapes will assist in shaping the body. The ability of materials to bend and return to their original shape is called *elasticity*.

The last test is an assembly exercise. Students should cut eight pieces of each material ½ inch by 3 inches. Then the design teams should use four different fastening techniques to assemble the materials.

Have students use glue, masking tape, scotch tape, and staples to fasten two pieces of like materials together. If the two materials join together, students should check this type of fastening technique on the Materials Testing Table. If the technique does not join the materials, students should leave the space blank. For example, newspaper glued to newspaper will bond very well; but aluminum foil will not glue well to itself.

As students conduct the material test, they will learn about the strength and nature of the materials. They will also learn the best techniques for assembling materials.

Next, have design teams investigate papier-mâché as a body material. Have students cut five pieces of newspaper 3 by 6 inches. Next, put a small amount of glue (1 tablespoon) in the bottom of a paper cup. Add a small amount of water to make the glue into a slurry. Then coat each piece of paper by dipping it in the glue mixture. Place the coated strips on a piece of plain white paper. Place one piece on top of the other. After the five pieces are pressed together, bend the papier-mâché at a right angle. Let the papier-mâché dry for 24 hours. After the papier-mâché has dried, students should sand it with fine sand paper.

Ask students: What happened to the paper as a result of papier-mâché? Did the sandpaper make the paper surface smooth?

You may want to decide as a class which materials you will use to construct the toy bodies. You may also want to allow students to choose from a variety of materials. You can ask design teams to make a list of materials they will need to construct the body of their toy.

FACILITATING STUDENT EXPLORATION

The design teams need to understand that this activity is exploratory. The materials used in the experiments will not necessarily be part of their toy. However, the knowledge they gain from performing the material tests will be used to construct their toy body.

As design teams complete their Materials Testing Tables, encourage them to try assembling unlike materials. For example, will aluminum foil glue to newspaper?

SHARING AND INTERPRETING

Ask students to present their Materials Testing Tables in class. Design teams may find that other teams discovered different characteristics of materials. Ask the design teams to post their results on a bulletin board so that everyone can see them.

NOTES

10

Supplemental Products

This chapter provides brief descriptions of thirteen supplemental products: seven for the elementary school grades and six others for the middle grades. Unfortunately, space considerations preclude us from including sample pages or tables of contents. Newer products are provided before older ones, and products for the elementary grades precede those for middle school. If more than one product is published the same year, reviews are ordered alphabetically by the last name of the lead author.

These materials typically are intended for the formal educational setting; however, they do not necessarily include a teacher component or package. Supplemental materials are often a collection of activities, design challenges, projects, and the like that give students practice and experience with only a limited range of technology content, covering only a few standards, and not necessarily in depth. These products are not intended to serve as a curriculum for an entire technology course at the middle grades or to provide the entire technology content needed for one or more elementary grades.

Before providing the reviews, we briefly describe some other products that were not reviewed for this book.

Late-Breaking or Other Products

The development of *TECH-Know* (www.ncsu.edu/techknow), a middle-grades technology product, is funded by the National Science Foundation (NSF). Eight design challenges provide instruction that supports the popular after-school competitions sponsored by the Technology Student Association (TSA): Cyberspace Pursuit, Dragster Design Challenge, Environmental Challenge, Flight Challenge, Graphic Design Challenge, Mechanical Challenge,

Structural Challenge, and Transportation Challenge. Although an accompanying textbook is planned for later phases of the development project, we mention *TECH-Know* among the supplemental products because its independent design challenges will be available sooner.

We do not provide a full description of the NSF-funded *Materials World Modules* (www.materialsworldmodules.org) because only some of these high school modules have been adapted for use in the middle grades. In high school, this product can be used as a curriculum, but it could only be used as a supplemental product at the middle grades. The interdisciplinary modules of hands-on projects are based on materials sciences and include composites, ceramics, biodegradable sensors, and sports materials. While this product inherently includes material very relevant to technology education (and science and mathematics), much of it was created prior to the *Standards for Technological Literacy*.

Kids Inventing Technology Series (KITS)

Developer/Author:	Ryan Brown, Phyllis Wright, Richard Seymour, and Josh Brown
Distributor/Publisher:	International Technology Education Association (ITEA)
Publication date:	2001–2003
Ordering information:	International Technology Education Association, 1914 Association Dr., Suite 201, Reston, VA 20191–1539; 1-703-860-2100; www.iteawww.org, $20 (members $15) per set; twelve to eighteen pages per activity

Kids Inventing Technology Series (KITS) is teacher materials comprised of four sets of five technology investigations each for standards-based instruction at the elementary level. Created expressly to address the Standards for Technological Literacy (STL), teachers can pick individual investigations that best support their curriculum or use sets to create a larger technology unit or curriculum. Some sets explore technologies in these areas: energy/power, information/communication, construction, manufacturing, and transportation. Others, particularly later in the series, define and develop the key concepts, characteristics, and processes of technology: engineering, design, research and development, systems and products, experimentation, and materials. The KITS series collectively addresses more than three-fourths of the standards. Each activity focuses on one or two of the benchmarks within a relevant standard.

Each investigation starts with an introduction containing background information, concepts, leading questions, and interesting facts that support a given technology standard. Two sets of activities, one appropriate for K–2 and another for 3–5, help students explore the ideas. Activities take from one to four or more class periods. Every investigation contains step-by-step teacher instructions, organized into the following sections:

- Introduction
- Teacher Preparation
- Benchmarks
- Supplies and Tools Needed
- Preparing the Students
- Conducting the Activity
- Checking for Understanding
- Masters for Student Handouts
- Extending the Activity
- Evidence of Attainment
- Connections to Other Subjects
- Resources

Each set of five units is loose-leaf bound with a glossy cover. Each unit is independent; there are no additional materials for use across the set.

Technology Starters:
A Standards-Based Guide

Developer/Author:	International Technology Education Association (ITEA)
Publication date:	2002
Funders/Contributors:	Technical Foundation of America
Ordering information:	International Technology Education Association, 1914 Association Dr., Suite 201, Reston, VA 20191–1539; 1-703-860-2100; www.iteawww.org, $29 (members $24), 180 pp.

This publication is part of *Advancing Technological Literacy: ITEA Professional Series*. The series is an addendum to *Standards for Technological Literacy* (STL) and offers background information and activities to start teaching technology in that vision. This teacher guide offers twelve investigations for the K–5 grade levels, grouped into three teaching-learning strategies: topic investigations, product generation, and ingenuity challenges. Activities require multiple days to weeks for completion, depending on the grade level and depth of investigation. Each teaching-learning strategy begins with the overview and intent of the strategy, followed by instructional procedures laying out student and teacher responsibilities and a list of possible student assessments.

Each investigation stands on its own and can be used in an order appropriate to a teacher's grade level and educational goals. A matrix shows which of the STL standards and benchmarks are covered in each investigation. The sets of activities address a page of benchmarks within each of Standards 1–13: with the exception of Standards 16–17 (energy, communication), the activities are less able to address the Design World standards (14–20).

Every investigation provides step-by-step instructions, suggestions (including a materials list), and photographs that illustrate student activities and their resulting products. Next are masters of any student handouts, often followed by an extension to the investigation and a page on connections to other curriculum areas.

The introductory chapter, Why Study Technology, has a lot of useful information for the teacher, including the basic rationale and research on teaching technology to primary students, and a pedagogical review of the implications for technology instruction of constructivism, multiple intelligences, and differentiated instruction. Additional sections discuss the role of technology curriculum in multiculturalism, interdisciplinary instruction, cooperative learning, project-based learning, problem solving, and assessment.

National Educational Technology Standards for Students: Multi-disciplinary Units for Grades 3–5

Developer/Author:	Larry Hannah, ed.
Publisher:	International Society for Technology in Education (ISTE) and the U.S. Department of Education
Publication date:	2002
Ordering information:	ISTE, www.iste.org/bookstore/detail.cfm?sku=nets35, $34.95 (nonmember price), 155 pp.

This compendium to the *National Educational Technology Standards for Students* (NETS) contains more than 200 lessons and activities that integrate the NETS with English language arts, math, science, and social studies. The book is organized into five themes: Form and Structure, Imagination, Perspectives, Movement, and Change. Each theme in turn offers five to ten activity-based units that contain background material for teachers, standards alignments, daily lesson plans, information about technology tools and software, Web-based and other resources, lesson extensions, and assessments for content and technology. The lessons and activities were developed by teachers, and tips and narrative from educators who have used the units in their own classrooms are highlighted. Introductory essays support teachers in classroom management, cooperative teaching, problem-based learning, Internet use, and assessment.

The NETS focus primarily on skills and understandings related to educational technology (see discussion of educational technology vs. technology education in Chapter 2). Although the focus of many concepts presented in the NETS and in this product is different from that found in the STL, there is nevertheless considerable crossover. STL Themes 3 (design), 4 (abilities for a technological world), and 5 (the designed world) receive particular attention.

The Great Technology Adventure: Technology Learning Activities Guide

Developer/Author:	Technology Student Association
Distributor/Publisher:	Scarecrow Education
Publication date:	2001
Ordering information:	Scarecrow Press, Inc., 4720 Boston Way, Lanham, MD 20706; 1-800-462-6420; www.scarecrowpress.com; $16.50; 104 pp.

This teacher monograph was developed by the Technology Student Association, a nonprofit educational organization of elementary, middle, and high school students. It offers 27 Technology Learning Activities (TLAs) designed to promote technology literacy in K–6 classrooms. Each has a real-world theme based on a current event, a literature or curriculum topic, or an event likely to be relevant to your students. This set of TLAs has multiple correlations to most of the technology standards. Fewer TLAs correspond to Standards 14, 16, 18, and 19.

The TLAs are designed for use by individuals or groups and can be presented in isolation, integrated into thematic units, or adapted to your own curriculum. A minimum time estimate is from three to five class periods, but they may take much longer when integrated into a rich curriculum. Each is presented on a single page, front and back, organized into the following sections:

- Situation—background
- Challenge—problem statement
- Criteria—parameters and/or restraints
- To Do—process used to complete TLA
- Background—topics to cover prior to beginning, or as augmentation
- Discussion Questions—prompts to initiate class discussions
- Correlation to Technology Standards—suggested standard tie-ins
- Related Curriculum—connections with math, science, social studies, art, and so on
- Resources—mostly topics and ideas to research in the library and on the Web

The guide begins with overviews and a listing of the Standards for Technological Literacy from the International Technology Education Association in 2000. Next are nine pages of Helpful Information, including terminology explanations, hints on integrating the TLAs into your curriculum, a guide for creating your own TLA, and a page on materials used. In the back of the guide is one page of resources, general and Internet resources, and literature listings.

Balancing the World of Technology in the Elementary Classroom

Developer/Author:	Kim Weaver
Distributor/Publisher:	Kim Weaver
Publication date:	1996–1997
Ordering information:	Kim Weaver, P.O. Box 2202, La Plata, MD 20646; www.angelfire.com/md2/storyweaver; $40 unit; 250–350 pp./unit

This series is six loose-leaf bound units of teacher materials for an integrated, thematic curriculum. Each unit requires two to three weeks of instruction. There is one for each grade K–5, plus an extra unit for Grades 1–2. Each unit has a theme centered on one of the following technology activities of construction: a bridge, a sailboat, a plane, a race car, a crane, or an elevator. The concepts focus on materials and mechanical, structural, and fluid technologies, and some lightly touch on optical and electrical technologies. The units require forty-five minutes to an hour of each day working on the construction—designing, building, testing, and modifying (redesign). The remainder of the school day is for thematically related activities in

- Reading, writing, language arts
- Mathematics
- Science
- Health and safety
- Social studies
- Careers

The unit is filled with ideas and duplicating masters for these activities, in addition to a classroom store—for construction materials, engineering portfolios, bulletin boards, and learning centers.

Each unit begins with eighteen pages of teacher materials discussingtechnology in general and in the elementary classroom, plus an overview of the series and the core technologies in the units. The bibliography lists children's literature relevant to the theme. Three companion videos are also available, for $14.95 to $19.95 each: one is for technology in the first grade (the bridge unit), another is an overview of the entire series, and the last is training for the tools and materials used in the series.

All Aboard! Cross-Curricular Design and Technology Strategies and Activities: Springboards for Teaching Series

Developer/Author:	The Metropolitan Toronto School Board
Distributor/Publisher:	Trifolium Books
Publication date:	1996
Ordering information:	U.S. distributor: Fitzhenry & Whiteside, 121 Harvard Avenue Suite 2, Allston, MA 02134; 1-800-387-9776; www.fitzhenry.ca, $18.95; 176 pp.

This teacher monograph offers 20 projects for Grades K–6, grouped under four themes—Human Achievement, Animal Shelters, the Built Environment, and Weather. They can be used in any combination or order that fits your curriculum.

Each project has a teacher planning page and a reproducible page for student use. The teacher page starts with a synopsis for each phase—Situation, Problem, Investigation, Construction, and Evaluation—followed by a Helping Hand section containing a concept web and suggestions for Internet searches. Next, a More Activity Ideas box lists activities relevant to the project. The main body of the teacher page starts with the problem statement and then has prompts and ideas to use with your students in the previously mentioned phases of the project. The student page varies from a page of illustrative graphics for the project to full pages of text, including the problem, related information, things to think about, and a group assessment.

Each thematic grouping of activities starts with a table giving grades recommended—either K–3 or 4–6—a simple project statement, recommended materials, and hints for possible advance preparations. Each grouping ends with two pages or more of additional activity ideas for that theme.

The 64 page Teacher Support section has everything to get you started teaching design and technology. The Your Classroom section discusses work area, safety, time, and materials needed, along with content and curriculum—technology concepts and skills, cross-curricular outcomes, and a guide to the basic concepts. The Making Your Own Activities section discusses how to use activities and ends with evaluation and assessment. The appendix to the book provides planning and product assessment sheets; safety quiz and contract forms for the teacher; self, peer, and group assessment; and resource Internet sites and suppliers.

Designing Everyday Things: Integrated Projects for the Elementary Classroom

Developer/Author:	Helen Clayfield and Robin Hyatt
Distributor/Publisher:	Heinemann
Publication date:	1994
Ordering information:	Heinemann, 361 Hanover Street, Portsmouth, NH 03801; 1-603-431-7894; www.heinemann.com; $16.20; 97 pp.

This teacher monograph consists of 24 activities designed to provide a starting point for teaching technology in the elementary classroom. It is organized by technology concepts into three chapters: Materials, Design, and Energy Sources. Each activity is brief, only two to five pages, often including reproducible student pages. They are self-contained, can be used by themselves or organized into integrated themes, and can range from one-day activities to multiple-day investigations. The activities are laid out step-by-step with the following sections:

- Design Brief—describes the problem
- Materials-Resources—lists what you need for the activity
- Teaching Points—helpful hints, prompts, and instructions
- Recording and Reporting—outcomes and assessments
- Further Investigations—extensions to the problem
- Did You Know?—interesting facts and, where needed, reproducible student pages

The text begins with 15 pages of teacher's information, which includes rationale and definition of teaching technology to primary students, organizational approaches for students and resources, safety guidelines, recording and reporting examples, and a section on how to use the book.

Humans Innovating Technology Series (HITS)

Developer/Author:	R. Thomas Wright, Richard Seymour, Josh Brown, Ryan Brown
Distributor/Publisher:	International Technology Education Association (ITEA)
Publication date:	2001–2003
Ordering information:	International Technology Education Association, 1914 Association Dr., Suite 201, Reston, VA 20191–1539; 1-703-860-2100; www.iteawww.org, $20 (members $15) per set; 14–20 pp. per activity

Humans Innovating Technology Series (HITS) is a teacher text comprised of four sets of five technology activities for standards-based instruction at the middle and high school levels. Created expressly to address the Standards for Technological Literacy (STL), some units explore technology in the fields of agriculture/biotechnology, information/communication, and transportation. Other units treat technology in general terms such as technology impacts and influences on history and society; technology and the environment; technology development, design, and use; and technology impacts on other fields of study. Another group focuses on the concepts, characteristics, and processes of technology such as design, engineering, products and systems, and maintenance. The HITS series to date collectively addresses more than three-fourths of the STL. Each activity focuses on one or two of the benchmarks within the relevant standard.

Activities take from three to six or more class periods. Teachers can pick activities that best support their curriculum or use activities to create a larger technology unit or curriculum. Every activity contains step-by-step teacher instructions, organized into the following sections:

- Introduction
- Technology Standard
- Grade Level Benchmarks
- Connections to Subjects
- Evidence of Attainment
- Key Terms

- Think About prompts
- Content Overview
- Problem/Challenge
- Context
- Resources
- Equipment/Supplies

- Teacher Preparation
- Getting Students Ready
- Conducting Activity
- Assessing Students
- Activity Handouts
- Assessment Rubrics

Each set of five units is loose-leaf bound with a glossy cover. Each unit is independent; there are no additional materials for use across the set.

Exploring Technology: A Standards-Based Middle School Model Course Guide

Developer/Author:	International Technology Education Association (ITEA)
Publication date:	2001
Funders/Contributors:	Technical Foundation of America
Ordering information:	International Technology Education Association, 1914 Association Dr., Suite 201, Reston, VA 20191–1539, 1-703-860-2100; www.iteawww.org, $25 (members $20), 80 pp.

This curriculum guide is part of *Advancing Technological Literacy: ITEA Professional Series*. It is designed to help teachers and curriculum developers make decisions about content, methods, activities, assessment strategies, and resources for a technology education course. The first chapter has ten pages of teacher information on the middle-level learner, their technological education, and a course framework that includes goals, planning and assessment, and a summary of the unit organization.

The second chapter offers five middle school technology units. The first two units start with the *Standards for Technological Literacy* (STL) standards and benchmarks addressed in the unit, an overview of the unit, and suggested learning experiences. These suggested learning experiences are summarized in a paragraph followed by a Web site URL or an ITEA publication citation as a source for the actual activity. The list of experiences is followed by the content outline and academic connections for math, science, social sciences, and language arts.

The last three units are technological theme units: (1) the scope of technology; (2) integration of various aspects of technology through events such as an automobile accident; and (3) the function, impact, and consequences of core technological principles—systems, resources, requirements, processes, optimization, trade-offs, and controls. Each unit starts with a general overview of the STL standards and benchmarks addressed, suggested learning experiences, general scenario, student preparation, unit sections, and academic connections to math, science, social science, and language arts. Each section of the unit has an overview, narrative, content outline, and a list of suggested learning experiences.

These units, particularly the thematic units, can be used in any order. If the objective is full coverage of the STL standards and benchmarks for middle school, then each and all the subsections should be completed. A matrix showing this coverage by unit is in the beginning of the guide, along with a compendium of major topics for the STL broken down by grade level.

Teaching Technology: Middle School Strategies for Standards-Based Instruction

Developer/Author:	International Technology Education Association (ITEA)
Publication date:	2000
Funders/Contributors:	Technical Foundation of America
Ordering information:	International Technology Education Association, 1914 Association Dr., Suite 201, Reston, VA 20191–1539, 1-703-860-2100; www.iteawww.org, $29 (members $24), 118 pp.

This publication is part of *Advancing Technological Literacy: ITEA Professional Series.* The series is an addendum to *Standards for Technological Literacy.* This teacher monograph offers 11 activities, which range from three days to six weeks in length (average two weeks) on these topics: technology and history, brainstorming, design, assessing technology, information technology, and biotechnology. A chart maps the activities against the standards for technology, math, and science. The sets of activities strongly address the standards for Design and for Abilities for Technological Design (8–13). Most activities also address one of the Designed World standards (14–20). Each activity is organized into these teacher sections:

- Purpose of Activity
- Standards Addressed
- Teaching Methods
- Prior Knowledge

- Resources, Time
- Description
- Summary
- Assessment

- Extensions (0–5 on each)
- Addressing Benchmarks
- Hand-out Masters (some)

An introductory chapter provides 25 pages of instructional guidance:

- Design Briefs Challenge Problem Solvers
- Teaching Students to Assess Impact
- Cooperative Learning and Leadership
- Assisting Students with Special Needs

- Enhancing Creative Thinking
- Sharing and Reporting Information
- Using Simulations to Teach Technology
- Using Concepts Maps to Facilitate Learning

- Standards-Based Student Assessment
- Engaging Community and Corporate Partners
- Using Modular Instruction

The book concludes with 20 pages of resources for teaching technology, including ten instructional materials (magazines, CD-ROMs, Web sites, etc.) and a list of several organizations having resources useful for technology education (ITEA, ASCD, etc.).

KidTech: Hands-On Problem Solving with Design Technology for Grades 5–8

Developer/Author:	Lucy Miller
Distributor/Publisher:	Dale Seymour Publications
Publication date:	1998
Ordering information:	Pearson Learning Group, 135 South Mount Zion Road, P.O. Box 2500, Lebanon, IN 46052; 1-800-526-9907; www.pearsonlearning.com; $22.50; 136 pp.

KidTech offers 60 design briefs of a range of difficulty levels in the following areas: communication, machines, toys, structures, energy, and transportation. Accordingly, *KidTech* could be useful for addressing Standards for Technological Literacy (STL) within Abilities for a Technological World and the Design World (Standards 11–20). Teachers can pick and choose which briefs would best complement their curriculum or could create a complete unit using an entire area or a combination of areas. For each design brief, Teacher Notes include

- Background information
- Cross-curricular extensions
- Materials needed
- Possible solutions

The twenty-seven-page Getting Started chapter provides a practical step-by-step approach for using design technology as an integral part of existing curriculum and educational goals. From basics for the beginning technology teacher to the latest ideas for the experienced teacher, it covers these topics:

- Setting up the classroom and an explanation of the tools needed
- A thorough explanation of the design process including roles and responsibilities of the various team members and a reproducible design brief recording sheet
- Planning and assessment strategies including knowledge and skills
- Sample assessments with quality criteria and a process rubric
- A student self-evaluation and sample design brief recording sheet and journal pages
- A practice design brief that focuses students on roles and responsibilities in the process

The eleven-page Basic Techniques chapter provides background information needed to complete the design briefs: basic construction techniques, methods for making creations move (wheels, pulleys, gears, drive belts, etc.), and harnessing power sources (propellers, rubber bands, electrical circuits, etc.).

By Design: Technology Exploration and Integration: Activities for Grades 6–9

Developer/Author:	Geoff Day, Julie Czerneda, and the Metropolitan Toronto School Board Teachers
Publisher:	Trifolium Books
Publication date:	1996
Ordering information:	Fitzhenry & Whiteside, 1-800-387-9776; www.fitzhenry.ca/1895579783.htm, $34.95 (U.S.), 166 pp.

By Design contains 40 activities that emphasize problem solving and integrating technology education concepts across the middle school curriculum. The activities employ the S.P.I.C.E. design model, which requires students to examine the **S**ituation, identify a resolvable **P**roblem or Possibility, **I**nvestigate and formulate ideas, **C**hoose and construct their design solutions, and **E**valuate their products and process. Each of the four units that make up this product integrates design and engineering technology with three other subject areas, drawing from English language arts, history, geography, mathematics, science, art, and social studies.

The activities are open-ended and generally involve students in designing and making products that are relevant to their world and lifestyles. They range in duration from three to twelve weeks and use about two to three class periods per week. Many of the activities require students to work in small groups. Each activity concludes with a student self-evaluation form that applies a five-point rating scale to five criteria for success. The activities are formatted as single-page, reproducible student handouts, accompanied on the facing page by teacher notes.

There are forty-eight pages of introductory teacher materials that provide information and support for understanding and implementing the S.P.I.C.E. model in the activities. Help with supporting classroom management, using planning guides, extending activities, and locating additional resources is also provided.

Many of the activities offer students experience with technology topics found in the *Standards for Technological Literacy* (STL), such as understanding the core concepts of technology (Standard 2), connections between technology and other fields (Standard 3), the attributes of design (Standard 8), problem solving (Standard 10), applying the design process (Standard 11), and using and maintaining technological products and systems (Standard 12). In addition, Standards 17 (information and communication technologies) and 20 (construction technologies) are also used.

Design Connections Through Science and Technology: National Science and Technology Week 1996

Developer/Author:	National Science and Technology Week
Distributor/Publisher:	National Science Foundation
Publication date:	1996
Funders/Contributors:	National Science Foundation
Ordering information:	National Science Foundation, 4201 Wilson Boulevard, Room 1245, Arlington, VA 22330; download all or any part for free at www.nsf.gov/od/lpa/nstw/teach/nstw 1996/start.htm; 50 pp.

The 1996 National Science Foundation National Science and Technology week focused on technology design activities. This teacher monograph offers five investigations that have students design a headband, a wind-powered vehicle, a snack mix including packaging, an earthquake-resistant house, and an Antarctic community. Lists of skills used, subject areas involved, and estimated times for each activity begin each investigation. These are followed by background for the investigation, some with additional information sources, and an early childhood opportunity for use with younger children. One to three activities accompany each investigation laid out with the following sections for ease of use:

- Time Frame—ranging from one to eight forty-five-minute sessions
- Suggested Age Level—as young as six and up to fifteen
- Materials—lists of everyday objects
- Preparation and Procedure—step-by-step guide including prompts, assessment ideas, and the source of this activity
- Resources—a list of relevant books. Some activities have an extension/homework master titled Home and Community Connection.

The investigations are independent, touch on many areas of science, technology, and mathematics and thus can be used in any order that works best for your curriculum. There is one page of introduction about this packet and six pages of resources relevant to teaching design including organizations, books listed by reader levels, curriculum guides, videos in various formats, software, Internet resources, and magazines.

11

Web Sites and Other Informal Resources

These resources for students and teachers are grouped into five broad categories:

- Compendiums and Encyclopedias
- Inventors and Inventions
- Activities
- Other Resources (including, Guides and Handbooks; Research and Teacher Instruction; and Magazines, Journals, and Newsletters)
- Web Sites

We call some of these resources informal because they were not expressly designed to be used in classroom instruction. The informal resources can be found primarily in the first three categories. Most of the resources in Research and Teacher Instruction; Magazines, Journals, and Newsletters; and Web Sites were developed for classroom teachers, curriculum developers, and administrators. We believe that all of these resources, whether informal or otherwise, are excellent sources of ideas, information, inspiration, and guidance for technology teachers and students. Annotations are based on information supplied by the publishers or material provided in the books themselves.

The resources included in this list come from many sources, but this list is not intended to be comprehensive. Some were suggested to us by colleagues, some are personal favorites that are part of our own libraries, some come from Web searches, and some are the suggestions of technology and science teachers.

For more comprehensive and continuously updated listings of informal resources, you may want to target specific topics or authors on your favorite search engine.

■ COMPENDIUMS AND ENCYCLOPEDIAS

Bloomfield, L. (1997). *How Things Work: The Physics of Everyday Life*. New York: John Wiley & Sons. www.wiley.com

This book presents the basic principles of physics in contexts that make them understandable and relevant. The book demonstrates the power of physics to explain and predict phenomena with just a few basic principles and shows how they are woven through the fabric of everyday life.

Bridgman, R. (1995). *Technology*. New York: Dorling Kindersley. http://us.dk.com

This book contains full-color photography of the machines that make, shape, test, and use materials, plus 3-D models that explain the principles involved, reveal the innovations, and help us understand the research that transforms our lives.

Bridgman, R. (2002). *1000 Inventions and Discoveries*. New York: Dorling Kindersley. http://us.dk.com/

This book contains 1,000 groundbreaking moments in history. From accidental discoveries to meticulously worked-out theories, this book highlights the record of human achievement from the dawn of man to the present.

Bunch, B., & Hellemans, A. (1993). *The Timetables of Technology*. New York: Simon & Schuster. www.simonsays.com

This book contains a chronological time line of significant events in the history of technology, plus profiles of important figures and essays on key subjects and trends.

Eyewitness Guides. (2000–2001). New York: Dorling Kindersley. http://us.dk.com

This family reference book series is structured so that individual themes make up a complete visual story and a self-contained module. The following listing includes books in this series that contain technology- related material of interest to children ages 8–12.

Adams, S. *World War I*	Langley, A. *Medieval Life*
Adams, S. *World War II*	Margeson, S. *Viking*
Baquedano, *E. Aztec, Inca, and Maya*	Nahum, A. *Flying Machine*
Gifford, C. *Media and Communications*	Pearson, A. *Ancient Greece*
Gravett, C. *Castle*	Platt, R. *Pirate*
Gravett, C. *Knight*	Platt, R. *Spy*
Gribbin, J. & M. *Time and Space*	Putnam, J. *Pyramid*
Hammond, T. *Sports*	Stanchak. J. *Civil War*
James, S. *Ancient Rome*	Stott, C. *Space Exploration*
	Sutton, R. *Car*

Goodman, N., Wulffson, D., Austin, A., & Pierce, A. (1996). *Discover How Things Work*. Lincolnwood, IL: Publications International, Ltd.

This book contains hundreds of bright, full-color illustrations showing the parts and inner workings of more than 100 common devices. Clear explanations make it easy to understand exactly how machines work.

Hawcock, D. (1998). *Amazing Pop-up Pull-out Space Shuttle*. New York: Dorling Kindersley. http://us.dk.com

This book is for children ages 9–12 and has a four-foot-long, 3-D paper-sculpted poster of the space shuttle. The book contains additional illustrations and space facts that explain how the space shuttle flies and what life is like for the astronauts on a mission. Children can remove the flight deck to examine the spacecraft's inner workings.

Kindersley, B., Kindersley, A., & Copsey, S. (1995). *Children Just Like Me*. New York: Dorling Kindersley. http://us.dk.com

This book is for children ages 8 to 11 and contains photographs and text that depict homes, schools, family life, and culture of young people around the world.

Macaulay, D. (1998). *The New Way Things Work*. Boston: Houghton Mifflin. www.hmco.com

This book is for readers of all ages and has been especially designed for those who find technology intimidating. The book provides comprehensive coverage of the workings of hundreds of machines. The book also provides explanations of the scientific principles behind each machine.

Panati, C. (1987). *Extraordinary Origins of Everyday Things*. New York: Harper & Row. www.harpercollins.com

Fascinating stories behind the origins of more than 500 everyday items, expressions, and customs.

Parsons, Jayne (Ed.). (1995). *The Way Science Works*. New York: Macmillan. www.macmillan.com

This book contains anatomical illustrations that explore how everything works in modern science and technology, from cars and helicopters to holography and gene splicing. Accompanying essays written by experts make all areas of technology, from the everyday to the exotic, accessible to the nonspecialist.

Porter, A. (2003). *How Things Work (Discovery Series)*. New York: Time Life Books. www.timelife.com

This reference series for children ages 8–12 contains atmospheric illustrations; strong photographs and lively text engage and encourage readers to discover the world around them.

Tambini, M. (1998). *Future*. New York: Alfred A. Knopf. www.random house.com

This book provides a glimpse of the twenty-first century with changes in weather, energy, and transportation on the horizon. Contains detailed photographs that illustrate the events, innovations, and achievements of the last 100 years.

Turvey, P. (1995). *The X-Ray Picture Book of Everyday Things & How They Work*. New York: Franklin Watts. www.wattspublishing.co.uk

This book explores the workings of machines designed for everyday life and discovers the scientific principles, technical secrets, and stories behind familiar things and how they work.

UNICEF. (2002). *A Life Like Mine*. New York: Dorling Kindersley. http://us.dk.com

This book shows how children live around the world, looks at what life is like for children of different countries, and shows how each child can fulfill his or her hopes and ambitions no matter how little or how much their human rights are infringed upon.

■ INVENTORS AND INVENTIONS

Bailey, J. (1984). *Small Inventions That Make a Big Difference*. Washington, DC: National Geographic Society. www.nationalgeographic.com

This book includes stories about inventors, the story of plastics, and descriptions of inventions from A to Z.

Bender, L. (1991). *Invention*. London: Dorling Kindersley. http://us.dk.com

This book examines more than 27 different types of inventions and their improvements over time.

Berger, M. & G. (1993). *Telephones, Televisions, and Toilets*. Nashville, TN: Ideals Children's Books.

This book provides explanations of how household items work and how a child can help ensure that they keep working.

Brockman, J. (2000). *The Greatest Inventions of the Past 2,000 Years*. New York: Simon & Schuster. www.simonsays.com

In this book the question "What is the greatest invention of the past 2,000 years?" was posed to some of the world's foremost scientific and creative thinkers, including several Nobel laureates. This book provides an opportunity to peek into the minds of some of the greatest thinkers of our time.

Caney, S. (1985). *Steven Caney's Invention Book*. New York: Workman Publishing. www.workman.com

This book leads children ages ten years and up directly into the world of creativity. The book combines stories behind many products that are household words and urges children to tinker on their own.

Casey, S. (1997). *Women Invent! Two Centuries of Discovery That Have Shaped Our World*. Chicago: Chicago Review Press.

This book contains stories of successful women and girl inventors and takes the reader on a journey through the process of inventing—from coming up with an idea and developing a model to gaining a patent and having it manufactured and sold.

Catlin, D. (1994). *Inventa Books of Mechanisms*. London: Valiant Technology, Ltd. www.valiant-technology.com

This book explores the world of mechanisms through humorous cartoon characters. It shows how mechanisms work, where they can be found, and why they are used.

Cousins, M. (1997). *The Story of Thomas Alva Edison*. New York: Random House. www.randomhouse.com

This is a biography of the great inventor whose creations have contributed to the comfort, convenience, and entertainment of people all over the world.

Davidson, M. (1988). *The Story of Benjamin Franklin, Amazing American*. New York: Bantam Doubleday Dell Books. www.randomhouse.com

The biography of the son of a Boston candle maker who became a scientist, writer, statesman, newspaperman, diplomat, and philosopher.

Davidson, M. (1990). *The Story of Thomas Alva Edison*. New York: Scholastic. www.scholastic.com

This simple biography of a genius may be the first step to learning about this brilliant man, who dedicated his time, ingenuity, and efforts toward achieving his dreams with an endless spirit of innovation.

Dunn, C. (1998). *The Giza Power Plant: Technologies of Ancient Egypt*. New York: Bear and Company.

An engineer takes a look at the Great Pyramid of Giza and the ancient technology behind it.

Egan, L. (1997). *Inventors and Inventions*. New York: Scholastic. www.scholastic.com

This book is filled with teaching ideas that help students explore the history of inventions and develop problem-solving skills that inventors use. Students explore the impact of inventions on history, create Inventor Trading Cards, and work cooperatively in an invention challenge.

Erlbach, A. (1997). *The Kids' Invention Book*. Minneapolis, MN: Lerner Learning Company.

This book takes kids through the step-by-step invention process. Children learn how to come up with an original idea, then how to test that idea and improve it until the product really works. Children learn how to protect their invention so no one else can make or sell it.

Flatow, I. (1992). *They All Laughed . . .* New York: HarperCollins Publishers. www.harpercollins.com

This book contains 24 biographies of inventors and some of their inventions and asks the question "Who is the real inventor?" The book attempts to demythologize the world of invention and discovery and prove that the real truth about inventors and their inventions is stranger than fiction.

Jones, C. (1991). *Mistakes That Worked*. New York: Doubleday. www.randomhouse.com

This book contains forty unusual stories about inventions we use almost every day that had surprisingly haphazard beginnings.

Jones, C. (1996). *Accidents May Happen.* New York: Bantam Doubleday Dell Publishing Group. www.randomhouse.com

This book contains 50 unusual stories about inventions we use almost every day that began by accident or mistake.

Karnes, F., et al. (1995). *Girls & Young Women Inventing: Twenty True Stories About Inventors Plus How You Can Be One Yourself.* Minneapolis, MN: Free Spirit Publishing. www.freespirit.com

This book profiles young female inventors showing how perseverance, ingenuity, common sense, and the enjoyment of problem solving leads to award-winning products and inventions. This book is for children in Grades 4–8.

Parker, S., & West, D. (1992). *53 ½ Things That Changed the World.* Brookfield, CT: Millbrook Press. www.millbrookpress.com

This book discusses topics ranging from the discovery of fire and the wheel to modern creations such as the jet engine and computers. Some of the world's great inventing disasters are described as well.

Perfect Inventions = Perfect World. (2000). New York: Scholastic. www.scholastic.com

A book of fanciful inventions written by the fifth-grade students of the Pickens Elementary School in South Carolina.

Petroski, H. (1992). *The Evolution of Useful Things: How Everyday Artifacts—From Forks and Pins to Paper Clips and Zippers—Came to Be As They Are.* New York: A. Knopf.

The human history behind common things we use every day, plus a new theory that technological innovation is the response to the perceived failures of existing products.

Platt, R. (1997). *Inventions Explained: A Beginner's Guide to Technological Breakthroughs.* New York: Henry Holt and Company. www.henryholt.com

This book provides an in-depth look at the earliest of tools, advancing through time and technology to highlight systems of measure, transportation, energy, medicine, machinery, and computing.

St. George, J. (2002). *So You Want to Be an Inventor?* New York: Philomel Books. www.penguinputnam.com

This book is an inspiring, witty look at history and inventions. A perfect introduction for children to the inventors and inventions that keep the world humming.

Sobel, D. (1996). *Longitude: The True Story of a Lone Genius Who Solved the Greatest Scientific Problem of His Time.* New York: Walker and Company. www.walkerbooks.com

This is a remarkable story of a clock maker who invented the chronometer, which revolutionized navigation at sea.

Sobey, E. (1996). *Inventing Stuff.* Palo Alto, CA: Dale Seymour Publications. www.pearsonpublishing.com

This book encourages young people (Grades 6–9) to use their creative talents to invent solutions to problems. Kids take time to ponder, tinker, experiment, play with ideas, and sharpen their critical thinking and problem-solving skills.

Sobey, E. (1999). *Young Inventors at Work! Learning Science by Doing Science.* New York: Addison-Wesley. www.awprofessional.com

This book challenges kids to use problem solving and critical thinking to design, build, and test model structures, games, and vehicles.

Sobey, E. (2001). *Inventing Toys: Kids Having Fun Learning Science.* Tucson, AZ: Zephyr Press. www.zephyrpress.com

This book provides a combination of invention and toy making to encourage students (age 12 and up) to design and fabricate working toys while learning the fundamentals of science, design, and the creative process. Toys range from cars to electric fans to rockets.

Taylor, B. (1995). *I Wonder Why Zippers Have Teeth and Other Questions About Inventions.* New York: Kingfisher. www.kingfisherpub.com

This book asks and answers 31 questions about inventions ranging from "Why do people invent things?" to "Are there insects on Mars?"

Thimmesh, C. (2000). *Girls Think of Everything.* Boston: Houghton Mifflin. www.hmco.com

This book chronicles women and their inventions. Women combine their curiosity and creativity to create cancer-fighting drugs, space helmets, coffeemakers, disposable diapers, and computer software.

Tomecek, S. (2003). *What a Great Idea! Inventions That Changed the World.* New York: Scholastic. www.scholastic.com

This book places significant inventions and discoveries in a historical context. The text is divided into five broad time periods and contains a series of essays on important advances that occurred in each "age." This book is for children in Grades 5–9.

Tucker, T. (1995). *Brainstorm! The Stories of Twenty American Kid Inventors.* New York: Farrar, Strauss and Giroux. www.fsgbooks.com

A book that shows serious inventors need not be adults and that inventions need not be complex, expensive machines to be patentable, marketable, and, sometimes, lucrative.

Williams, T. (2000). *A History of Invention: From Stone Axes to Silicon Chips.* New York: Facts on File, Inc. www.factsonfile.com

This book familiarizes the reader with the technological process and discusses how each technological innovation met a critical need while creating the demand and opportunity for the next breakthrough.

Wood, R. (1995). *Great Inventions.* Time Life Books. www.timelife.com

This book is part of The Nature Company Discoveries Library series for children. Illustrations, photographs, and lively text engage and encourage children to discover for themselves the world around them.

Wulffson, D. (2001). *The Kid Who Invented the Trampoline.* New York: Dutton Children's Books. www.penguinputnam.com

This book contains 50 stories about how things we take for granted came to be. Stories are presented in alphabetical order.

Wyatt, V. (2003). *Invention (FAQ)*. Tonawanda, NY: Kids Can Press. www.ibby-canada.org

This book features the Frequently Asked Questions (FAQ) format often used on the Internet along with activities and fascinating facts. It is for children ages 9–12 and answers questions and provides inspiration for them to come up with bright ideas of their own.

■ ACTIVITIES—COLLECTIONS, INDIVIDUAL, AND SERIES

Ardley, N. (1995). *How Things Work*. Pleasantville, NY: Reader's Digest Publications. www.rd.com

This book for children age 12 and up contains step-by-step experiments that investigate different aspects of technology and how machines work. Students can build machines and devices that actually work, such as microphones and simple computers. Each experiment contains a listing of materials, colorful photographs, diagrams, illustrations, clear instructions, and useful background information.

Berenstain, J. & S. (1996). *The Berenstain Bears Fly-It!* New York: Random House. www.randomhouse.com

A reading and activity book for young readers with activities involving air-powered (balloon engines) paper airplanes, an ascension balloon, and a space station.

Carrow, R. (1997). *Put a Fan in Your Hat!* New York: McGraw-Hill. www.mcgraw-hill.com

This book for children in Grades 3–8 explores concepts in electricity and physics through twelve activities.

Challenges in Physical Science, DESIGNS Project (2004). Dubuque, IA: Kendall/Hunt. www.kendallhunt.com. Or e-mail: hcoyle@cfa.harvard.edu

Six science engineering modules from the DESIGNS Project (**D**oable **E**ngineering **S**cience **I**nvestigations **G**eared for **N**on-science **S**tudents) at the Science Education Department, Harvard-Smithsonian Center for Astrophysics. The Grades 5–9 modules focus on batteries, bridges, electromagnets, gravity cars, solar houses, and windmills.

City Technology Curriculum Guides, Center for Children and Technology (CDE), Educational Development Center (EDC). (1997–2002). New York: City College of New York.

These guides are a collaborative effort to create field-tested, integrated design and technology curricular materials for elementary-level teachers.

Gregson, R. (2001). *Archigames: 50 Activities to Build Creative Thinkers*. New York: McGraw-Hill. www.mcgraw-hill.com

This book contains innovative, simple games and projects that explore how human-constructed environments affect the world around us and direct our everyday decisions and movement. This is for children in Grades 3–5.

Nelson, D. (1984). *Transformations: Process and Theory.* Order through Web site at www.csupomona.edu/~dnelson/ordering.html

A curriculum guide giving step-by-step details and ideas for implementing City Building Education in the classroom.

Nolan, A. (1998). *Understand Garbage and Our Environment.* New York: McGraw-Hill. www.mcgraw-hill.com

This book contains thought-provoking, cutting-edge activities and builds middle-schoolers' science while promoting awareness of complex environmental issues, including recycling, waste reduction, and other topics.

O'Brien-Palmer, M. (2002). *How the Earth Works: 60 Fun Activities for Exploring Volcanoes, Fossils, Earthquakes and More.* Chicago: Chicago Review Press.

This book contains activities, games, and experiments for children ages 6–9 that explore the Earth's structure, features, and changing landscape. Children explore the causes of earthquakes and make model volcanoes with lava flows.

Press, J., & Williamson, S. (1996). *Vroom! Vroom! Making Dozers, 'Copters, Trucks & More.* Charlotte, VT: Williamson Publishing. www. idealspubli cations.com

This book for children ages 5–11 provides instructions for using milk cartons, egg cartons, and other materials to make cars, buses, sailboats, and more.

Romanek, T. (2001). *The Technology Book for Girls and Other Advanced Beings.* Tonawanda, NY: Kids Can Press. www.ibby-canada.org/

This book contains interactive activities and shows how everyday technology works. Children learn how infrared light opens an automatic door, how light travels through fiber-optic cables, and how to test the power of radio waves in a microwave oven.

Smyth, I. (1998). *The Amazing Inventions of Professor Screwloose.* Santa Fe, NM: Envision Publishing LLC.

This mechanical pop-up book provides some scientific experiments and the construction of a 3D barking model of a robot-like dog.

Ultimate LEGO Book. (1999). New York: Dorling Kindersley. http://us. dk.com

Introduces the world of model making with LEGOs, featuring life-size sculptures of dinosaurs, monuments, buildings, and other items. This book is for children ages 12 and up.

VanCleave, J. (1993). *Machines.* New York: John Wiley & Sons. www. wiley.com

This book includes 20 simple and fun experiments using inexpensive materials with minimum preparation and clean up. Also includes additional suggestions on how students can develop their own science fair project.

Vecchione, G. (1999). *100 First-Prize Make-It-Yourself Science Fair Projects.* New York: Sterling. www.sterlingpub.com

This book contains science and technology projects for children ages 8 to 12. Projects include solar-powered machines and a kite sighter.

Wiese, J. (1995). *Rocket Science: 50 Flying, Floating, Spinning Gadgets Kids Create Themselves.* New York: John Wiley & Sons. www.wiley.com

This book contains projects to teach children the science behind everyday things. Topics covered include mechanics, air and waterpower, electricity and magnetism, chemistry, and optics. Each activity features step-by-step instructions and a list of inexpensive materials found at home or in neighborhood stores.

Woelfle, G. (1997). *The Wind at Work: An Activity Guide to Windmills.* Chicago: Chicago Review Press.

This guide provides activities and explains how the wind works, what windmills have contributed in the past, and why they offer environmental promise today as a source of clean, renewable energy.

Zubrowski, B. (1986). *Wheels at Work: Building and Experimenting with Models of Machines,* New York: William Morrow. www.harpercollins.com

This is a book for children in Grades 5–9 containing experiments using wheels as part of simple machines. Children learn how to build models of pulley systems, gear systems, water wheels, windmills, paddle wheels, and the windlass. All materials are common household objects.

Zubrowski, B. (1989). *Tops: Building and Experimenting With Spinning Toys.* New York: William Morrow. www.harpercollins.com

This book for children Grades 5–9 promotes the fun and enjoyment of constructing toys and experimenting with them. Directions are given for building these toys in such a way that one characteristic can be changed, allowing experimenters to compare the behavior of two objects. Construction materials may be found at home or purchased at a nearby store.

Zubrowski, B. (1990). *Balloons: Building and Experimenting With Inflatable Toys.* New York: William Morrow. www.harpercollins.com

This book for children ages 9–12 introduces them to the physical properties of gases and the scientific concepts of force and pressure.

Zubrowski, B. (1991). *Blinkers and Buzzers: Building and Experimenting With Electricity and Magnetism.* New York: Beech Tree Books. www.harpercollins.com

This book contains fifty creative experiments that show how and why traffic lights, telegraphs, and burglar alarms work while providing hands-on learning.

Zubrowski, B. (1993). *Mobiles: Building and Experimenting with Balancing Toys.* Oxford, UK: Beech Tree Books. www.harpercollins.com

This book for children in Grades 3–7 contains simple activities to demonstrate various concepts of balance. The book contains more than fifty experiments demonstrating how toys and sculptures that defy gravity actually work.

Zubrowski, B. (1995). *Shadow Play: Making Pictures With Light and Lenses.* Oxford, UK: Beech Tree Books. www.harpercollins.com

This book offers activities for children ages 4–8 designed to help children learn through playing with light. The book contains more than 50 experiments grouped into three sections: shadows in natural and artificial light, construction of a shadow box and associated activities, and the construction of a camera box.

OTHER RESOURCES—GUIDES AND HANDBOOKS; RESEARCH AND TEACHER INSTRUCTION; MAGAZINES, JOURNALS, AND NEWSLETTERS ■

Guides and Handbooks

Balkwill, R. (1999). *The Best Book of Trains.* Boston: Houghton Mifflin & Company. www.hmco.com

This book for children ages 5–8 introduces all sorts of trains from around the world, explaining how they are constructed and how they run, and who drives them.

Bingham, C. (1998). *Big Book of Monster Machines.* New York: Dorling Kindersley. http://us.dk.com

Photographs and text examine the parts and functions of such large machines as trucks, jets, supertankers, tractors, bulldozers, and fire engines. This book is for children ages 5 to 8.

Nelson, D. (1982). *City Building Education: A Way to Learn.* Order through Web site at www.csupomona.edu/~dnelson/ordering.html

The theory behind City Building methodology and an introduction to the work of Doreen Nelson. Still timely and useful.

Norman, D. (1990). *The Design of Everyday Things.* New York: Doubleday. www.randomhouse.com

This book is a collection of examples of good and bad design that includes some simple rules for designers and prompts readers to think about how they interact with their surroundings.

Sonenklar, C. (1999). *Robots Rising.* New York: Henry Holt & Company. www.henryholt.com

This book defines and describes current and future robot technology for children age 10 and up. The book includes robots that defuse bombs, assist with medical procedures, explore volcanoes, and more. There is a glossary with many different robotic terms.

Research and Teacher Instruction

Brooks-Young, S. (2002). *Making Technology Standards Work for You: A Guide for School Administrators.* Eugene, OR: International Society for Technology in Education (ISTE). www.iste.org

This resource offers a step-by-step approach to help administrators develop and implement a vision for using educational technology more effectively. Each chapter focuses on an element of educational leadership—planning, curriculum and instruction, assessment, staff development, and legal and social issues—showing how to assess what is in place already and determine what needs to be done next.

Cross, G. (1994). *Technology and American Society: A History.* Upper Saddle River, NJ: Pearson Educational. www.pearsonpublishing.com

This book contains a survey of the history of technology in America, from 1700 to the present. It covers the history of inventions with discussions of the social, economic, and cultural effects of technology.

Eggleston, J. (1992). *Teaching Design and Technology.* Buckingham, UK: Open University Press. www.mcgraw-hill.com

Design and technology is one of the fastest growing areas of the contemporary school curriculum. The author shows how this area has come to occupy a new and central place in the school curriculum and highlights the higher status and new identity now accorded to technology.

International Society for Technology in Education (ISTE). (2000). *National Educational Technology Standards for Students: Connecting Curriculum and Technology.* Eugene, OR: Author. www.iste.org

This edition of the *National Educational Technology Standards for Students* (NETS) offers more than 36 teacher-created lesson plans and activities for Grades K–12 that connect NETS with multiple subject areas and their content standards. Units for each grade range provide developmentally appropriate themes, tools, and resources from which teachers can choose when developing specific learning experiences for their classrooms. Also includes the full text of the National Educational Technology Standards for Students.

International Technology Education Association (ITEA). (2000). *Standards for Technological Literacy: Content for Study of Technology.* Reston, VA: Author. www.iteawww.org

This book describes what students should know and be able to do in order to be technologically literate. Standards include specific benchmarks for knowledge and abilities for 20 technology education standards for Grades K–2, 3–5, 6–8, and 9–12.

International Technology Education Association (ITEA). (2003). *Advancing Excellence in Technological Literacy: Student Assessment, Professional Development, and Program Standards.* Reston, VA: Author. www.iteawww.org

A companion document to *Standards for Technological Literacy: Content for Study of Technology,* this book presents standards and enabling guidelines for student assessment, professional development of teachers, and the program infrastructure associated with the study of technology in Grades K–12.

International Technology Education Association (ITEA), *Professional Publications Series.* (2000–2004). Web site: www.iteawww.org/H1d.html

From the ITEA Center to Advance the Teaching of Technology and Science (CATTS), this series of professional publications is based on

Standards for Technological Literacy: Content for the Study of Technology and is designed for developing contemporary, standards-based K–12 technology education programs. Titles include

Exploring Technology: A Standards-Based Middle School Model Course Guide

Foundations of Technology: A Standards-Based High School Model Course Guide

A Guide to Develop Standards-Based K–12 Technology Education

Measuring Progress: A Guide to Assessing Students for Technological Literacy

Models for Introducing Technology: A Standards-Based Guide

Planning Learning: A Guide to Developing Technology Curricula

Realizing Excellence: A Guide for Exemplary Programs in Technological Literacy

Teaching Technology: High School Strategies for Standards-Based Instruction

Teaching Technology: Middle School Strategies for Standards-Based Instruction

Technology Starters Guide: A Standards-Based Guide

Johnsey, R. (1991). *Design and Technology Through Problem Solving.* London: Simon & Schuster. www.simonsays.com

Nonspecialist teachers will find that this handbook helps teachers introduce design and technology into the primary/middle school classroom. Using an open-ended problem-solving approach, this book describes projects that may be undertaken by children of varying abilities. Although these projects increase in their complexity as the book proresses, they do not require expensive or complicated equipment.

Petroski, H. (1985). *To Engineer Is Human: The Role of Failure in Successful Design.* New York: St Martin's Press. www.stmartins.com

The author uses several examples to demonstrate that engineering successes are often the result of a long succession of spectacular, but forgotten, failures.

Pool, R. (1997). *Beyond Engineering: How Society Shapes Technology.* Oxford, UK: Oxford University Press. www.oup-usa.org

This book presents the often-complex ways machines and society interact. The author demonstrates that technology is shaped not only by engineering but also by cultural values, economics, management, and history.

Ross, C. (1994). *Girls as Constructors in the Early Years: Promoting Equal Opportunity in Math, Science and Technology.* Stoke on Trent, UK: Trentham Books. www.trentham-books.co.uk

This handbook sets out ways of involving girls in constructional activities and analyzes the management issues that determine their achievement.

Tenner, E. (1996). *Why Things Bite Back: Technology and the Revenge of Unanticipated Consequences.* New York: Cambridge University Press.www.cup.org

This book presents basic economic issues and technological change that have had the greatest impact on society since 1750.

Wright, R., Israel, E., & Lauda, D. (1993). *A Decision-Maker's Guide to Technology Education.* Reston, VA: ITEA. www.iteawww.org

This is a concise and helpful booklet that provides educators and policymakers with a rationale for studying technology education, a description of what technology education is (including goals for the field and content), guidance for teaching technology, how to structure programs and courses in technology education, and a call for action.

Magazines, Journals, and Newsletters

Bright Ideas Magazine. www.iteawww.org/brightideasform.html

Bright Ideas is a service provided by the International Technology Education Association (ITEA), with the intent of promoting technological literacy in our school systems. This online publication is e-mailed four times per year and is free to subscribers.

Edutopia. www.glef.org/php/magform.php

Edutopia is the George Lucas Education Foundation's magazine (paper and online) that gives practical, hands-on insight into what works now, what's on the horizon, and who's shaping the changing future of education. Free to qualified subscribers.

Journal of Technology Education. http://scholar.lib.vt.edu/ejournals/JTE/v15n1/editor.html

This e-journal from Virginia Polytechnic Institute and State University contains articles, reviews, and information about current technology education practices and research. Free.

Learning and Leading With Technology. www.techlearning.com

This publication from the International Society for Technology in Education (ISTE) features practical, useable ideas for improving educational outcomes with technology.

Teacher Chronicles. www.iteawww.org/TeacherChronicles/teachchron.html

These online stories follow technology teachers throughout the school year, showing readers the real-life challenges, triumphs, and insights of teachers "in the trenches." Free.

Techniques. www.acteonline.org

Published eight times a year by the Association for Career and Technical Education, this magazine brings news of legislation affecting technical education, in-depth features on issues and programs, profiles of educators, and more.

Technology and Children. www.iteawww.org/F2.html

T&C is packed with practical, innovative, and creative articles and activities for the elementary teacher. Interdisciplinary learning program successes and other current issues are addressed. Each issue delivers fresh ideas for classroom use. Published four times per year. Available to ITEA members only.

The Technology Teacher. www.iteawww.org/F1.html

Published eight times a year, this journal is for technology education professionals from elementary school teachers to middle school, junior high, and high school classroom teachers, as well as educators of teachers. Articles cover many issues, including technology learning activities, new programs, and reports of current trends in technological education. Available to ITEA members only.

T.H.E. Journal (Technological Horizons in Education). www.thejournal.com/

This journal covers issues and information about the current state of technology education and educational technology. Subscription only.

ties Magazine. www.tiesmagazine.org/

This online Magazine of Design & Technology Education (*ties*) provides stories and ideas for integrating math, science, and technology primarily in middle, junior, and senior high school curricula. Articles emphasize design and problem solving as instructional techniques. Subscription only.

TrendScout. www.iteawww.org

ITEA's *TrendScout* is one electronic service provided by ITEA to keep members up-to-date with the latest information, directions, and activities of the technology education profession. *TrendScout* is offered as a PDF that can be viewed, downloaded, or printed. Available only to current ITEA members.

WEB SITES ■

Association for Career and Technical Education (ACTE). www.acteonline.org

ACTE is the largest national education association dedicated to the advancement of education that prepares youth and adults for careers. This area offers information about the history, mission, and structure of ACTE, as well as details on their annual awards program and information about how you can participate in the annual observance of Career and Technical Education Week.

Eisenhower National Clearinghouse (ENC). www.enc.org/

The Eisenhower National Clearinghouse for Mathematics and Science Education (ENC) identifies effective curriculum resources, creates high-quality professional development materials, and disseminates useful information and products to improve K–12 mathematics and science teaching and learning. ENC Online features Web links, curriculum resources, professional development, and education topics.

EngineerGirl. www.engineergirl.org

This site for girls about engineers and engineering careers features a Gallery of Women Engineers, an Ask an Engineer option, a career quiz, and an increasing number of engineering links.

Gateway to Educational Materials (GEM). www.thegateway.org/

The Gateway to Educational Materials (GEM) is a Consortium effort to provide educators with quick and easy access to thousands of educational resources found on various federal, state, university, nonprofit, and commercial Internet sites. Funded by the U.S. Department of Education. Teachers, parents, and administrators can search or browse GEM and find thousands of educational materials, including lesson plans, activities, and projects from more than 500 of the 700+ GEM Consortium members.

Innovative Curriculum Online Network (ICON). http://icontechlit. enc.org/external/icon_mission/0,4898,,00.shtm

The National Science Foundation has provided funding to establish a central source and comprehensive digital collection for technological literacy resources. The International Technology Education Association (ITEA) and the Eisenhower National Clearinghouse (ENC) created ICON, The National Digital Library for Technological Literacy, so that K–12 classroom teachers and college and university faculty will be able to locate digital resources concerned with technological literacy content and pedagogy The site currently contains more than 2,200 entries for materials in the public domain.

International Technology Education Association (ITEA). www.iteawww.org

This site is an exhaustive source of information, publications, links, resources, news, professional development, threaded conversation groups, and the latest updates on the Standards for Technological Literacy (STL).

National Science Teachers Association (NSTA). www.nsta.org/ostbs04

This site features a wide variety of resources, information, and related links for science educators. The Teacher Resources subsite offers a very large annotated listing of trade books for K–12 children, including a sizeable section on technology trade books.

Teaching and learning through design, creativity, and technology. http:// www.csupomona.edu/~dnelson/doreen.html

This is the official site of the Center for City Building Education. The Center was founded by Doreen Nelson more than thirty years ago with the goal to help children develop and unleash their creative skills, to improve teaching skills, and to raise the standards in academic performance in reading, math, language, science, and cognitive skills, with technology as a tool to manipulate those subjects. Aimed at elementary and secondary students, project-based activities merge the practical with the theoretical.

Technology Student Association (TSA). www.tsawww.org/

The Technology Student Association (TSA) is a national nonprofit organization devoted exclusively to the needs of elementary, middle, and high school students with a dedicated interest in technology. The site features information, resources, and Web links to conferences and programs, competitive events, and forums.

T.H.E. Online. www.thejournal.com

This is a great "one-stop shop" for teachers interested in technology in education, including T.H.E. (Technological Horizons in Education) Journal, EduHound, e-newsletters, and Web links to other technology and education resources.

Appendix A

MORE BENCHMARK-LEVEL ANALYSES ■

Can the textbooks in Chapter 8 give middle school students a foundation for becoming technologically literate by the end of high school? As noted in a Chapter 5 discussion, the glass is both half-empty, half-full.

Given the heft of textbooks, in theory they have the room to cover everything essential, but do they? The individual reviews in Chapter 8 spell out the books' standard-by-standard coverage of the Standards for Technological Literacy (STL), in more detail than publishers do, based on our page-by-page, line-by-line inspection. (Chapter 4 introduces our study methods, and Appendix B provides a few specifics.)

However, the most exacting and most meaningful level of determining whether the textbooks are standards-based is checking to see which of the STL benchmarks they address. "*Benchmarks* . . . provide the *fundamental* content elements for the broadly stated Standards; The Benchmarks are *required* for students to meet the Standards" (emphasis added; ITEA, 2000, pp. 14–15). Yet, in our experience, the benchmarks mostly are overlooked in discussions about products' alignment with the STL.

In Chapter 8 we provided two kinds of information about benchmark coverage within each of the standards: the percentage of material that covers at least one benchmark (standards-based) and which benchmark(s) are most prevalent in the textbook.

For those interested in digging a little deeper on their own, Table A.1 provides more specifics about benchmark coverage for each of the twenty standards in each of the five textbooks, including:

- A listing of all the benchmarks present,
- The number of times that we find these benchmarks in the textbook, and
- The grade range of the benchmark (K–5 versus 6–8 versus 9–12).

From Table A.1, one can start to investigate how *broad* a range of benchmarks is covered within each standard. Using a common refrain of the Third International Mathematics and Science Study (TIMSS), is the curriculum a "mile wide and an inch deep," or "a mile deep and an inch wide?" (Schmidt, Raizen, Britton, Bianchi, & Wolfe, 1997). The optimal approach lies somewhere between these extremes.

The textbooks generally struck a reasonable balance. Among the set of the textbooks, 55 to 66 percent of the standards are addressed by a range of their benchmarks. Even for those "balanced" standards, however, each book still left out at least one of the corresponding benchmarks. For the other third to almost

Table A.1 Benchmark-level analysis

STL standard	Technology: Shaping Our World John B. Gradwell, Malcolm Welch, and Eugene Martin		Technology Education: Learning by Design Michael Hacker and David Burghardt		Technology: Design and Applications R. Thomas Wright and Ryan A. Brown		Technology Interactions Henry R. Harms and Neal R. Swernofsky		Technology in Action Brad and Terry Thode	
	Benchmarks covered by text	Benchmarks covered by activities	Benchmarks covered by text	Benchmarks covered by activities	Benchmarks covered by text	Benchmarks covered by activities	Benchmarks covered by text	Benchmarks covered by activities	Benchmarks covered by text	Benchmarks covered by activities
1	F G K (15)	F G J (15)	C F G H K L (15)	F G H (5)	D F G H I M (18)	D F (2)	F (1)	—	*D F G H J (13)	*F (3)
2	D F H I J K L M N O P Q R S T V CC EE (124)	H I J K N O T V (46)	*D F H I J K M N O P R S T U V X Y Z BB EE (169)	H J M N R S V Z EE (120)	H I J K M N O P Q S T U V EE (84)	*H I J K N V (18)	B F H I K M N S T V CC DD (38)	J K Q V (8)	F H I J K M P R S DD EE (47)	B D E F I J K M N S DD EE (23)
3	E F H (24)	F (3)	*E F I (32)	D F (23)	D E F (17)	*E F (10)	E F (86)	F (12)	C E F I J (38)	C E F I (25)
4	D E F G I J K (43)	D (4)	C D E F G I (29)	D E I (8)	C D E G (28)	*D E (8)	D E F G (35)	—	*D E F H (15)	*D E (6)
5	B D E F J K L (27)	*B D J (6)	D E F K (8)	F (1)	D E F (6)	*D (8)	C D E F I J K L (44)	D I (5)	C D F (12)	D F J (16)
6	D E F G (7)	E J (5)	D E F G I (8)	E (3)	*D E F G (30)	D (3)	D E F (8)	G (2)	D F (3)	* (1)
7	D F H I N (10)	B (2)	*B E G H I K N O (32)	—	*B C D E F H J K N O (25)	*G J K N O (9)	D I O (16)	D (1)	*B C D E J N O (9)	* (1)
8	*E G H (13)	*G (24)	G H J (5)	E G H J (145)	C D E F G H (56)	*E F G (8)	*E F G (14)	E F G (9)	E G (11)	E (10)

296

9	FHI (22)	GHIK (7)	GHK (4)	FGH (108)	*DFGHIKL (137)	FHIL (15)	CFGH (28)	FGHI (65)	FGHI (14)	CGIK (6)
10	(0)	GIJ (12)	HI (2)	H (6)	EFGHIJ (23)	GH (6)	FGH (5)	H (17)	FGHI (7)	*GH (13)
11	(0)	HIJKL MN (169)	HIJKL (7)	HIJKLOP (345)	(0)	HIJKLN (87)	HJL (4)	HIJKL (333)	— (0)	*BHIJ KLR (228)
12	EH (111)	EGHIJLP (73)	HJLP (53)	DHJKLP (173)	EHK (86)	*DEGHIJ KLP (76)	EHIJLP (71)	ADEH JKLP (88)	HIJ (30)	ADE HIJKLP (135)
13	G (1)	CFGJ (19)	GIL (7)	FGHIJL (19)	FGHI (7)	DFGH (21)	FGH (3)	*DFGHK (16)	— (0)	EFGHI (25)
14	*GJKL (11)	C (4)	*EGJK (12)	EFG (4)	CFGHIJ (11)	CG (4)	GIJ (16)	G (2)	GJ (6)	G (1)
15	DFG HIJLM (11)	DIJL (4)	DFGHIL (18)	DHIJ (4)	FGHIJ (23)	* (2)	FGHI (22)	HI (3)	DGHI (5)	— (0)
16	*CDEFG HJKLM (106)	*DFHKM (19)	*EFGHIJ KMN (71)	*FGHK (10)	EFGHI JKMN (66)	*DFIK (12)	*EFGHIN (47)	*EFGH (13)	*CEFG HIJKM (39)	*FHIKM (17)
17	*FHIJKN OPQ (31)	*IJKNP (36)	HIJK LNOP (90)	HIJKNP (25)	*AHIJKNP (94)	*AFHI JKMP (28)	*HIJ KLNP (62)	JKNP (18)	*EHIJKNP (41)	*HIJKP (28)
18	*DEF GHIK (24)	(2)	*FGHIKL (24)	GHI (4)	FGHIK (26)	*FG (4)	FHIK (5)	*GH (5)	*DEFGI (20)	*DFGI (9)
19	*CFH IJMOP (64)	*FHKO (7)	*ADEFG HIJKMO PQR (94)	FHIKM (12)	FGHIJ KMOP (41)	FHKO (9)	FHIJ KMOP (34)	FHK (5)	DFGH IKMO (19)	*HJKO (9)
20	*ACFG IKLMN (37)	*CFGH (9)	*AFGH IJKMN (32)	ADFL (9)	CFGHI (22)	*CFG (7)	BFGHKN (39)	F (4)	*CFILN (12)	*BCDF (14)

Benchmarks in boldface indicate the Grades 6–8 benchmarks. Benchmarks left of bold are Grades K–2 or 3–5. Benchmarks right of bold are Grades 9–12.

Values in parentheses indicate the total number of times that any benchmark occurred.

An asterisk (*) in front of benchmarks indicates instances when no specific benchmarks were covered, but the broad topic of the standard was addressed.

half of the standards (33 to 45 percent), their content focused on just one or a couple of benchmarks and ignored the rest.

The next two tables illustrate a balanced or broad range of benchmarks covered within a standard and a narrow benchmark coverage within a standard, respectively. In Table A.2, a range of benchmarks are covered within Standard 16. In Table A.3, the books' attention is placed almost solely on one benchmark (5D) and barely touches on Benchmarks 5E or 5F, if at all.

Table A.2   Number of instances that textbooks addressed each benchmark of Standard 16 (broad benchmark coverage)

Benchmark	Total	Book 1	Book 2	Book 3	Book 4	Book 5
16E—energy is the capacity to do work	17	2	7	5	2	1
16F—energy can be used in many processes	87	10	28	9	10	30
16G—power is the rate at which energy is converted	21	1	10	3	1	6
16H—power systems drive other technology systems	43	7	10	11	4	11
16I—energy is not used efficiently in our environment	34	17	1	1	15	0

Table A.3   Number of instances that textbooks addressed each benchmark of Standard 5 (narrow benchmark coverage)

Benchmark	Total	Book 1	Book 2	Book 3	Book 4	Book 5
5D—importance of waste management to society	71	24	20	3	15	9
5E—technology use to repair damage from natural disasters	9	0	3	3	0	3
5F—using technologies often puts environment/ economic concerns in competition	7	2	1	2	1	1

Appendix B

A LITTLE MORE ABOUT METHODS ■

Some readers and researchers in particular may want to know a little more about our methods of analyzing the products. Most of the following information pertains to how we analyzed a product's alignment with the Standards for Technological Literacy (STL) standards and benchmarks.

The three authors initially spent weeks becoming thoroughly familiar with every page of the STL document. All of us then spent two more weeks coding the content of the same product against the STL benchmarks.

Typically, we coded a chapter or two, compared and discussed our results, and coded some more. We continued this for the better part of four more products to attain an interrater reliability in our coding of 93 percent at the standards level and 82 percent at the benchmarks level when examining the text, or prose, portions of the books. Our training process for coding the activities was similar to the previously mentioned one, except we sampled activities across many products. The interrater reliability was 91 percent. From then on, we individually coded products, but consulted with each other almost daily, especially whenever any new issue arose.

We developed this approach in part by drawing on our work in previous, similar research studies. During the Third International Mathematics and Science Study (TIMSS), McKnight and Britton (1992) developed empirical procedures for analyzing the content of mathematics and science curricular resources of more than twenty-five countries. The method involved comparing topics covered to the science and mathematics frameworks of TIMSS. For *Connecting Mathematics and Science Curricula to Workplace Contexts*, Britton and colleagues (1999) employed a more qualitative inspection. They evaluated the ways in which curricula illustrated how mathematics and science are used in various vocations and workplaces. De Long-Cotty and colleagues recently evaluated hundreds of curricular resources that utilize a project-based-learning design (or PBL, see www.pblnet.org).

In addition to our prior methods, we considered curriculum analysis methods developed by other leading organizations. For example, Project 2061 at the American Association for the Advancement of Science (AAAS) uses a rigorous process for empirically examining mathematics and science curricula (AAAS, 2000). The Education Development Center created a detailed framework for selecting mathematics curricula (Goldsmith, Mark, & Kantrov,

2000). Our colleagues at WestEd along with those at BSCS recently created an analytical process for choosing science curricula: the AIMS process.

For judging the readability of textbooks, Lexile scores were computed using the Lexile Framework for Reading. Grade-level ratings were awarded based on the Fry Readability Graph.

References

American Association for the Advancement of Science, Project 2061. (1989). *Science for all Americans*. Washington, DC: Author.

American Association for the Advancement of Science, Project 2061. (1993a). *Technology: A panel report*. Washington, DC: Author.

American Association for the Advancement of Science, Project 2061. (1993b). *Benchmarks for Science Literacy*. New York: Oxford University Press.

American Association for the Advancement of Science, Project 2061. (2000). *Research priorities for technology education*. Washington, DC: Author.

Benson, C., & Till, W. (1999). *Second international primary design and technology conference*. Birmingham, UK: Centre for Research in Primary Technology, University of Central England.

Britton, E., De Long-Cotty, B., & T. Levenson. (2004). Approaching the Standards? A review of new textbooks for the middle grades. *Technology Teacher, 63*(8), 30–33.

Britton, E., Huntley, M., Jacobs, G., & Shulman-Weinberg, A. (1999). *Connecting mathematics and science to workplace contexts*. Thousand Oaks, CA: Corwin Press.

Britton, E., & Raizen, S. (Eds.). (1996). *Examining the examinations*. Dordrecht, Netherlands: Kluwer Academic Publishers.

Chamblis, M., & Calfee, R. (1998). *Textbooks for learning: Nurturing children's minds*. Malden, MA: Blackwell.

De Vries, M., & Tamir, A. (1995). *Shaping concepts of technology*. Dordrecht, Netherlands: Kluwer Academic Publishers.

Goldsmith, L., Mark, J., & Kantrov, I. (2000). *Choosing a standards-based mathematics curriculum*. Westport, CT: Heinemann.

International Society for Technology in Education (ISTE). (2000). *National education technology standards for teachers*. Washington, DC: Author.

International Technology Education Association (ITEA). (2000). *Standards for technological literacy: Content for the study of technology*. Reston, VA: Author.

International Technology Education Association (ITEA). (2004). *Advancing excellence in technological literacy: Assessment, professional development, and program standards*. Reston, VA: Author.

McKnight, C., & Britton, E. (1992). *Training manual for content analysis of textbooks and curriculum guides: Survey of mathematics and science opportunity, third international mathematics and science study*. Lansing: TIMSS Center, Michigan State University.

Morse, M. P., & the AIBS Review Team. (2001). *A review of biological instructional materials for secondary schools*. Washington, DC: American Institute of Biological Sciences.

Muther, C. (1999). *Curriculum decisions? Materials selection?* Manchester, CT: Connie Muther and Associates, Inc.

National Academy of Engineering and National Research Council. (2002). *Technically speaking: Why all Americans need to know more about technology* (G. Peason & T. Young, Eds.). Washington, DC: Author.

National Research Council. (1996). *National science education standards*. Washington, DC: National Academy Press.

Raizen, S., Sellwood, P., Todd, R., & Vickers, M. (1995). *Technology education in the classroom: The designed world*. San Francisco: Jossey-Bass.

Rose, L., & Dugger, W. (2003). *ITEA/Gallup poll reveals what Americans think about technology*. Retrieved December 29, 2004, from www.iteawww.org/TAA/PDFs/Gallupreport.pdf

Schmidt, W., Raizen, S., Britton, E., Bianchi, L., & Wolfe, R. (1997). *Many visions, many aims: A cross-national investigation of curricular intentions in school science*. Dordrecht, Netherlands: Kluwer Academic Publishers.

CORWIN PRESS

The Corwin Press logo—a raven striding across an open book—represents the union of courage and learning. Corwin Press is committed to improving education for all learners by publishing books and other professional development resources for those serving the field of K–12 education. By providing practical, hands-on materials, Corwin Press continues to carry out the promise of its motto: **"Helping Educators Do Their Work Better."**

WestEd is a nonprofit research, development and service agency that works with educators and other communities to promote excellence, achieve equity, and improve learning for children, youth, and adults.

The International Technology Education Association (ITEA) is the professional organization of technology teachers. Our mission is to promote technological literacy for all by supporting the teaching of technology and promoting the professionalism of those engaged in this pursuit. ITEA strengthens the profession through leadership, professional development, membership services, publications, and classroom activities. Contact ITEA at itea@iris.org.

NSTApress®
NATIONAL SCIENCE TEACHERS ASSOCIATION

The National Science Teachers Association is the largest professional organization in the world promoting excellence and innovation in science teaching and learning for all. NSTA's membership includes more than 55,000 science teachers, science supervisors, administrators, scientists, business and industry representatives, and others involved in science education.